DISCRIMINATION

A GUIDE TO THE RELEVANT CASE LAW

TWENTY-FOURTH EDITION

Michael Rubenstein

Michael
Rubenstein
Publishing

Published by Michael Rubenstein Publishing Ltd

PO Box 61064
Southwark
London
SE1P 5BQ

www.rubensteinpublishing.com
www.eordirect.co.uk

© Michael Rubenstein Publishing Ltd 2011

ISBN: 978-0-9558224-3-8

Printed by Hobbs the Printers Ltd, Totton, Hampshire

CONTENTS

Contents continued

CASE INDEX

INTRODUCTION

The 24th edition of the Discrimination Guide takes into account the effect on the case law of 57 discrimination cases reported during 2010.

Discrimination has assumed ever-increasing prominence in the world of employment law. This was one of the main reasons why we launched *Equality Law Reports* (EqLR) in October 2010. This edition of the Guide covers both cases reported in *Industrial Relations Law Reports* (IRLR) during 2010 and also employment discrimination cases included in EqLR.

A major purpose of this Guide is to extract from the thousands of discrimination cases decided over the years the main principles concerning employment discrimination that still can be regarded as binding authority. My hope is that this will assist those advising, acting or adjudicating in this jurisdiction on the current approach of the courts to the range of problems of interpretation posed by the statutes.

2010 was an historic year for discrimination law with the passage of the Equality Act, and the coming into force of most of its employment provisions. Cases under the Equality Act are unlikely to reach the appellate courts, however, before the second half of 2011 at the earliest. Most of the reported decisions in coming months will still be interpreted in accordance with the legacy legislation and, therefore, it seemed sensible not to restructure the whole of the Guide, but instead to retain the division according to strands – or protected characteristics – for at least another year.

What I have done, however, is add to each of the statutory references in the Guide their "destination" in the Equality Act 2010. In doing this, I have been greatly assisted by EmpLaw's "Equality Act 2010 x-ref tool for employment law professionals" (www.emplaw.co.uk).

In 2009, equal pay was the most prominent cause of action among the discrimination cases reported. This changed markedly in 2010, with equal pay falling to sixth of the seven strands. There were 16 cases reported raising sex discrimination issues, 12 disability discrimination cases, 11 age discrimination cases, 10 race discrimination cases, six cases concerned with discrimination on grounds of religion or belief, five to do with equal pay and two sexual orientation discrimination cases. The total number exceeds 52 because some cases concerned more than one protected characteristic.

During 2010, IRLR and/or EqLR reported six judgments of the European Court of Justice on discrimination law, one judgment of the Supreme Court, 16 discrimination law judgments of the Court of Appeal, and 34 judgments from the EAT on aspects of discrimination law. The reported EAT judgments came from courts presided over by 13 different judges: 10 judgments from the current President, Mr Justice Underhill; four judgments from Mrs Justice Cox and four from Lady Smith; three from Mr Justice Wilkie; two from Mr Justice Burton, HH Judge McMullen QC, HH Judge Richardson and Mrs Justice Slade; and one judgment each from HH Judge Ansell, HH Judge Birtles, Mr Justice Keith, Mr Justice Langstaff, and HH Judge Serota QC.

To take the judgments reported in 2010 into account has meant deleting 43 entries which appeared in the 23rd edition of the Guide, but which are no longer considered relevant, while adding 88 new principles in light of the new case law.

Where essentially the same point has been enunciated in more than one reported case, the highest authority has been cited or, where that is not possible, the most recent or the most frequently quoted decision. For this and other purposes, therefore, the Guide distinguishes between the principle and the case. The principle, if still relevant, should be found in the Guide. A particular case may not be referred to either because it is no longer relevant or because the principle enunciated is better captured by another reference.

Conflicting lines of authority inevitably present a difficult problem for an exercise such as this. Where the issue can be said to be open to serious doubt, I have included both conflicting sets of decisions. On the other hand, where a case has clearly been overruled implicitly, the principle has been removed even though the case has not been expressly disapproved.

Finally, since there has to be a cut-off point in preparing a publication such as this, I have only included cases reported in IRLR or EqLR up to the end of 2010. Inevitably, however, because this area of the law is developing so rapidly, the Guide may include some principles which been have overruled by the courts by the time this edition reaches your hands. For those who wish to keep up to date, the Guide thus should be seen as an adjunct to *Industrial Relations Law Reports* and *Equality Law Reports*, rather than a replacement for regular perusal of these journals. *Equal Opportunities Review* will continue to provide expert analysis of many of these key decisions.

Michael Rubenstein
January 2011

1. SEX AND RACE DISCRIMINATION

EC SEX DISCRIMINATION LAW

Remedies under EC law

In order to carry out their task the Council and the Commission shall in accordance with the provisions of this Treaty, make regulations, issue directives, take decisions, make recommendations or deliver opinions.

A regulation shall have general application. It shall be binding in its entirety and directly applicable in all Member States.

A directive shall be binding, as to the result to be achieved, upon each Member State to which it is addressed, but shall leave to the national authorities the choice of form and methods.

A decision shall be binding in its entirety upon those to whom it is addressed.

Recommendations and opinions shall have no binding force.

EC TREATY – Article 189

1. Member States shall ensure that, after possible recourse to other competent authorities including where they deem it appropriate conciliation procedures, judicial procedures for the enforcement of obligations under this Directive are available to all persons who consider themselves wronged by failure to apply the principle of equal treatment to them, even after the relationship in which the discrimination is alleged to have occurred has ended.

2. Member States shall ensure that associations, organisations or other legal entities which have, in accordance with the criteria laid down by their national law, a legitimate interest in ensuring that the provisions of this Directive are complied with, may engage, either on behalf or in support of the complainant, with his/her approval, in any judicial and/or administrative procedure provided for the enforcement of obligations under this Directive.

3. Paragraphs 1 and 2 are without prejudice to national rules relating to time limits for bringing actions as regards the principle of equal treatment.

EQUAL TREATMENT DIRECTIVE 2006/54 – Article 17

Member States shall introduce into their national legal systems such measures as are necessary to ensure real and effective compensation or reparation as the Member States so determine for the loss and damage sustained by a person injured as a result of discrimination on grounds of sex, in a way which is dissuasive and proportionate to the damage suffered. Such compensation or reparation may not be restricted by the fixing of a prior upper limit, except in cases where the employer can prove that the only damage suffered by an applicant as a result of discrimination within the meaning of this Directive is the refusal to take his/her job application into consideration.

EQUAL TREATMENT DIRECTIVE 2006/54 – Article 18

Direct enforcement

Marshall v   **[1986] IRLR 140 ECJ**
Southampton and South-West
  Hampshire Area Health Authority
A Directive may not of itself impose obligations on an individual, as opposed to a State authority, and a provision of a Directive may not be relied upon as against an individual. According to Article 189 of the EC Treaty, the binding nature of a Directive, which constitutes the basis for the possibility of relying on the Directive before a national court, exists only in relation to "each Member State to which it is addressed". Whether a respondent must be regarded as having acted as an individual is for the national court to determine according to the circumstances of each case.

Marshall v   **[1986] IRLR 140 ECJ**
Southampton and South-West
  Hampshire Area Health Authority
Wherever the provisions of an EC Directive appear, as far as their subject-matter is concerned, to be unconditional and sufficiently precise, those provisions may be relied upon by an individual against the State where that State fails to implement the Directive in national law by the end of the period prescribed, or where it fails to implement the Directive correctly.

Verholen v   **[1992] IRLR 38 ECJ**
Sociale Verzekeringsbank Amsterdam
Community law does not preclude a national court from examining of its own motion whether national legal rules comply with the precise and unconditional provisions of a Directive, the period for whose implementation has elapsed.

Marshall v   **[1986] IRLR 140 ECJ**
Southampton and South-West
  Hampshire Area Health Authority
Where a person involved in legal proceedings is able to rely on a Directive as against the State, he may do so regardless of the capacity in which the latter is acting, whether employer or public authority.

Foster v   **[1990] IRLR 354 ECJ**
British Gas plc
Unconditional and sufficiently precise provisions of a Directive can be relied on against an organisation, whatever its legal form, which is subject to the authority or control of the State or which has been made responsible, pursuant to a measure adopted by the State, for providing a public service under the control of the State and has for that purpose special powers beyond those which result from the normal rules applicable in relations between individuals.

Foster v   **[1991] IRLR 268 HL**
British Gas plc
The sole questions under the test laid down by the Euro-

pean Court are whether the employer, pursuant to a measure adopted by the State, provides a public service under the control of the State and exercises special powers. That the employer engages in commercial activities, does not perform any of the traditional functions of the State and is not the agent of the State is not relevant to this test.

Foster v　　　　　　　　　　　　　**[1991] IRLR 268 HL**
British Gas plc
The principle laid down by the European Court of Justice was that the State must not be allowed to take advantage of its own failure to comply with Community law. There is no justification for a narrow or strained construction of the ruling of the European Court, which was couched in terms of broad principle and purposive language.

Doughty v　　　　　　　　　　　　**[1992] IRLR 126 CA**
Rolls-Royce plc
The three criteria formulated by the European Court in *Foster* for determining whether a particular entity is such that the provisions of a Directive are directly enforceable against it are cumulative requirements rather than alternative. The power of control is only one of the cumulative criteria.

Cotter v　　　　　　　　　　　　**[1991] IRLR 380 ECJ**
Minister for Social Welfare
In the absence of measures implementing a directly enforceable provision of an EC Directive, women are entitled to have the same rules applied to them as are applied to men who are in the same situation since, where the Directive has not been implemented, those rules remain the only valid point of reference. This principle applies even if it infringes a prohibition on unjust enrichment laid down by national law.

Jesuthasan v　　　　　　　　　　　**[1998] IRLR 372 CA**
London Borough of Hammersmith & Fulham
Legislative measures which have been declared incompatible with EC law on account of their indirectly discriminatory effects must be disapplied in respect of all employees, regardless of sex. Therefore, even though the claimant is a man, he was entitled to rely on the decision of the House of Lords in *R v Secretary of State for Employment ex parte EOC* that the hours per week qualifying thresholds to claim unfair dismissal were incompatible with EC law because they indirectly discriminated against women.

Secretary of State for Scotland v　　　**[1991] IRLR 187 EAT**
Wright
An employment tribunal has jurisdiction to hear a claim brought under directly applicable provisions of the Equal Treatment Directive in circumstances where the claimant has no remedy under domestic legislation. Accordingly, the tribunal had jurisdiction to hear the employees' complaint that their exclusion from the right to a contractual redundancy payment contravened the Equal Treatment Directive.

Blaik v　　　　　　　　　　　　　**[1994] IRLR 280 EAT**
Post Office
If there is a sufficient remedy given by domestic law, it is unnecessary and impermissible to explore the same complaint under the equivalent provisions in a Directive. It is only if there is a disparity between the two that it becomes necessary to consider whether the provisions in EC law are directly enforceable by the complainant in his proceedings against the respondent.

Time limits

Emmott v　　　　　　　　　　　　**[1991] IRLR 387 ECJ**
Minister for Social Welfare
In the absence of Community rules on the subject, it is for the domestic legal system of each Member State to determine the procedural conditions governing actions at law intended to ensure the protection of rights which individuals derive from the direct effect of Community law, provided that such conditions are not less favourable than those relating to similar actions of a domestic nature, nor framed so as to render virtually impossible the exercise of rights conferred by Community law. The laying down of reasonable time limits, which if unobserved bar proceedings, in principle satisfies these two conditions.

Emmott v　　　　　　　　　　　　**[1991] IRLR 387 ECJ**
Minister for Social Welfare
Until such time as a Directive has been properly transposed into domestic law, a defaulting Member State may not rely on an individual's delay in initiating proceedings against it in order to protect rights conferred upon him by the provisions of the Directive, and a period laid down by national law within which proceedings must be initiated cannot begin to run before that time.

Bulicke v　　　　　　　　　　　　**[2010] EqLR 105 ECJ**
Deutsche Büro Service GmbH
The fixing of a period of two months for submitting a claim did not appear liable to render practically impossible or excessively difficult the exercise of rights conferred by EU law because the starting point for the time limit was at the point at which the worker has knowledge of the alleged discrimination.

Steenhorst-Neerings v　　　　　　　**[1994] IRLR 244 ECJ**
Bestuur van de Bedrijfsvereniging
　voor Detailhandel, Ambachten en
　Huisvrouwen
A national rule of law restricting the retroactive effect of claims is not precluded by EC law where an individual seeks to rely on rights conferred directly by an EC Directive and where on the date the claim for benefit was made the Member State concerned had not yet properly transposed that provision into national law. The principle set out by *Emmott*,

that the time limits for proceedings brought by individuals seeking to avail themselves of their rights are applicable only when a Member State has properly transposed the Directive, did not apply in such a case. The right to claim benefits conferred upon women by the direct effect of a Directive must be exercised under the conditions determined by national law, provided those conditions are no less favourable than those relating to similar domestic actions and that they are not framed so as to render virtually impossible the exercise of rights conferred by Community law.

Johnson v   **[1995] IRLR 157 ECJ**
Chief Adjudication Officer (No.2)
It is compatible with European Community law to apply a national rule, which limits the period in respect of which arrears of benefit are payable, to a claim based on the direct effect of an EC Directive, even where that Directive has not been properly transposed within the prescribed period in the Member State. The solution adopted in *Emmott* was justified by the particular circumstances of that case, in which a time bar had the result of depriving the claimant of any opportunity whatever to rely on her right to equal treatment under the Directive. This was to be contrasted with application of a rule which merely limited the retroactive effect of claims for benefits to one year, and therefore did not make it virtually impossible to exercise rights based on the Directive.

Setiya v   **[1995] IRLR 348 EAT**
East Yorkshire Health Authority
The principle laid down in *Emmott* relates only to time limits for initiating proceedings, and has no application to national time limits for appealing against a decision.

Agreement precluding complaint

Livingstone v   **[1992] IRLR 63 EAT**
Hepworth Refractories plc
The procedural provisions of UK domestic law comply with the conditions indicated by the European Court in *Emmott*. Therefore, the proper approach is to apply the procedures of the Sex Discrimination Act, including that relating to time limits and the code intended to protect employees against bad bargains, to claims of sex discrimination brought directly under Community law.

Grounds of race

2(a). Direct discrimination shall be taken to occur where one person is treated less favourably than another is, has been or would be treated in a comparable situation on grounds of racial or ethnic origin.

RACE DISCRIMINATION DIRECTIVE 2000/43 – Article 2

Centrum voor Gelijkheid van Kansen   **[2008] IRLR 732 ECJ**
en voor Racismebestrijding v
Firma Feryn NV
The fact that an employer states publicly that it will not recruit employees of a certain ethnic or racial origin constitutes direct discrimination in respect of recruitment within the meaning of Article 2(2)(a) of the EC Race Discrimination Directive, such statements being likely strongly to dissuade certain candidates from submitting their candidature and, accordingly, to hinder their access to the labour market. The existence of such direct discrimination is not dependent on the identification of a complainant who claims to have been the victim.

Grounds of sex

1. For the purposes of this Directive, the following definitions shall apply:
(a) "direct discrimination": where one person is treated less favourably on grounds of sex than another is, has been or would be treated in a comparable situation;
(b) "indirect discrimination": where an apparently neutral provision, criterion or practice would put persons of one sex at a particular disadvantage compared with persons of the other sex, unless that provision, criterion or practice is objectively justified by a legitimate aim, and the means of achieving that aim are appropriate and necessary;
(c) "harassment": where unwanted conduct related to the sex of a person occurs with the purpose or effect of violating the dignity of a person, and of creating an intimidating, hostile, degrading, humiliating or offensive environment;
(d) "sexual harassment": where any form of unwanted verbal, non-verbal or physical conduct of a sexual nature occurs, with the purpose or effect of violating the dignity of a person, in particular when creating an intimidating, hostile, degrading, humiliating or offensive environment;
(e) "pay": the ordinary basic or minimum wage or salary and any other consideration, whether in cash or in kind, which the worker receives directly or indirectly, in respect of his/her employment from his/her employer;
(f) "occupational social security schemes": schemes not governed by Council Directive 79/7/EEC of 19 December 1978 on the progressive implementation of the principle of equal treatment for men and women in matters of social security whose purpose is to provide workers, whether employees or self-employed, in an undertaking or group of undertakings, area of economic activity, occupational sector or group of sectors, with benefits intended to supplement the benefits provided by statutory social security schemes or to replace them, whether membership of such schemes is compulsory or optional.

2. For the purposes of this Directive, discrimination includes:
(a) harassment and sexual harassment, as well as any less favourable treatment based on a person's rejection of or submission to such conduct;
(b) instruction to discriminate against persons on grounds of sex;
(c) any less favourable treatment of a woman related to pregnancy or maternity leave within the meaning of Directive 92/85/EEC.

EQUAL TREATMENT DIRECTIVE 2006/54 – Article 2

P v   **[1996] IRLR 347 ECJ**
S

The scope of the Equal Treatment Directive cannot be confined simply to discrimination based on the fact that a person is one or other sex. In view of its purpose and the fundamental nature of the rights which it seeks to safeguard, the scope of the Directive also applies to discrimination based essentially, if not exclusively, on the sex of the person concerned.

Pregnancy

Dekker v   **[1991] IRLR 27 ECJ**
VJV-Centrum

Whether a refusal to employ results in direct discrimination on grounds of sex depends on whether the most important reason is one which applies without distinction to employees of both sexes or whether it exclusively applies to one sex. As employment can only be refused because of pregnancy to women, such a refusal is direct discrimination on grounds of sex. Therefore, an employer is acting in direct contravention of the principle of equal treatment embodied in the EC Equal Treatment Directive if he refuses to enter into a contract of employment with a female claimant, found suitable by him for the post in question, because of the possible adverse consequences to him of employing a pregnant woman.

Handels- og Kontorfunktionærernes   **[1991] IRLR 31 ECJ**
  Forbund i Danmark
  (acting for Hertz) v
Dansk Arbejdsgiverforening
  (acting for Aldi Marked K/S)

The dismissal of a female worker because of her pregnancy constitutes direct discrimination on grounds of sex, in the same way as does the refusal to recruit a pregnant woman. Therefore, a woman is protected from dismissal because of her absence during the maternity leave from which she benefits under national law.

Webb v   **[1994] IRLR 482 ECJ**
EMO Air Cargo (UK) Ltd

Dismissal of a woman on grounds of pregnancy constitutes direct discrimination on grounds of sex. In determining whether there is discrimination on grounds of sex contrary to the Directive, the situation of a woman who finds herself incapable by reason of pregnancy of performing the task for which she was recruited cannot be compared with that of a man similarly incapable for medical or other reasons.

Mayr v   **[2008] IRLR 387 ECJ**
Bäckerei und Konditorei Gerhard
  Flöckner OHG

The prohibition of dismissal of pregnant workers pro-

vided for in the Pregnant Workers Directive 92/85 does not extend to a female worker who is undergoing in vitro fertilisation treatment where, on the date she is given notice of her dismissal, her ova have already been fertilised by her partner's sperm cells, so that in vitro fertilised ova exist, but they have not yet been transferred into her uterus. However, dismissal of a female worker essentially because she is at an advanced stage of in vitro fertilisation treatment, between the follicular puncture and the immediate transfer of the in vitro fertilised ova into her uterus, constitutes direct discrimination on grounds of sex contrary to the Equal Treatment Directive since such treatment directly affects only women.

Sexual orientation

Grant v   **[1998] IRLR 206 ECJ**
South-West Trains Ltd

Discrimination based on sexual orientation does not constitute discrimination based on the sex of the worker within the meaning of Article 141.

Gender reassignment

P v   **[1996] IRLR 347 ECJ**
S

Where such discrimination arises from the gender reassignment of the person concerned, he or she is treated unfavourably by comparison with persons of the sex to which he or she was deemed to belong before undergoing gender reassignment.

Exclusions

Perceval-Price v   **[2000] IRLR 380 NICA**
Department of Economic Development

The term "worker" in the context of Community law must be interpreted broadly and in a purposive fashion so as to include within the definition all persons who are engaged in a relationship which is broadly that of employment rather than being self-employed or independent contractors.

Perceval-Price v   **[2000] IRLR 380 NICA**
Department of Economic Development

Tribunal chairmen are "workers" who are in "employment" within the meaning of European Community law, and are therefore entitled to bring equal pay and sex discrimination complaints, notwithstanding that they do not fall within the definition of "employment" under domestic equal pay and sex discrimination legislation because they are holders of statutory office.

Sex as determining factor

2. Member States may provide, as regards access to employment including the training leading thereto, that a difference of treatment which is based on a characteristic related to sex shall not constitute discrimination where, by reason of the nature of the particular occupational activities concerned or of the context in which they are carried out, such a characteristic constitutes a genuine and determining occupational requirement, provided that the objective is legitimate and the requirement is proportionate.

EQUAL TREATMENT DIRECTIVE 2006/54 – Article 14

Johnston v   **[1986] IRLR 263 ECJ**
The Chief Constable of the Royal
  Ulster Constabulary
[Article 14(2)] of the Equal Treatment Directive, being a derogation from an individual right laid down in the Directive, must be interpreted strictly, and in determining the scope of any derogation, the principle of proportionality must be observed. That principle requires that derogations remain within the limits of what is appropriate and necessary for achieving the aim in view and requires the principle of equal treatment to be reconciled as far as possible with the requirement which constituted the decisive factor as regards the context of the activity in question. It is for the national court to ensure that the principle of proportionality is observed.

Sirdar v   **[2000] IRLR 47 ECJ**
The Army Board
There is no general exception in the EC Treaty covering all measures taken by Member States for reasons of public security. Therefore, application of the principle of equal treatment is not subject to any general reservation as regards measures for the organisation of the armed forces. However, the UK Government might be entitled under the Equal Treatment Directive to exclude women from service in special combat units such as the Royal Marines.

Commission of the European   **[1984] IRLR 29 ECJ**
  Communities v
United Kingdom of Great Britain
  and Northern Ireland
Reconciliation of the principle of equality of treatment with the principle of respect for private life is one of the factors which must be taken into consideration in determining the scope of the exception provided for in [Article 14(2)] of the Equal Treatment Directive.

Positive action

(4) With a view to ensuring full equality in practice between men and women in working life, the principle of equal treatment shall not prevent any Member State from maintaining or adopting measures providing for specific advantages in order to make it easier for the underrepresented sex to pursue a vocational activity or to prevent or compensate for disadvantages in professional careers.

EC TREATY – Article 141

Member States may maintain or adopt measures within the meaning of art. 141(4) of the Treaty with a view to ensuring full equality in practice between men and women in working life.

EQUAL TREATMENT DIRECTIVE 2006/54 – Article 3

Abrahamsson v   **[2000] IRLR 732 ECJ**
Fogelqvist
The Equal Treatment Directive does not preclude a rule of national case law under which a candidate belonging to the underrepresented sex may be granted preference over a competitor of the opposite sex, provided that the candidates possess equivalent or substantially equivalent merits and the candidatures are subjected to an objective assessment which takes account of the specific personal situations of all the candidates.

Abrahamsson v   **[2000] IRLR 732 ECJ**
Fogelqvist
The Equal Treatment Directive precludes national legislation which provides for positive discrimination in recruitment in favour of candidates of the under-represented sex by automatically granting preference to candidates belonging to the under-represented sex, so long as they are sufficiently qualified, subject only to the proviso that the difference between the merits of the candidates of each sex is not so great as to result in a breach of the requirement of objectivity in making appointments. Such legislation was ultimately based on the mere fact of belonging to the under-represented sex.

Abrahamsson v   **[2000] IRLR 732 ECJ**
Fogelqvist
Although Article 141(4) allows the Member States to maintain or adopt measures providing for special advantages intended to prevent or compensate for disadvantages in professional careers in order to ensure full equality between men and women in professional life, it cannot be inferred that it allows a selection method which is disproportionate to the aim pursued.

Kalanke v   **[1995] IRLR 660 ECJ**
Freie Hansestadt Bremen
National rules which guarantee women absolute and unconditional priority for appointment or promotion go beyond promoting equal opportunities and overstep the limits of the exception to the principle of equal treatment in the Equal Treatment Directive.

EFTA Surveillance Authority v   **[2003] IRLR 318 EFTA Ct**
Kingdom of Norway
The Equal Treatment Directive is based on the recognition of the right to equal treatment as a fundamental right of the individual. National rules and practices derogating from that right can only be permissible when they show sufficient flexibility to allow a balance between the need for the promotion of the under-represented gender and the opportunity for candidates of the opposite gender to

have their situation objectively assessed. There must, as a matter of principle, be a possibility that the best-qualified candidate obtains the post. Therefore, national legislation which allows a number of academic posts to be reserved exclusively for women because they are under-represented in the particular post went beyond the scope of the Directive insofar as it gave absolute and unconditional priority to female candidates.

Marschall v   **[1998] IRLR 39 ECJ**
Land Nordrhein-Westfalen
It is not contrary to the Equal Treatment Directive for equally-qualified women to be given preference for promotion where there are fewer women than men in the relevant post, so long as male candidates are guaranteed that women are not to be given priority if reasons specific to an individual equally-qualified man tilt the balance in his favour.

Application by Badek   **[2000] IRLR 432 ECJ**
A measure which is intended to give priority in promotion to women in sectors of the public service where they are underrepresented is compatible with Community law if it does not automatically and unconditionally give priority to women when women and men are equally qualified, and the candidatures are the subject of an objective assessment which takes account of the specific personal situations of all candidates.

Application by Badek   **[2000] IRLR 432 ECJ**
The Equal Treatment Directive does not preclude a rule for the public service which allocates at least half the training places to women in occupations in which women are under-represented and for which the State does not have a monopoly of training. Nor does it preclude a rule for the public service which guarantees, in sectors in which women are underrepresented, that where male and female candidates have equal qualifications, either all women who are qualified will be given an interview, or that no more male candidates than female candidates will be interviewed.

Lommers v   **[2002] IRLR 430 ECJ**
Minister van Landbouw,
  Natuurbeheer en Visserij
Provision of a limited number of subsidised nursery places to female staff only is permissible in principle under the Equal Treatment Directive, where the scheme has been set up by the employer to tackle extensive under-representation of women, in a context characterised by a proven insufficiency of proper, affordable child-care facilities, so long as male employees who take care of their children by themselves are allowed to have access to the scheme on the same conditions as female employees. The fact that the policy did not guarantee access to nursery places to employees of both sexes on an equal footing was not contrary to the principle of proportionality.

Access to jobs

1. There shall be no direct or indirect discrimination on grounds of sex in the public or private sectors, including public bodies, in relation to:
(a) conditions for access to employment, to self-employment or to occupation, including selection criteria and recruitment conditions, whatever the branch of activity and at all levels of the professional hierarchy, including promotion;
    EQUAL TREATMENT DIRECTIVE 2006/54 – Article 14

Johnston v   **[1986] IRLR 263 ECJ**
The Chief Constable of the Royal
  Ulster Constabulary
The application of the principle of equal treatment to the conditions governing access to jobs, as set out in [Article 14(1)] of the Equal Treatment Directive, is unconditional and sufficiently precise so that it may be relied upon by individuals as against a Member State where that Member State fails to implement it correctly.

Gerster v   **[1997] IRLR 699 ECJ**
Freistaat Bayern
Legislation which treats part-time employees less favourably than full-time employees by providing for them to accrue length of service more slowly, and perforce gain promotion later, results in discrimination against women as compared with men and must in principle be regarded as contrary to the Equal Treatment Directive, unless the distinction is justified by objective reasons unrelated to any discrimination on grounds of sex. There would be no infringement of the Equal Treatment Directive if the national court found that part-time employees are generally slower than full-time employees in acquiring job-related abilities and skills, and that the competent authorities were in a position to establish that the measures chosen reflected a legitimate social policy aim, were an appropriate means of achieving that aim and were necessary in order to do so. However, a requirement that part-time employees must complete a longer period of service than a full-time employee in order to have approximately the same chance of promotion must be regarded as contrary to the Equal Treatment Directive if the national court concludes that there is no special link between length of service and acquisition of a certain level of knowledge or experience.

Kording v   **[1997] IRLR 710 ECJ**
Senator Für Finanzen
Legislation which treats a part-time employee less favourably than a full-time employee, by providing that the total length of professional experience required for exemption from a qualifying examination is to be extended on a pro rata basis for part-time workers, gives rise to indirect discrimination against women if substantially fewer men than women work part-time and must in principle be regarded as contrary to the Equal Treatment Directive. However, such inequality of treatment would be compatible with the Directive if it were

justified by objective factors unrelated to any discrimination on grounds of sex.

Meyers v [1995] IRLR 498 ECJ
Adjudication Officer
A benefit such as family credit in the UK falls within the scope of [Article 14(1)] of the Equal Treatment Directive, since its subject-matter is access to employment in that the benefit is intended to keep poorly-paid workers in employment. The fact that a scheme of benefits is part of a national social security system cannot exclude it from the scope of the Directive.

Pregnancy discrimination

2. For the purposes of this Directive, discrimination includes:
(c) any less favourable treatment of a woman related to pregnancy or maternity leave within the meaning of Directive 92/85/EEC.
EQUAL TREATMENT DIRECTIVE 2006/54 – Article 2

Dekker v [1991] IRLR 27 ECJ
VJV-Centrum
A refusal to employ because of the financial consequences of absence connected with pregnancy must be deemed to be based principally on the fact of the pregnancy. Such discrimination cannot be justified by the financial detriment that would be suffered by the employer during the woman's maternity leave.

Dekker v [1991] IRLR 27 ECJ
VJV-Centrum
If the reason a woman is not selected is because she is pregnant, the decision is directly related to the claimant's sex and it is not important that there were no male claimants.

Mahlburg v [2000] IRLR 276 ECJ
Land Mecklenburg-Vorpommern
It is contrary to the Equal Treatment Directive for an employer to refuse to appoint a pregnant woman to a post of an unlimited duration on the ground that a statutory prohibition on employment arising on account of her pregnancy would prevent her from being employed in that post from the outset and for the duration of the pregnancy.

Sarkatzis Herrero v [2006] IRLR 296 ECJ
Instituto Madrileño de la Salud
When a female employee is on maternity leave at the time of her appointment, deferring the start of her career, for the purposes of calculating her seniority, to the date on which she actually took up the post constitutes discrimination on grounds of sex contrary to European Community law.

Busch v [2003] IRLR 625 ECJ
Klinikum Neustadt GmbH & Co Betriebs-KG
It is contrary to the Equal Treatment Directive to require an employee who wishes to return to work before the end of

parental leave to inform her employer that she is pregnant, even though she will be unable to carry out all of her duties because of legislative provisions. Such discrimination cannot be justified by the fact that a woman is temporarily prevented from performing all of her duties by a legislative prohibition imposed because of pregnancy. That would be contrary to the objective of protection pursued by the Equal Treatment Directive and the Pregnant Workers Directive and would rob them of any practical effect.

Access to training

1. There shall be no direct or indirect discrimination on grounds of sex in the public or private sectors, including public bodies, in relation to:
(b) access to all types and to all levels of vocational guidance, vocational training, advanced vocational training and retraining, including practical work experience;
EQUAL TREATMENT DIRECTIVE 2006/54 – Article 2

Johnston v [1986] IRLR 263 ECJ
The Chief Constable of the Royal
  Ulster Constabulary
The application of the principle of equal treatment to the conditions governing access to training, as set out in [Article 14(1)] of the Equal Treatment Directive, is unconditional and sufficiently precise so that it may be relied upon by individuals as against a Member State where that Member State fails to implement it correctly.

Working conditions and dismissal

1. There shall be no direct or indirect discrimination on grounds of sex in the public or private sectors, including public bodies, in relation to:
(c) employment and working conditions, including dismissals, as well as pay as provided for in Article 141 of the Treaty;
EQUAL TREATMENT DIRECTIVE 2006/54 – Article 2

Marshall v [1986] IRLR 140 ECJ
Southampton and South-West
  Hampshire Area Health Authority
[Article 2(1)] of the Equal Treatment Directive may be relied upon as against a State authority acting in its capacity as employer, in order to avoid the application of any national provision which does not conform to [Article 2(1)]. [Article 2(1)] is sufficiently precise and unconditional to be relied on by individuals and to be applied by national courts. The provision, taken by itself, prohibits any discrimination on grounds of sex with regard to working conditions in a general manner and in unequivocal terms. It does not confer on Member States the right to limit the application of the principle of equality of treatment in its field of operation or to subject it to conditions.

Meyers v   **[1995] IRLR 498 ECJ**
Adjudication Officer
To confine the concept of a working condition within the meaning of [Article 2(1)] solely to those working conditions which are set out in the contract of employment or applied by the employer in respect of a worker's employment would remove situations directly covered by an employment relationship from the scope of the Directive. Therefore, a benefit such as family credit, which is necessarily linked to an employment relationship, constitutes a working condition within the meaning of [Article 2(1)] of the Directive.

Discriminatory retirement ages

Burton v   **[1982] IRLR 116 ECJ**
British Railways Board
"Dismissal" for the purposes of [Article 2(1)] of the Equal Treatment Directive must be widely construed.

Marshall v   **[1986] IRLR 140 ECJ**
Southampton and South-West
   Hampshire Area Health Authority
A general policy concerning dismissal involving the dismissal of a woman solely because she has attained the qualifying age for a State pension, which age is different under national legislation for men and women, constitutes discrimination on grounds of sex contrary to [Article 2(1)] of the Equal Treatment Directive. In accordance with the decision of the European Court in *Burton v British Railways Board*, the term "dismissal" in [Article 2(1)] must be given a wide meaning. An age limit for the compulsory dismissal of workers pursuant to an employer's general policy concerning retirement relates to the conditions governing dismissal, to be determined in accordance with the Equal Treatment Directive, even if the dismissal involved the grant of a retirement pension.

Pregnancy

Brown v   **[1998] IRLR 445 ECJ**
Rentokil Ltd
Dismissal of a woman at any time during her pregnancy for absences due to incapacity for work caused by an illness resulting from that pregnancy is direct discrimination on grounds of sex contrary to the EC Equal Treatment Directive.

Webb v   **[1994] IRLR 482 ECJ**
EMO Air Cargo (UK) Ltd
It is contrary to the Equal Treatment Directive to dismiss a woman employed for an unlimited term who, shortly after her recruitment is found to be pregnant, even though she was recruited initially to replace another employee during the latter's maternity leave and notwithstanding that the employer would have dismissed a male employee engaged for this purpose who required leave of absence at the relevant time for medical or other reasons.

Webb v   **[1994] IRLR 482 ECJ**
EMO Air Cargo (UK) Ltd
Dismissal of a pregnant woman recruited for an indefinite period cannot be justified on grounds relating to her inability to fulfil a fundamental condition of her contract of employment.

Tele Danmark v   **[2001] IRLR 853 ECJ**
HK (acting on behalf of Brandt-Nielsen)
[Article 2] of the Equal Treatment Directive and Article 10 of the Pregnant Workers Directive preclude a worker from being dismissed on the ground of pregnancy, notwithstanding that she was recruited for a fixed period, failed to inform the employer that she was pregnant even though she was aware of this when the contract of employment was concluded, and because of her pregnancy was unable to work during a substantial part of the term of that contract. Dismissal of a worker on account of pregnancy constitutes direct discrimination on grounds of sex, whatever the nature and extent of the economic loss incurred by the employer as a result of her absence because of pregnancy. Whether the contract was concluded for a fixed or an indefinite period has no bearing on the discriminatory character of the dismissal. In either case the employee's inability to perform her contract of employment is due to pregnancy.

Brown v   **[1998] IRLR 445 ECJ**
Rentokil Ltd
It is direct discrimination on grounds of sex to dismiss a pregnant woman because of absences resulting from pregnancy in accordance with a contractual term providing that an employer may dismiss workers of either sex after a stipulated number of weeks of continuous absence.

Brown v   **[1998] IRLR 445 ECJ**
Rentokil Ltd
The Equal Treatment Directive affords a woman protection against dismissal on grounds of her absence throughout the period of pregnancy and during the maternity leave accorded to her under national law. Where a woman is absent owing to illness resulting from pregnancy or childbirth, and that illness arose during pregnancy and persisted during and after maternity leave, her absence not only during maternity leave but also during the period extending from the start of her pregnancy to the start of her maternity leave cannot be taken into account for computation of the period justifying her dismissal under national law. Absence after maternity leave may be taken into account under the same conditions as a man's absence through incapacity for work of the same duration.

Habermann-Beltermann v   **[1994] IRLR 364 ECJ**
Arbeiterwohlfahrt, Bezirksverband
   Ndb/Opf eV
Termination of a contract without a fixed term on account of a woman's pregnancy cannot be justified on the ground that a statutory prohibition, imposed because of pregnancy, temporarily prevents the employee from performing night work.

Jiménez Melgar v   **[2001] IRLR 848 ECJ**
Ayuntamiento de Los Barrios
Non-renewal of a fixed-term contract is a refusal of employ-ment and, where non-renewal of a fixed-term contract is based on the worker's pregnancy, it constitutes direct dis-crimination on grounds of sex contrary to Articles 2(1) and 3(1) of the Equal Treatment Directive.

Handels- og Kontorfunktionærernes   **[1991] IRLR 31 ECJ**
   Forbund i Danmark
   (acting for Hertz) v
Dansk Arbejdsgiverforening
   (acting for Aldi Marked K/S)
The Equal Treatment Directive does not preclude dismiss-als resulting from absence due to an illness which origi-nated in pregnancy or confinement and which appears after maternity leave.

CNAVTS v   **[1998] IRLR 399 ECJ**
Thibault
The principle of non-discrimination on grounds of sex in working conditions requires that a woman who continues to be bound to her employer by her contract of employment during maternity leave should not be deprived of the benefit of working conditions which apply to both men and women and are the result of that employment relationship. The exer-cise by women of pregnancy and maternity rights cannot be the subject of unfavourable treatment regarding their access to employment or their working conditions.

Land Brandenburg v   **[2005] IRLR 147 ECJ**
Sass
A woman who is treated unfavourably because of absence on maternity leave suffers discrimination on the ground of her pregnancy and of that leave. Community law requires that taking such statutory protective leave should interrupt neither the employment relationship of the woman con-cerned nor the application of the rights derived from it and cannot lead to discrimination against that woman.

Álvarez v   **[2010] EqLR 238 ECJ**
Sesa Start España ETT SA
The Equal Treatment Directive precludes a Spanish nation-al law which provides that female workers who are mothers and whose status is that of an employed person are entitled to time off to feed an unweaned child whereas male work-ers who are fathers with that same status are not entitled to the same leave unless the child's mother is also an employed person. The fact that the leave might be taken by the employed father or the employed mother without dis-tinction meant that feeding and devoting time to the child could be carried out just as well by the father as by the mother. Since their positions were comparable with regard to their possible need to reduce their daily working time in order to look after their child, this precluded a finding that the measure ensured the protection of a woman's biological condition following pregnancy. To hold that only a mother

whose status is that of an employed person is the holder of the right to qualify for such leave, whereas a father with the same status could only enjoy this right but not be the holder of it, would be liable to perpetuate a traditional distribution of the roles of men and women by keeping men in a role subsidiary to that of women in relation to the exercise of their parental duties.

Gillespie v   **[1996] IRLR 214 ECJ**
Northern Health and Social
   Services Board
The Equal Treatment Directive does not apply to pay. Since the benefit paid during maternity leave constitutes pay and falls within the scope of Article 141 and the Equal Pay Direc-tive, it cannot be covered by the Equal Treatment Directive as well.

CNAVTS v   **[1998] IRLR 399 ECJ**
Thibault
It is contrary to the Equal Treatment Directive for a woman to be accorded unfavourable treatment regarding her work-ing conditions by being deprived of the right to an annual assessment of her performance and, therefore, of the oppor-tunity of qualifying for promotion to a higher pay grade as a result of her absence on account of maternity leave.

Boyle v   **[1998] IRLR 717 ECJ**
Equal Opportunities Commission
A contractual term according to which a worker who does not return to work after childbirth is required to repay the difference between the pay received by her during her mater-nity leave and the Statutory Maternity Pay to which she was entitled does not constitute discrimination on grounds of sex contrary to EC law, notwithstanding that for other forms of paid leave, such as sick leave, workers are entitled to their salary without having to undertake to return to work at the end of their leave. The situation of a pregnant woman cannot be compared to that of a man or a woman on sick leave.

Boyle v   **[1998] IRLR 717 ECJ**
Equal Opportunities Commission
EC law does not preclude a clause in a contract of employ-ment which requires a woman who is on sick leave with a pregnancy-related illness to take paid maternity leave if the period of sick leave occurs within six weeks of the expect-ed date of childbirth, notwithstanding that any other worker who is sick is entitled to exercise their right to uncondi-tional paid sick leave.

Boyle v   **[1998] IRLR 717 ECJ**
Equal Opportunities Commission
EC law does not preclude a clause in a contract of employ-ment which limits the period during which annual holiday accrues to the statutory minimum 14 weeks' maternity leave period and which provides that annual holiday ceases to accrue during any period of supplementary maternity leave granted by the employer.

Land Brandenburg v   **[2005] IRLR 147 ECJ**
Sass

The fact that legislation grants women maternity leave of more than the minimum period of 14 weeks laid down by the Pregnant Workers Directive does not preclude that leave from being considered to be maternity leave as referred to in Article 8 of that Directive and, therefore, a period during which the rights connected with the employment contract must be ensured. The decision in *Boyle v Equal Opportunities Commission* did not prejudge this since *Boyle* concerned additional leave granted by an employer rather than statutory leave.

Gender reassignment

P v   **[1996] IRLR 347 ECJ**
S

Dismissal of a transsexual for a reason related to a gender reassignment must be regarded as contrary to [Article 2(1)] of the Directive.

Indirect discrimination under EC law

R v   **[1999] IRLR 253 ECJ**
Secretary of State for Employment
    ex parte Seymour-Smith

In order to establish whether a measure adopted by a Member State has disparate effect as between men and women to such a degree as to amount to indirect discrimination for the purposes of Article 141, the national court must verify whether the statistics indicate that a considerably smaller percentage of women than men is able to satisfy the condition required. That would be evidence of apparent sex discrimination. That could also be the case if the statistical evidence revealed a lesser but persistent and relatively constant disparity over a long period between men and women who satisfy the requirement.

R v   **[1999] IRLR 253 ECJ**
Secretary of State for Employment
    ex parte Seymour-Smith

The best approach for determining whether a rule has a more unfavourable impact on women than on men is to consider the respective proportions of men in the workforce able to satisfy the requirement and those unable to do so, and to compare those proportions as regards women in the workforce.

Jørgensen v   **[2000] IRLR 726 ECJ**
Foreningen af Speciallæger

In order to determine whether a collective agreement indirectly discriminates on grounds of sex, the Equal Treatment Directive requires a separate assessment to be made of each of the key conditions laid down in the contested provisions, in so far as those key elements constitute in themselves specific measures based on their own criteria of application and affecting a significant number of persons

belonging to a determined category. An overall assessment of all the elements which might be involved in a scheme or a set of provisions would not allow effective review of the application of the principle of equal treatment and might not comply with the rules governing the burden of proof in matters relating to indirect discrimination on grounds of sex.

R v   **[1999] IRLR 253 ECJ**
Secretary of State for Employment
    ex parte Seymour-Smith

If a considerably smaller percentage of women than men is capable of fulfilling a statutory requirement, such as the service qualification for unfair dismissal, it is for the Member State, as the author of the allegedly discriminatory rule, to show that the said rule reflects a legitimate aim of its social policy, that that aim is unrelated to any discrimination based on sex, and that it could reasonably consider that the means chosen were suitable for attaining that aim.

Nolte v   **[1996] IRLR 225 ECJ**
Landesversicherrungsanstalt
    Hannover

A legislative measure is based on objective factors unrelated to discrimination on grounds of sex where the measure chosen reflects a legitimate social policy of the Member State, is appropriate to achieve that aim and necessary in order to do so. However, social policy is a matter for the Member States. Consequently, the Member States have a broad margin of discretion in exercising their competence to choose the measures capable of achieving the aim of their social and employment policy.

Kruger v   **[1999] IRLR 808 ECJ**
Kreiskrankenhaus Ebersberg

The exclusion of persons in "minor" employment from the scope of a collective agreement providing for the grant of a special annual bonus was indirect discrimination within the meaning of Article 141 where it affected a considerably higher percentage of women than men. The exclusion was not justified since an exclusion from the benefit of a collective agreement is a different situation from that in *Nolte* and *Megner*, in which the Court held that the exclusion of persons in minor employment from social insurance fell within the broad margin of discretion of Member States to choose the measures for achieving the aims of their social and employment policy.

R v   **[1999] IRLR 253 ECJ**
Secretary of State for Employment
    ex parte Seymour-Smith

In order to show that a measure is justified by objective factors unrelated to any discrimination based on sex, it is not sufficient for a Member State to show that it was reasonably entitled to consider that the measure would advance a social policy aim. Although, in the *Nolte* case, the Court observed that, in choosing the measures capable of achieving the aims of their social and employment policy, the Member States have a broad margin of discretion, that cannot have the effect of frustrating the implementation of a fundamental principle of Community law such as that of equal pay for men and women. Mere generalisations concerning the capacity of a specific measure to encourage recruitment are not enough to show that the aim of the disputed rule is unrelated to any discrimination based on sex nor to provide evidence on the basis of which it could reasonably be considered that the means chosen were suitable for achieving that aim.

Jørgensen v   **[2000] IRLR 726 ECJ**
Foreningen af Speciallæger
Budgetary considerations cannot in themselves justify discrimination on grounds of sex. Although budgetary considerations may underlie a Member State's choice of social policy and influence the nature or scope of the social protection measures which it wishes to adopt, they do not in themselves constitute an aim pursued by that policy and cannot therefore justify discrimination against one of the sexes.

Kutz-Bauer v   **[2003] IRLR 368 ECJ**
Freie und Hansestadt Hamburg
An employer cannot justify discrimination solely because avoidance of such discrimination would involve increased costs.

Kachelmann v   **[2001] IRLR 49 ECJ**
Bankhaus Hermann Lampe KG
The Equal Treatment Directive does not preclude a selection process for dismissal when a part-time job is abolished on economic grounds that does not compare full-time workers with part-time workers, even though this may create an indirect disadvantage for part-time workers. If comparability between full-time and part-time workers were to be introduced in the selection process, that would have the effect of placing part-time workers at an advantage, while putting full-time workers at a disadvantage since, in the event of their jobs being abolished, part-time workers would have to be offered a full-time job, even if their employment contract did not entitle them to one.

Sanctions

Member States shall introduce into their national legal systems such measures as are necessary to ensure real and effective compensation or reparation as the Member States so determine for the loss and damage sustained by a person injured as a result of discrimination contrary to Article 3, in a way which is dissuasive and proportionate to the damage suffered; such compensation or reparation may not be restricted by the fixing of a prior upper limit, except in cases where the employer can prove that the only damage suffered by a claimant as a result of discrimination within the meaning of this Directive is the refusal to take his/her job application into consideration.

EQUAL TREATMENT DIRECTIVE 2006/54 – Article 18

Coote v   **[1998] IRLR 656 ECJ**
Granada Hospitality Ltd
By virtue of [Article 18], all persons have the right to obtain an effective remedy in a competent court against measures which they consider interfere with the equal treatment for men and women laid down in the Directive. It is for the Member States to ensure effective judicial control of compliance with the applicable provisions of Community law and of national legislation intended to give effect to the rights for which the Directive provides.

Marshall v   **[1993] IRLR 445 ECJ**
Southampton and South-West Hampshire
   Area Health Authority (No.2)
[Article 18] of EC Equal Treatment Directive 76/207 must be interpreted as meaning that compensation for the loss and damage sustained by a victim of discrimination may not be limited by national law to an upper limit fixed a priori or by excluding an award of interest to compensate for the loss sustained by the recipient as a result of the effluxion of time until the capital sum awarded is actually paid. Financial compensation must be adequate, in that it must enable the loss and damage actually sustained as a result of discrimination to be made good in full in accordance with the applicable national rules.

Marshall v   **[1993] IRLR 445 ECJ**
Southampton and South-West Hampshire
   Area Health Authority (No.2)
[Article 18] of the Equal Treatment Directive may be relied upon by individuals before the national courts as against an authority of the State acting in its capacity as an employer in order to set aside a national provision which imposes limits on the amount of compensation recoverable by way of reparation.

Dekker v   **[1991] IRLR 27 ECJ**
VJV-Centrum
The Equal Treatment Directive does not make the liability of the discriminator in any way dependent upon evidence of fault on the part of the employer, nor require that it be established that there are no grounds for justification which he can take advantage of. Accordingly, where a Member State chooses a civil law sanction, any breach of the prohibition of discrimination must in itself be sufficient to impose full liability on the discriminator and no account can be taken of grounds for justification provided for under national law.

Dræhmpæhl v   **[1997] IRLR 538 ECJ**
Urania Immobilenservice ohG
The Equal Treatment Directive precludes provisions of domestic law which, unlike other provisions of domestic civil and labour law, place an upper limit of three months' salary for the job in question as the amount of compensation which may be claimed by a claimant discriminated against on grounds of sex in the making of an appointment, where that claimant would have obtained the vacant position if the

selection process had been carried out without discrimination. A Member State must ensure that infringements of Community law are penalised under procedural and substantive conditions which are analogous to those applicable to infringements of domestic law of a similar nature and importance.

EC law and UK law

General principles

Webb v   [1993] IRLR 27 HL
EMO Air Cargo (UK) Ltd
Although an EC Directive does not have direct effect upon the relationship between a worker and an employer who is not an emanation of the State, it is for a United Kingdom court to construe domestic legislation in any field covered by a Community Directive so as to accord with the interpretation of the Directive as laid down by the European Court, if that can be done without distorting the meaning of the domestic legislation. That is so whether the domestic legislation came after or preceded the Directive. However, as the European Court said in the *Marleasing* case, a national court must construe a domestic law to accord with the terms of a Directive in the same field only if it is possible to do so. That means that the domestic law must be open to an interpretation consistent with the Directive.

Porter v   [1993] IRLR 329 NICA
Cannon Hygiene Ltd
If in a given situation there are two possible interpretations of a provision in national law and one of them accords with the wording and purpose of a relevant EC Directive while the other does not do so, the national court's duty under the EC Treaty is to prefer the interpretation which accords with the Directive. However, there is no "usual method of interpretation" which enables or permits a court simply to disregard a statutory provision or interpret it in a sense directly opposite to that which the House of Lords has said is the correct interpretation.

EXCLUSIONS AND EXCEPTIONS

Meaning of "employment"

(1) In this Act, unless the context otherwise requires –
  "employment" means employment under a contract of service or of apprenticeship or a contract personally to execute any work or labour, and related expressions shall be construed accordingly;
                    SEX DISCRIMINATION ACT – s.82
                         RACE RELATIONS ACT – s.78
                    ➡ EQUALITY ACT 2010 – s.83

Muschett v   [2010] IRLR 451 CA
HM Prison Service
Mutuality of obligation is not a condition of a contract for services.

Mirror Group Newspapers Ltd v   [1986] IRLR 27 CA
Gunning
The words "a contract personally to execute any work or labour" in the extended definition of "employment" in s.82(1) of the Sex Discrimination Act contemplates a contract whose dominant purpose is that the party contracting to provide services under it performs personally the work or labour which forms the subject-matter of the contract. What falls to be determined, therefore, looking at the contract as a whole, is firstly whether there is some obligation by one contracting party personally to execute any work or labour and, secondly, whether that is the dominant purpose of the contract. The word "any" in the phrase "a contract personally to execute any work or labour" refers to the kind of work or labour to be performed rather than the amount or quantity. Therefore, it could not be accepted that any obligation personally to execute any work or labour, however limited in amount the work or labour might be, is sufficient to bring the contract containing that obligation within the statutory definition.

Mingeley v   [2004] IRLR 373 CA
Pennock and Ivory
On the plain words of the statute and the authorities, a claimant has to establish that his contract placed him under an obligation "personally to execute any work or labour".

Quinnen v   [1984] IRLR 227 EAT
Hovells
The inclusion in the definition of "employment" in s.82(1) of the Sex Discrimination Act of a third limb covering employment under "a contract personally to execute any work or labour" is a wide and flexible concept and was intended to enlarge upon the ordinary connotation of "employment" so as to include persons outside the master-servant relationship.

BP Chemicals Ltd v   **[1995] IRLR 128 EAT**
Gillick

The extended definition of "employment" in s.82, referring to employment under a contract personally to execute work, must be taken to refer to a contract between the party doing the work and the party for whom the work is done. A contract worker does not enter into an "employment" relationship with the principal.

Percy v   **[2006] IRLR 195 HL**
Church of Scotland Board of National Mission

An associate minister's relationship with the Church of Scotland constituted "employment" within the meaning of s.82(1) of the Sex Discrimination Act in that she was employed under a contract "personally to execute" work. Accordingly, she was entitled to bring her claim of sex discrimination against the church in an employment tribunal.

Percy v   **[2006] IRLR 195 HL**
Church of Scotland Board of National Mission

Holding an office and being an employee are not inconsistent. A person may hold an "office" on the terms of, and pursuant to, a contract of employment.

Hall v   **[2000] IRLR 578 CA**
Woolston Hall Leisure Ltd

Where the performance by the employer of a contract of employment involves illegality of which the employee is aware, public policy does not bar the employee, when discriminated against on grounds of sex by dismissal, from recovering compensation under the Sex Discrimination Act. A complaint of sex discrimination by dismissal is not based on the contract of employment. Although the employee must establish that she was employed and was dismissed from that employment, it is the sex discrimination which is the core of the complaint. The correct approach is for the tribunal to consider whether the claimant's claim arises out of or is so inextricably bound up with her illegal conduct that the court could not permit the claimant to recover compensation without appearing to condone that conduct.

Claim in time

An employment tribunal shall not consider a complaint under [s.63 – SDA; s.54 – RRA] unless it is presented to the tribunal before the end of the period of three months beginning when the act complained of was done . . .

A court or tribunal may nevertheless consider any such complaint, claim or application which is out of time if, in all the circumstances of the case, it considers that it is just and equitable to do so.

For the purposes of this section –

> *(a) When the inclusion of any term in a contract renders the making of the contract an unlawful act, that act shall be treated as extending throughout the duration of the contract; and*

> *(b) any act extending over a period shall be treated as done at the end of that period; and*

> *(c) a deliberate omission shall be treated as done when the person in question decided upon it;*

and in the absence of evidence establishing the contrary a person shall be taken for the purposes of this section to decide upon an omission when he does an act inconsistent with doing the omitted act or, if he has done no such inconsistent act, when the period expires within which he might reasonably have been expected to do the omitted act if it was to be done.

SEX DISCRIMINATION ACT – s.76(1), (5), (6)
RACE RELATIONS ACT – s.68(1), (6), (7)
➡ EQUALITY ACT 2010 – s.123

Dodd v   **[1988] IRLR 16 EAT**
British Telecom plc

An originating application is "presented" when the application arrives at the Office of Employment Tribunals. In order to commence proceedings, it is not necessary for the application to be registered by the Office of Employment Tribunals.

Dodd v   **[1988] IRLR 16 EAT**
British Telecom plc

In order to be a valid complaint sufficient to stop time running, the written application must contain sufficient to identify who is making it and against whom it is made, and must contain sufficient to show what sort of complaint it is. An application whose contents did not comply with those broad minimum requirements would not be capable of being described as an originating application at all. However, the requirements of rule 1(a), (b) and (c) of the Employment Tribunals Rules of Procedure, which specify that an originating application shall set out the name and address of the claimant and of the person against whom relief is sought and the grounds, with particulars thereof, on which relief is sought, are not mandatory but are directory only. Therefore, where an application indicates that the claimant is making a complaint of discrimination in relation to her rejection for a particular post, a failure to specify whether the complaint is of sex discrimination or race discrimination or both is not fatal to the efficacy of the originating application.

Ali v   **[2005] IRLR 201 CA**
Office of National Statistics

Direct discrimination is one type of unlawful act and indirect discrimination is a different type of unlawful act. Accordingly, a claimant who alleged on his originating application that he had been less favourably treated on racial grounds needed permission to amend his claim of race discrimination to add a claim of indirect discrimination since this was a new claim, which was brought out of time.

Clarke v   **[1991] IRLR 490 EAT**
Hampshire Electro-plating Co Ltd

In determining when "the act complained of was done", the question is whether the cause of action had crystallised on the relevant date, not whether the complainant felt that he had suffered discrimination on that date. The phrase "the act complained of was done" indicates that there was at that time an act of discrimination and that the cause of action could properly be said to be complete at that time, because otherwise there would be no point in bringing proceedings. Every case must depend upon its own facts as to the clarity of the crystallisation of any cause of action.

Virdi v   **[2007] IRLR 24 EAT**
Commissioner of Police of the Metropolis
An act is "done" when it is completed and the act is complete for the purpose of the time limitation when the decision is taken rather than when it is communicated.

Cast v   **[1998] IRLR 318 CA**
Croydon College
A decision by an employer may be a separate act of discrimination for time limit purposes, whether or not it is made on the same facts as before, providing it results from a further consideration of the matter and is not merely a reference back to an earlier decision. If the matter is reconsidered in response to a further request, time begins to run again. Therefore, the appellant's complaint that the respondents had discriminated against her on grounds of sex by refusing to permit her to work part-time after she returned from maternity leave was not out of time, even though her request to work part-time was first refused prior to her maternity leave, and her originating application was not submitted until after she returned from maternity leave when her further requests to work part-time were again refused. Each decision amounted to a fresh refusal of a fresh request to work part time.

Swithland Motors plc v   **[1994] IRLR 276 EAT**
Clarke
An unlawful act of discrimination by omitting to offer employment cannot be committed until the alleged discriminator is in a position to offer such employment. Accordingly, the only sensible construction of s.76(6)(c) of the Sex Discrimination Act, which provides that "a deliberate omission shall be treated as done when the person in question decided upon it", is that "decides" means "decides at a time and in circumstances when he is in a position to implement that decision" and not "decides on the hypothetical basis that he will implement the decision when and if circumstances arise in which he is able to do so".

Aniagwu v   **[1999] IRLR 303 EAT**
London Borough of Hackney
A claimant must be able to identify the detriment to which he has been subjected before he can present a complaint. Therefore, the time limit for bringing a complaint of discrimination in respect of an employer's refusal to accept a grievance began to run from the date the decision of a grievance panel was communicated to the employee rather than the date on which that decision was taken.

Adekeye v   **[1993] IRLR 324 EAT**
Post Office
If a dismissed black employee complains that he or she did not succeed upon an internal appeal in circumstances where a white comparator would have succeeded such that there is an allegation of unlawful discrimination on racial grounds in the result of the appeal, that is an "act complained of".

Extension

Robertson v   **[2003] IRLR 434 CA**
Bexley Community Centre
An employment tribunal has a very wide discretion in determining whether or not it is just and equitable to extend time. It is entitled to consider anything that it considers relevant. However, time limits are exercised strictly in employment cases. When tribunals consider their discretion to consider a claim out of time on just and equitable grounds, there is no presumption that they should do so unless they can justify failure to exercise the discretion. On the contrary, a tribunal cannot hear a complaint unless the claimant convinces it that it is just and equitable to extend time. The exercise of discretion is thus the exception rather than the rule.

Chief Constable of Lincolnshire   **[2010] IRLR 327 CA**
   Police v
Caston
The statement in *Robertson v Bexley Community Centre* has been latched on to by commentators as offering "guidance", but in essence is an elegant repetition of well-established principles relating to the exercise of a judicial discretion. What the case does is to emphasise the employment tribunal's wide discretion.

Hutchison v   **[1977] IRLR 69 EAT**
Westward Television Ltd
The formula provided by s.76(5) of the Sex Discrimination Act allowing an employment tribunal to consider a complaint which is out of time "if, in all the circumstances of the case, it considers that it is just and equitable to do so", entitles the tribunal to take into account anything which it judges to be relevant. The employment tribunal is to do what it thinks is fair in the circumstances.

Mills v   **[1998] IRLR 494 EAT**
Marshall
The words "just and equitable" in the discrimination legislation giving power to extend time could not be wider or more general. The discretion to extend time is unfettered and may include a consideration of the date from which the complainant could reasonably have become aware of her right to present a worthwhile complaint.

London Borough of Southwark v   **[2003] IRLR 220 CA**
Afolabi
In considering whether it is just and equitable to extend

time, a tribunal is not required to go through the matters listed in s.33(3) of the Limitation Act 1980, provided that no significant factor has been left out of account by the tribunal in exercising its discretion.

Mills v Marshall [1998] IRLR 494 EAT

Where a person was reasonably unaware of the fact that they had the right to being proceedings until shortly before the complaint was filed, whether it is just and equitable to extend time is for the employment tribunal to determine, balancing all the relevant factors, including whether it is possible to have a fair trial of the issues raised by the complaint. Unawareness of the right to sue might stem from a failure by the lawyers to appreciate that a claim lay, or because the law "changed" or was differently perceived after a decision of another court.

Chohan v Derby Law Centre [2004] IRLR 685 EAT

Delay in bringing a claim in time due to incorrect legal advice ought not defeat a claimant's contention that the claim ought to be heard. The failure by a legal adviser to enter proceedings in time should not be visited upon the claimant for otherwise the defendant would be in receipt of a windfall.

British Coal Corporation v Keeble [1997] IRLR 336 EAT

It was "just and equitable" to allow the claimants to bring their complaints under Sex Discrimination Act concerning a discriminatory voluntary redundancy payment scheme outside the requisite three-month time limit, notwithstanding that the reason for the delay was the claimants' mistake of law as to their position. If the only reason for a long delay is a wholly understandable misapprehension of the law, that must have been a matter which Parliament intended the tribunal to take into account when considering "all the circumstances of the case". The statement in *Biggs v Somerset County Council* that "it would be contrary to the principle of legal certainty to allow past transactions to be reopened and limitation periods to be circumvented because the existing law at the relevant time had not been explained or had not been fully understood" was intended to apply only in the context of the time limit provisions relating to unfair dismissal and the consideration of whether it was "reasonably practicable" for the claimant to present her complaint in time. The discretion conferred by s.76(5) of the Sex Discrimination Act is very much wider than relating to unfair dismissal.

Apelogun-Gabriels v London Borough of Lambeth [2002] IRLR 116 CA

The correct law for whether it is just and equitable to extend the time limit for presenting a discrimination complaint which is out of time because the claimant was pursuing internal proceedings was laid down by *Robinson v Post*

Office rather than by *Aniagwu v London Borough of Hackney*. The fact, if it be so, that the employee had deferred proceedings in the tribunal while awaiting the outcome of domestic proceedings is only one factor to be taken into account. To the extent that *Aniagwu* lays down some general principle that one should always await the outcome of internal grievance procedures before embarking on litigation, it was plainly wrong.

Robinson v Post Office [2000] IRLR 904 EAT

When delay on account of an incomplete internal appeal is relied upon as a reason for failing to lodge a tribunal application in time, it will ordinarily suffice for the employment tribunal to put this into the balance when the justice and equity of the matter is being considered.

Hutchison v Westward Television Ltd [1977] IRLR 69 EAT

The words "in all the circumstances of the case" in s.76(5) refer to the actual facts of the matter in so far as they are relevant to the matter under consideration in s.76(5). The employment tribunal is not required to hear the entire case before making its decision as to whether time should be extended, although it may want to form some fairly rough idea as to whether it is a strong complaint or a weak complaint.

Dimtsu v Westminster City Council [1991] IRLR 450 EAT

An employment tribunal is not obliged to raise the question of whether a complainant wishes to apply under s.68(6) of the Race Relations Act for an extension of the time limit, so as to enable events which took place more than three months before the originating application was presented to form part of the substantive complaint, in circumstances in which the complainant's representative had not requested an extension of the time limit.

Continuing discrimination

Barclays Bank plc v Kapur [1991] IRLR 136 HL

To maintain a continuing regime which adversely affects an employee is an act which continues so long as it is maintained.

Hendricks v Commissioner of Police for the Metropolis [2003] IRLR 96 CA

In determining whether there was "an act extending over a period", as distinct from a succession of unconnected or isolated specific acts, for which time would begin to run from the date when each specific act was committed, the focus should be on the substance of the complaints that the employer was responsible for an ongoing situation or a continuing state of affairs. The concepts of policy, rule, practice, scheme or regime in the authorities were given as examples of when an act extends over a period. They should not be treated as a complete and constricting statement of the indicia of "an act extending over a period".

Robertson v   **[2003] IRLR 434 CA**
Bexley Community Centre
To establish a continuing act it must be shown that the employer had a practice, policy, rule or regime governing the act said to constitute it.

Cast v   **[1998] IRLR 318 CA**
Croydon College
Application of a discriminatory policy or regime pursuant to which decisions may be taken from time to time is an act extending over a period. There can be a policy even though it is not of a formal nature or expressed in writing, and even though it is confined to a particular post or role.

Cast v   **[1997] IRLR 14 EAT**
Croydon College
The mere repetition of a request cannot convert a single managerial decision into a policy, practice or rule.

Hendricks v   **[2003] IRLR 96 CA**
Commissioner of Police for the Metropolis
The burden is on the claimant to prove, either by direct evidence or by inference from primary facts, that alleged incidents of discrimination were linked to one another and were evidence of a continuing discriminatory state of affairs covered by the concept of "an act extending over a period."

Tyagi v   **[2001] IRLR 465 CA**
BBC World Service
A job claimant cannot complain of a policy of "continuing discrimination" extending over a period. The statutory language relating to selection arrangements, which refers to discrimination in the arrangements which the employer makes "for the purpose of determining who should be offered that employment", makes it clear that what is being complained about is not employment generally but the particular employment that is being offered.

Examples

Barclays Bank plc v   **[1991] IRLR 136 HL**
Kapur
An employer's refusal to allow an employee's previous service to count towards a pension is an "act extending over a period" within the meaning of s.68(7)(b) of the Race Relations Act rather than a "deliberate omission" within the meaning of s.68(7)(c). A man works not only for his current wage but also for his pension and to require him to work on

less favourable terms as to pension is as much a continuing act as to require him to work for lower wages.

Sougrin v   **[1992] IRLR 416 CA**
Haringey Health Authority
In *Kapur*, in stating that there would be a continuing act lasting throughout the period of employment if an employer continued to pay lower wages to coloured employees, Lord Griffiths was clearly referring to the case of an employer who has a policy of paying coloured employees less than their white counterparts.

Sougrin v   **[1992] IRLR 416 CA**
Haringey Health Authority
A grading decision is a one-off act with continuing consequences rather than a continuing act of discrimination.

Rovenska v   **[1997] IRLR 367 CA**
General Medical Council
If the General Medical Council's regime for exemption from a test set for registration as a medical practitioner was indirectly discriminatory, then it would be committing an act of unlawful discrimination on every occasion that it refused to allow the claimant limited registration without first taking the test.

Owusu v   **[1995] IRLR 574 EAT**
London Fire & Civil Defence Authority
In alleging a failure by the employers over a number of years to re-grade him and a failure to give him an opportunity to act-up when such opportunities arose, the complainant was alleging a continuing act in the form of maintaining a practice which resulted in consistent discriminatory decisions.

Calder v   **[1989] IRLR 55 EAT**
James Finlay Corporation Ltd
By constituting a mortgage subsidy scheme under the rules of which a woman could not obtain benefit, the employers were discriminating against the appellant woman in the way they afforded her "access" to the benefit. It followed that so long as she remained in the employers' employ, there was a continuing discrimination against her. Alternatively, it could be said that so long as her employment continued, the employers were subjecting her to "any other detriment". As the rule of the scheme constituted a discriminatory act extending over the period of the appellant's employment, it was therefore to be treated as having been done at the end of her employment rather than on the last occasion on which she was deliberately refused access to the scheme. Consequently, as her complaint had been presented within three months of leaving her employment, the employment tribunal had jurisdiction to entertain it.

Littlewoods Organisation plc v   **[1993] IRLR 154 EAT**
Traynor
A complaint of racial discrimination in respect of alleged racial abuse was not out of time, notwithstanding that the last

incident took place more than three months before the complaint was filed, in circumstances in which remedial measures promised by the employers had not been fully implemented when the respondent resigned and made his complaint to the tribunal. So long as the remedial measures which had been agreed on were not actually taken, a situation capable of involving racial discrimination continued and allowing that situation to continue amounted to a continuing act.

Barclays Bank plc v   **[1991] IRLR 136 HL**
Kapur
A "deliberate omission" in s.68(7)(c) of the Race Relations Act was included by the draftsman as a sweeping-up provision intended for the protection of employees and addressed to activities peripheral to the employment rather than to the terms of the employment itself. It was intended to cover a one-off, rather than a continuing situation.

Agreement precluding complaint

(3) A term in a contract which purports to exclude or limit any provision of this Act [or the Equal Pay Act 1970 – SDA] is unenforceable by any person in whose favour the term would operate apart from this subsection.
(4) Subsection (3) does not apply –
> *(a) to a contract settling a complaint to which [s.63(1) of this Act or s.2 of the Equal Pay Act – SDA; s.54(1) – RRA] applies where the contract is made with the assistance of a conciliation officer;*
> *(aa) to a contract settling a complaint to which [s.63(1) of this Act or s.2 of the Equal Pay Act – SDA; s.54(1) – RRA] applies if the conditions regulating compromise contracts under this Act are satisfied in relation to the contract;*
> *(b) to a contract settling a claim which [s.66 – SDA; s.57 – RRA] applies.*
(4A) The conditions regulating compromise contracts under this Act are that –
> *(b) the contract must relate to the particular complaint.*
> > **SEX DISCRIMINATION ACT – s.77**
> > **RACE RELATIONS ACT – s.72**
> > ➡ **EQUALITY ACT 2010 – s.144, s.147**

Clarke v   **[2006] IRLR 324 EAT**
Redcar & Cleveland Borough Council
Where the parties make a contract that follows any attempt by an ACAS conciliation officer to promote a settlement, the contract is made with the assistance of that ACAS officer. Whether a settlement is effective to preclude a claim being brought before a tribunal depends on whether what the ACAS officer has done corresponds to the functions which a conciliation officer has a duty, or power, to discharge. In determining whether the conciliation officer exercised her functions in order to effect a valid conciliation contract, the following principles apply:

a. The ACAS officer has no responsibility to see that the terms of the settlement are fair on the employee.

b. The expression "promote a settlement" must be given a liberal construction capable of covering whatever action by way of such promotion as is applicable in the circumstances of the particular case.

c. The ACAS officer must never advise as to the merits of the case.

d. It is not for the tribunal to consider whether the officer correctly interpreted her duties; it is sufficient that the officer intended and purported to act under the section.

e. If the ACAS officer were to act in bad faith or adopt unfair methods when promoting a settlement, the agreement might be set aside and might not operate as a bar to proceedings.

Clarke v   **[2006] IRLR 324 EAT**
Redcar & Cleveland Borough Council
An ACAS conciliation officer is not under a duty to give advice, to evaluate the claims or to ensure that the claimants understand the nature and extent of all their potential claims.

Lunt v   **[1999] IRLR 458 EAT**
Merseyside TEC Ltd
The requirement in s.77(4A)(b) of the Sex Discrimination Act that a compromise agreement "must relate to the particular complaint" is not limited to complaints that have been presented to an employment tribunal. However, a "blanket" agreement compromising claims which had never been indicated in the past is not permitted.

Lunt v   **[1999] IRLR 458 EAT**
Merseyside TEC Ltd
A single compromise agreement can cover claims under more than one statute.

Mayo-Deman v   **[2005] IRLR 845 EAT**
University of Greenwich
There is nothing in law which requires an employment tribunal to ensure that settlement terms agreed between the parties amount to a compromise agreement complying with the terms of s.77(4A) of the Sex Discrimination Act and s.72(4A) of the Race Relations Act before it permits a claim to be dismissed when the parties have reached what is otherwise a contractual agreement.

Work ordinarily outside Great Britain

(1) For the purposes of this Part and s.1 of the Equal Pay Act 1970 ("the relevant purposes"), employment is to be regarded as being at an establishment in Great Britain if –
> *(a) the employee does his work wholly or partly in Great Britain, or*
> *(b) the employee does his work wholly outside Great Britain and subsection (1A) applies.*

(1A) This subsection applies if –
  (a) the employer has a place of business at an establishment in Great Britain,
  (b) the work is for the purposes of the business carried on at that establishment, and
  (c) the employee is ordinarily resident in Great Britain –
    (i) at the time when he applies for or is offered the employment, or
    (ii) at any time during the course of the employment.

SEX DISCRIMINATION ACT 1975 (as amended) – s.10
[Note: These provisions remain in force only for seamen.]

(1) For the purposes of this Part, employment is to be regarded as being at an establishment in Great Britain if the employee –
  (a) does his work wholly or partly in Great Britain; or
  (b) does his work wholly outside Great Britain and subsection (1A) applies.

(1A) This subsection applies if, in a case involving discrimination on grounds of race or ethnic or national origins, or harassment –
  (a) the employer has a place of business at an establishment in Great Britain;
  (b) the work is for the purposes of the business carried on at that establishment; and
  (c) the employee is ordinarily resident in Great Britain –
    (i) at the time when he applies for or is offered the employment, or
    (ii) at any time during the course of the employment.

RACE RELATIONS ACT 1976 (as amended) – s.8
[Note: These provisions remain in force only for seamen.]

Neary v   **[2010] EqLR 26 EAT**
Service Children's Education
A person's "ordinary residence" is the place or country that a person has adopted voluntarily and for settled purposes as part of the regular order of his life.

Ministry of Defence v   **[2010] EqLR 33 EAT**
Wallis
Where an employee of international schools had directly effective rights under the Equal Treatment Directive, it was necessary for the court to qualify the territorial limitation in the Sex Discrimination Act in order to give effect to those EU law rights.

Saggar v   **[2005] IRLR 618 CA**
Ministry of Defence
In determining whether or not a claimant worked wholly outside Great Britain, the relevant period is the whole period of employment.

Deria v   **[1986] IRLR 108 CA**
General Council of British Shipping
Whether there has been a refusal to offer employment "at an establishment in Great Britain" so as to confer jurisdiction under the Race Relations Act is to be determined by what was contemplated by the parties at the date of the act complained of. Therefore, s.8(1) and (2) of the Act can be construed as meaning that "employment is to be regarded as being at an establishment in Great Britain unless the employee does *or is to do* his work wholly outside Great Britain".

Tradition Securities and   **[2008] IRLR 934 EAT**
Futures SA v
X
The right to bring a discrimination claim before an employment tribunal is determined by reference to the claimant's situation at the time of the alleged unlawful discrimination. The concept of a continuing act of discrimination cannot confer jurisdiction retrospectively. Therefore, a tribunal had no jurisdiction to consider a claim by a French employee of a French company that she was unlawfully sexually harassed when she was employed wholly outside Great Britain prior to transferring to England.

Bossa v   **[1998] IRLR 284 EAT**
Nordstress Ltd
Article 48 of the EC Treaty, which provides that freedom of movement of workers entails "the abolition of any discrimination based on nationality between workers of the Member States" as regards employment, has direct effect. The provisions of the Race Relations Act excluding a complaint relating to employment outside Great Britain must be disapplied where there is a conflict with the right to freedom of movement established by Article 48. Therefore, a tribunal had jurisdiction to hear the appellant's complaint that he had been discriminated against on grounds of nationality contrary to the Race Relations Act when he was not interviewed by an employer in Great Britain for a post based in Italy because he held Italian nationality.

Immunity

Heath v   **[2005] IRLR 270 CA**
Commissioner of Police for the
  Metropolis
Proceedings before a police disciplinary board constituted under the Police (Discipline) Regulations are sufficiently "judicial" to fall within the rule of absolute immunity from suit that attaches to judicial or quasi-judicial proceedings and excludes complaints about unlawful discriminatory conduct in the course of such proceedings to other judicial bodies, including employment tribunals.

Death of claimant

Harris v   **[2000] IRLR 320 CA**
Lewisham & Guys
  Mental Health NHS Trust
A complaint brought under the discrimination statutes survives the death of the complainant.

Bankruptcy of claimant

Khan v   **[2004] IRLR 961 CA**
Trident Safeguards Ltd

A claim for race discrimination is a "hybrid" claim, since it includes both a claim for pecuniary loss, which is property that is part of the bankrupt's estate, and a claim for injury to feelings, which is "personal" and does not form part of the bankrupt's estate, and therefore the whole of the hybrid claim vests in the trustee in bankruptcy in accordance with the decision in *Ord v Upton*. However, there is a public interest in claims of race discrimination being fully examined. Therefore, a bankrupt should be permitted to limit their claim for relief to a declaration and compensation for injury to feelings only. If that is done, the claim ceases to be a hybrid one.

Acts done under statutory authority

(1) Nothing in the following provisions, namely –
    (a) Part II,
    (b) Part III so far as it applies to vocational training, or
    (c) Part IV so far as it has effect in relation to the provisions mentioned in paragraphs (a) and (b),
shall render unlawful any act done by a person in relation to a woman if –
    (i) it was necessary for that person to do it in order to comply with a requirement of an existing statutory provision concerning the protection of women, or
    (ii) it was necessary for that person to do it in order to comply with a requirement of a relevant statutory provision (within the meaning of Part I of the Health and Safety at Work etc Act 1974) and it was done by that person for the purpose of the protection of the woman in question (or of any class of women that included that woman).

(2) In subsection (1) –
    (a) the reference in paragraph (i) of that subsection to an existing statutory provision concerning the protection of women is a reference to any such provision having effect for the purpose of protecting women as regards –
    (i) pregnancy or maternity, or
    (ii) other circumstances giving rise to risks specifically affecting women,
whether the provision relates only to such protection or to the protection of any other class of persons as well; and
    (b) the reference in paragraph (ii) of that subsection to the protection of a particular woman or class of women is a reference to the protection of that woman or those women as regards any circumstances falling within paragraph (a)(i) or (ii) above.

(3) In this section "existing statutory provision" means (subject to subsection (4)) any provision of –
    (a) an Act passed before this Act, or
    (b) an instrument approved or made by or under such an Act (including one approved or made after the passing of this Act).

(4) Where an Act passed after this Act re-enacts (with or without modification) a provision of an Act passed before this Act, that provision as re-enacted shall be treated for the purpose of subsection (3) as if it continued to be contained in an Act passed before this Act.

A(1) Nothing in –
    (a) the relevant provisions of Part III, or
    (b) Part IV so far as it has effect in relation to those provisions,
shall render unlawful any act done by a person if it was necessary for that person to do it in order to comply with a requirement of an existing statutory provision within the meaning of s.51.

(2) In subsection (1) "the relevant provisions of Part III" means the provisions of that Part except so far as they apply to vocational training.

SEX DISCRIMINATION ACT – s.51
➡ **EQUALITY ACT 2010 – Sch. 23, para. 1**

(1) Nothing in Parts II to IV shall render unlawful any act of discrimination done –
    (a) in pursuance of any enactment or Order in Council; or
    (b) in pursuance of any instrument made under any enactment by a Minister of the Crown; or
    (c) in order to comply with any condition or requirement imposed by a Minister of the Crown (whether before or after the passing of this Act) by virtue of any enactment.
References in this section to an enactment, Order in Council or instrument include an enactment, Order in Council or instrument passed or made after the passing of this Act.

(1A) Subsection (1) does not apply to an act which is unlawful, on grounds of race or ethnic or national origins, by virtue of a provision referred to in section 1(1B).

(2) Nothing in Parts II to IV shall render unlawful any act whereby a person discriminates against another on the basis of that other's nationality or place of ordinary residence or the length of time for which he has been present or resident in or outside the United Kingdom or an area within the United Kingdom, if that act is done –
    (a) in pursuance of any enactment or Order in Council; or
    (b) in pursuance of any instrument made under any enactment by a Minister of the Crown; or
    (c) in order to comply with any requirement imposed by a Minister of the Crown (whether before or after the passing of this Act) by virtue of any enactment; or
    (d) in pursuance of any arrangements made (whether before or after the passing of this Act) by or with the approval of, or for the time being approved by, a Minister of the Crown; or
    (e) in order to comply with any condition imposed (whether before or after the passing of this Act) by a Minister of the Crown.

RACE RELATIONS ACT 1976 (as amended) – s.41
➡ **EQUALITY ACT 2010 – Sch. 23, para. 1**

Hampson v   **[1990] IRLR 302 HL**
Department of Education and Science
The words "in pursuance of any instrument" are confined to acts done in necessary performance of an express obligation contained in the instrument and do not also include acts done in exercise of a power or discretion conferred by the instrument. An act is done "in pursuance of" an enactment, order or instrument only if it is specified in the enactment, order or instrument.

Page v   **[1981] IRLR 13 EAT**
Freighthire (Tank Haulage) Ltd
The interests of safety are not a justification for discrimination on grounds of sex unless the act was done to comply with a pre-existing statutory requirement within the meaning of s.51 of the Sex Discrimination Act.

Page v   **[1981] IRLR 13 EAT**
Freighthire (Tank Haulage) Ltd
In order to satisfy the test of s.51, an employer does not have to show that debarring a woman from taking up a job was inexorably the only method available to him of satisfying the requirements of the Health and Safety at Work Act to ensure, so far as is reasonably practicable, the health, safety and welfare at work of his employees. It is important to consider all the circumstances of the case, the risk involved and the measures which it can be said are reasonably necessary to eliminate the risk. There may be cases where one course which is suggested as being sufficient may leave open some doubt as to whether it is going to achieve the desired level of protection. In such a case, it may be that an employer is complying with the requirements of the legislation if, in all the circumstances, he thinks it right not to allow an employee, for his (or her) own protection or safety, to do the particular job.

Amnesty International v   **[2009] IRLR 884 EAT**
Ahmed
The effect of s.41(1A) is to disapply s.41(1) in the case of all discrimination (direct or indirect) within the scope of the Race Directive.

> **Race discrimination**

Genuine occupational requirements

(1) In relation to discrimination on grounds of race or ethnic or national origins –
    (a) section 4(1)(a) or (c) does not apply to any employment; and
    (b) section 4(2)(b) does not apply to promotion or transfer to, or training for, any employment; and

    (c) section 4(2)(c) does not apply to dismissal from any employment;
where subsection (2) applies.

(2) This subsection applies where, having regard to the nature of the employment or the context in which it is carried out –
    (a) being of a particular race or of particular ethnic or national origins is a genuine and determining occupational requirement;
    (b) it is proportionate to apply that requirement in the particular case; and
    (c) either –
        (i) the person to whom that requirement is applied does not meet it, or
        (ii) the employer is not satisfied, and in all the circumstances it is reasonable for him not to be satisfied, that that person meets it.".
        RACE RELATIONS ACT 1976 (as amended) – s.4A
        ➡ **EQUALITY ACT 2010 – Sch. 9, para. 1**

(1) In relation to racial discrimination in cases where s.4A does not apply –
    (a) s.4(1)(a) or (c) does not apply to any employment where being of a particular racial group is a genuine occupational qualification for the job; and
    (b) s.4(2)(b) does not apply to opportunities for promotion or transfer to, or training for, such employment.

(2) Being of a particular racial group is a genuine occupational qualification for a job only where –
    (a) the job involves participation in a dramatic performance or other entertainment in a capacity for which a person of that racial group is required for reasons of authenticity; or
    (b) the job involves participation as an artist's or photographic model in the production of a work of art, visual image or sequence of visual images for which a person of that racial group is required for reasons of authenticity; or
    (c) the job involves working in a place where food or drink is (for payment or not) provided to and consumed by members of the public or a section of the public in a particular setting for which, in that job, a person of that racial group is required for reasons of authenticity; or
    (d) the holder of the job provides persons of that racial group with personal services promoting their welfare, and those services can most effectively be provided by a person of that racial group.

(3) Subsection (2) applies where some only of the duties of the job fall within paragraph (a), (b), (c) or (d) as well as where all of them do.

(4) Paragraph (a), (b), (c) or (d) of subsection (2) does not apply in relation to the filling of a vacancy at a time when the employer already has employees of the racial group in question –
    (a) who are capable of carrying out the duties falling within that paragraph; and
    (b) whom it would be reasonable to employ on those duties; and
    (c) whose numbers are sufficient to meet the employer's likely requirements in respect of these duties without undue inconvenience.
        RACE RELATIONS ACT – s.5
        ➡ **EQUALITY ACT 2010 – Sch. 9, para. 1**

London Borough of Lambeth v   **[1989] IRLR 379 EAT**
CRE

Section 5 provides an exception to s.4, and as a matter of principle should be narrowly or strictly construed. Section 5(2), in setting out the genuine occupational qualification exceptions, uses the word "only".

Tottenham Green Under-Fives'   **[1989] IRLR 147 EAT**
    Centre v
Marshall

In construing s.5 an employment tribunal needs to carry out a delicate balancing exercise, bearing in mind the need to guard against discrimination and the desirability of promoting racial integration. It is important not to give s.5 too wide a construction, which would enable it to provide an excuse or cloak for undesirable discrimination. On the other hand, where genuine attempts are being made to integrate ethnic groups into society, too narrow a construction might stifle such initiatives.

London Borough of Lambeth v   **[1989] IRLR 379 EAT**
CRE

In exercising their jurisdiction in s.5 cases, tribunals should take a broad commonsense approach on matters which are largely issues of fact. It should not be too difficult to identify genuine defences, and to distinguish specious defences which cloak undesirable discrimination.

Tottenham Green Under-Fives'   **[1991] IRLR 162 EAT**
    Centre v
Marshall (No.2)

It is not open to an employment tribunal to disregard a duty in determining whether a genuine occupational qualification exception applies, unless the matter is de minimis or is a sham duty invented for the purpose of qualifying for the exception. Provided the employment tribunal is satisfied that the relevant duty is not so trivial that it can properly be disregarded altogether, it is not for the tribunal to make an evaluation of the importance of the duty. Section 5(3) indicates clearly that one of the duties of the job, if it falls within any of the relevant paragraphs, will operate to make the exception available.

London Borough of Lambeth v   **[1990] IRLR 230 CA**
CRE

The use of the word "personal" in s.5(2)(d), where the holder of the job provides "personal services", indicates that the identity of the giver and the recipient of the services is important and appears to contemplate direct contact between the giver and the recipient – mainly face to face or where there could be susceptibility in personal, physical contact.

London Borough of Lambeth v   **[1990] IRLR 230 CA**
CRE

If a person is providing persons of a racial group defined by colour (eg black people) with personal services promoting their welfare, it is open to an employment tribunal on the particular facts of the case to find that those services can be most effectively provided by a person of that colour, from whatever ethnic group he comes, and even though some of his clients may belong to other ethnic groups.

Tottenham Green Under-Fives'   **[1989] IRLR 147 EAT**
    Centre v
Marshall

Where a defence is raised under s.5(2)(d), the holder of the post must be directly involved in the provision of the services, although this need not necessarily be on a one-to-one basis. If the post-holder provides several personal services to the recipient, the defence is established provided one of those genuinely falls within s.5(2)(d).

Tottenham Green Under-Fives'   **[1989] IRLR 147 EAT**
    Centre v
Marshall

The phrase "promoting their welfare" in s.5(2)(d) is a very wide expression and it would be undesirable to seek to narrow the width of those words.

Tottenham Green Under-Fives'   **[1989] IRLR 147 EAT**
    Centre v
Marshall

The phrase "those services can most effectively be provided by a person of that racial group" in s.5(2)(d) assumes that the personal services could be provided by others. The words are not "must be provided" nor "can only be provided". Whether the services can be "most effectively provided" by a person of that racial group and whether they would be less effective if provided by others is a matter of fact for the tribunal. However, if a tribunal accepts that the conscious decision of a responsible employer to commit an act of discrimination and to rely upon s.5(2) is founded upon a genuinely held and reasonably based opinion that a genuine occupational requirement will best promote the welfare of the recipient, considerable weight should be given to that decision when reaching a conclusion whether or not the defence succeeds.

> **Sex discrimination**

Genuine occupational qualifications

(1) In relation to sex discrimination –
> *(a) s.6(1)(a) or (c) does not apply to any employment where being a man is a genuine occupational qualification for the job; and*
> *(b) s.6(2)(a) does not apply to opportunities for promotion or transfer to, or training for, such employment.*

(2) Being a man is a genuine occupational qualification for a job only where –

(a) the essential nature of the job calls for a man for reasons of physiology (excluding physical strength or stamina) or, in dramatic performances or other entertainment, for reasons of authenticity, so that the essential nature of the job would be materially different if carried out by a woman; or

(b) the job needs to be held by a man to preserve decency or privacy because –

   (i) it is likely to involve physical contact with men in circumstances where they might reasonably object to its being carried out by a woman, or

   (ii) the holder of the job is likely to do his work in circumstances where men might reasonably object to the presence of a woman because they are in a state of undress or are using sanitary facilities; or

[(ba) the job is likely to involve the holder of the job doing his work, or living in a private home and needs to be held by a man because objection might reasonably be taken to allowing a woman –

   (i) the degree of physical or social contact with a person living in the home, or

   (ii) the knowledge of intimate details of such a person's life, which is likely, because of the nature or circumstances of the job or of the home, to be allowed to, or available to, the holder of the job; or]

(c) the nature or location of the establishment makes it impracticable for the holder of the job to live elsewhere than in premises provided by the employer, and –

   (i) the only such premises which are available for persons holding that kind of job are lived in, or normally lived in, by men and are not equipped with separate sleeping accommodation for women and sanitary facilities which could be used by women in privacy from men, and

   (ii) it is not reasonable to expect the employer either to equip those premises with such accommodation and facilities or to provide other premises for women; or

(d) the nature of the establishment, or of the part of it within which the work is done, requires the job to be held by a man because –

   (i) it is, or is part of, a hospital, prison or other establishment for persons requiring special care, supervision or attention, and

   (ii) those persons are all men (disregarding any women whose presence is exceptional), and

   (iii) it is reasonable, having regard to the essential character of the establishment or that part, that the job should not be held by a woman; or

(e) the holder of the job provides individuals with personal services promoting their welfare or education, or simlar personal services, and those services can most effectively be provided by a man; or

(f) . . . [repealed].

(g) the job needs to be held by a man because it is likely to involve the performance of duties outside the United Kingdom in a country whose laws or customs are such that the duties could not, or could not effectively, be performed by a woman; or

(h) the job is one of two to be held by a married couple.

(3) Subsection (2) applies where some only of the duties of the job fall within paragraphs (a) to (g) as well as where all of them do.

(4) Paragraph (a), (b), (c), (d), (e), (f) or (g) of subsection (2) does not apply in relation to the filling of a vacancy at a time when the employer already has male employees –

   (a) who are capable of carrying out the duties falling within that paragraph; and

   (b) whom it would be reasonable to employ on those duties; and

   (c) whose numbers are sufficient to meet the employer's likely requirements in respect of those duties without undue inconvenience.

SEX DISCRIMINATION ACT – s.7

➡ **EQUALITY ACT 2010 – Sch. 9, para. 1; Sch. 23, para. 3**

Timex Corporation v   **[1981] IRLR 530 EAT**
Hodgson
Where a man is selected for redundancy on grounds of his sex in circumstances in which a woman has been retained because her job has been given additional duties of a kind where being a woman may be a genuine occupational qualification, the discrimination by the employers is in selecting the woman to do the revised job, not in dismissing the man who is not selected. Therefore, although the defence under s.7 of the Sex Discrimination Act that there was a genuine occupational qualification does not extend to conduct falling within s.6(2)(b), in such a case the discrimination lies either in failing to "transfer" the man to the revised job within s.6(2)(a) or in "deliberately omitting to offer" the man employment in the revised job within s.6(1)(c), so that the exceptions in s.7(2) can apply.

Sisley v   **[1983] IRLR 404 EAT**
Britannia Security Systems Ltd
Section 7(2)(b)(ii) of the Sex Discrimination Act is not confined to cases where the job itself requires the holder to be in a state of undress. The reference in the subsection to "sanitary facilities" shows that the subsection is not confined to job duties. It deals with the situation where the holder of a particular job is likely to do his work, and all matters reasonably incidental to it, in circumstances where the holder might reasonably object to the presence of a member of the opposite sex because the holder is in a state of undress or is using sanitary facilities.

Sisley v   **[1983] IRLR 404 EAT**
Britannia Security Systems Ltd
Section 7(2)(b)(ii) does not extend to circumstances where someone other than the holder of the job might object to the presence of a member of the opposite sex, so that it does not cover cases where the holder of the job (for example, a man employed in a dress shop) is working in circumstances where women customers might object to a man doing that job because the women are in a state of undress.

Sisley v   **[1983] IRLR 404 EAT**
Britannia Security Systems Ltd
The words "to live in" in s.7(2)(c) of the Sex Discrimination Act involve the concept of residence either permanent

or temporary and do not cover cases where an employee is obliged to remain on the premises for a limited period of time, eating and taking a period of rest. Whether there is the necessary feature of residence is a question of fact and degree in every case.

Timex Corporation v   **[1981] IRLR 530 EAT**
Hodgson
Once an employment tribunal is satisfied that additional duties have been genuinely added to a job, its function is to look at the duties involved in the job and, under s.7(3), to see whether some of those duties fall within s.7(2). The employment tribunal cannot tell the employers how to manage their business and that they need not have included the additional duties in the revised job.

Etam plc v   **[1989] IRLR 150 EAT**
Rowan
Being a woman was not a genuine occupational qualification for a sales assistant's job in a women's clothing shop so as to entitle the appellants to refuse to consider a man for the post, notwithstanding that it would have been impossible for a man to carry out the functions of a sales assistant within the shop's fitting room, where the case fell within the circumstances envisaged by s.7(4) in that a man would have been able to adequately carry out the bulk of the job of sales assistant, and such parts as he could not carry out could easily have been done by one of the female sales assistants without causing any inconvenience or difficulty for the appellants.

Lasertop Ltd v   **[1997] IRLR 498 EAT**
Webster
The relevant time under s.7(4), which refers to the filling of a vacancy "at a time when the employer already has [female] employees", is when the prima facie discrimination takes place. The employer must already have sufficient female employees at that time who are capable of carrying out the prohibited duties and whom it would be reasonable to employ on those duties without undue inconvenience.

Lasertop Ltd v   **[1997] IRLR 498 EAT**
Webster
The provisions of s.7(4), which provide that s.7(2) does not apply when the employer already has sufficient male employees who could reasonably carry out the relevant duties, focuses solely on the contractual duties falling within s.7(2). The remaining contractual duties are irrelevant. In this case, the job in question required a salesperson to take prospective members on a tour of a women-only health club and that part of the post-holder's selling duties which took him into the changing room, sauna area, sunbed room and toilet could not be allocated to female members of staff without undue inconvenience.

Contractual benefits

(6) Subsection (2) does not apply to benefits consisting of the payment of money when the provision of those benefits is regulated by the woman's contract of employment.

SEX DISCRIMINATION ACT 1975 – s.6
➡ **EQUALITY ACT 2010 – s.71**

Hoyland v   **[2006] IRLR 468 CS**
Asda Stores Ltd
The important word in s.6(6) is "regulated". For s.6(6) to apply in a given situation, it is not necessary that the entitlement in question should be part of the formal contract of employment. It is sufficient if it arises out of the contract of employment and is regulated by it in the sense that but for the existence of the contract of employment, it would not be paid.

Hoyland v   **[2006] IRLR 468 CS**
Asda Stores Ltd
A claim relating to a deduction in annual bonus from a woman who was absent on maternity leave fell within the exclusion in s.6(6) as regards claims relating to "benefits consisting of the payment of money when the provision of those benefits is regulated by the woman's contract of employment", notwithstanding that the bonus was stated to be "discretionary".

DIRECT DISCRIMINATION

(1) A person discriminates against another in any circumstances relevant for the purpose of any provision of this Act if –

(a) on racial grounds he treats that other less favourably than he treats or would treat other persons . . .

RACE RELATIONS ACT – s.1

➡ **EQUALITY ACT 2010 – s.13**

(1) A person discriminates against a woman in any circumstances relevant for the purposes of any provision of this Act if –

(a) on the ground of her sex he treats her less favourably than he treats or would treat a man . . .

SEX DISCRIMINATION ACT – s.1

➡ **EQUALITY ACT 2010 – s.13**

(1) This section applies where a complaint is presented under section 54 and the complaint is that the respondent –

(a) has committed an act of discrimination, on grounds of race or ethnic or national origins, which is unlawful by virtue of any provision referred to in section 1(1B)(a), (e) or (f), or Part IV in its application to those provisions, or

(b) has committed an act of harassment.

(2) Where, on the hearing of the complaint, the complainant proves facts from which the tribunal could, apart from this section, conclude in the absence of an adequate explanation that the respondent –

(a) has committed such an act of discrimination or harassment against the complainant, or

(b) is by virtue of section 32 or 33 to be treated as having committed such an act of discrimination or harassment against the complainant,

the tribunal shall uphold the complaint unless the respondent proves that he did not commit or, as the case may be, is not to be treated as having committed, that act.

RACE RELATIONS ACT 1976 (as amended) – s.54A

➡ **EQUALITY ACT 2010 – s.136**

(1) This section applies to any complaint presented under section 63 to an employment tribunal.

(2) Where, on the hearing of the complaint, the complainant proves facts from which the tribunal could, apart from this section, conclude in the absence of an adequate explanation that the respondent –

(a) has committed an act of discrimination or harassment against the complainant which is unlawful by virtue of Part 2, or

(b) is by virtue of section 41 or 42 to be treated as having committed such an act of discrimination or harassment against the complainant,

the tribunal shall uphold the complaint unless the respondent proves that he did not commit, or, as the case may be, is not to be treated as having committed, that act.

SEX DISCRIMINATION ACT (as amended) – s.63A

➡ **EQUALITY ACT 2010 – s.136**

Burden of proof

Igen Ltd v Wong   **[2005] IRLR 258 CA**

The statutory amendments to the burden of proof altered the pre-existing position established by the case law relating to direct discrimination. They require the employment tribunal to go through a two-stage process. The first stage requires the claimant to prove facts from which the tribunal could, apart from the section, conclude in the absence of an adequate explanation that the respondent has committed, or is to be treated as having committed, the unlawful act of discrimination against the complainant. The tribunal is required to make an assumption at the first stage which may be contrary to reality, the plain purpose being to shift the burden of proof at the second stage so that unless the respondent provides an adequate explanation, the complainant will succeed. It would be inconsistent with that assumption to take account of an adequate explanation by the respondent at the first stage. The second stage, which only comes into effect if the complainant has proved those facts, requires the respondent to prove that he did not commit or is not to be treated as having committed the unlawful act, if the complaint is not to be upheld. If the second stage is reached, and the respondent's explanation is inadequate, it will be not merely legitimate but also necessary for the tribunal to conclude that the complaint should be upheld.

St Christopher's Fellowship v Walters-Ennis   **[2010] EqLR 82 CA**

The words "could conclude" in the burden of proof provisions – which provide that where the claimant proves facts from which the tribunal could conclude in the absence of an adequate explanation that the respondent has committed an act of discrimination against the claimant, the tribunal shall uphold the complaint unless the respondent proves that he did not commit the act – mean that "a reasonable employment tribunal could properly conclude" from all the evidence before them, including all the evidence given by the respondent as well as the claimant.

Igen Ltd v Wong   **[2005] IRLR 258 CA**

Although there are two stages in the tribunal's decision-making process, tribunals should not divide hearings into two parts to correspond to those stages. Tribunals will generally wish to hear all the evidence, including the respondent's explanation, before deciding whether the requirements at the first stage are satisfied and, if so, whether the respondent has discharged the onus which has shifted.

Abbey National plc v Chagger   **[2009] IRLR 86 EAT**

Although the provisions of s.54A on the burden of proof do not expressly apply to claims of discrimination on grounds of colour, the different kinds of discrimination referred to in s.3(1) overlap to a very considerable extent, and in many cases they will be practically indistinguishable. Thus claimants who formulate their claim on the basis of "colour discrimination" will inevitably in fact be complaining, whether or not they appreciate it, of discrimination on the ground of race and ethnic origin, and therefore of two of the factors which explicitly attract the operation of s.54A.

Meaning of "less favourable"

R v   **[1989] IRLR 173 HL**
Birmingham City Council ex parte
   Equal Opportunities Commission
In order to establish that there was less favourable treatment of members of one sex by reason of their having been denied the same opportunities as the other sex, it is enough that they are deprived of a choice which was valued by them and which (even though others may take a different view) is a choice obviously valued, on reasonable grounds, by many others. It is not necessary to prove that that which was lost was "better".

Simon v   **[1987] IRLR 307 CA**
Brimham Associates
Words or acts of discouragement can amount to treatment of the person discouraged which is less favourable than that given to other persons.

Burrett v   **[1994] IRLR 7 EAT**
West Birmingham Health
   Authority
The fact that a complainant honestly considers that she is being less favourably treated does not of itself establish that there is "less favourable treatment" within s.1(1)(a). Whether there is less favourable treatment is for the employment tribunal to decide.

Stewart v   **[1994] IRLR 440 EAT**
Cleveland Guest (Engineering) Ltd
There is room for disagreement as to what is or is not less favourable treatment and the employment tribunal, as industrial jury, is best placed to make a decision on the facts of a particular case. If the error of law relied upon is the argument that the employment tribunal reached a decision which no reasonable tribunal, on a proper appreciation of the facts and law, would have reached, an overwhelming case to that effect must be made out.

Discriminatory treatment

James v   **[1990] IRLR 288 HL**
Eastleigh Borough Council
The question to be considered under s.1(1)(a) is: "would

the complainant have received the same treatment from the defendant but for his or her sex?" This test embraces both the case where the treatment derives from the application of a gender-based criterion and the case where it derives from the selection of the complainant because of his or her sex.

Nagarajan v   **[1999] IRLR 572 HL**
London Regional Transport
The crucial question in a case of direct discrimination is why the complainant received less favourable treatment. Was it on grounds of race? Or was it for some other reason? If racial grounds were the reason for the less favourable treatment, direct discrimination under s.1(1)(a) is established. The reason why the discriminator acted on racial grounds is irrelevant when deciding whether an act of racial discrimination occurred.

Shamoon v   **[2003] IRLR 285 HL**
Chief Constable of the Royal Ulster Constabulary
Per Lord Nicholls: Employment tribunals may sometimes be able to avoid arid and confusing disputes about the identification of the appropriate comparator by concentrating primarily on why the claimant was treated as she was, and postponing the less favourable treatment issue until after they have decided why the treatment was afforded. Was it on the proscribed ground or was it for some other reason? If the former, there will usually be no difficulty in deciding whether the treatment afforded to the claimant on the proscribed ground was less favourable than was or would have been afforded to others.

Amnesty International v   **[2009] IRLR 884 EAT**
Ahmed
There is no real difficulty in reconciling *James v Eastleigh* and *Nagarajan*. In some cases, such as *James*, the ground for the treatment complained of is inherent in the act itself. In cases of this kind, what was going on inside the head of the putative discriminator will be irrelevant. In other cases, of which *Nagarajan* is an example, the act complained of is not in itself discriminatory but is rendered so by a discriminatory motivation – ie by the mental processes (whether conscious or unconscious) that led the putative discriminator to do the act. In both cases, the ultimate question is what was the ground of the treatment complained of, or the reason why it occurred. The difference between them simply reflects the different ways in which conduct may be discriminatory.

James v   **[1990] IRLR 288 HL**
Eastleigh Borough Council
Since the statutory pensionable age is itself a criterion which directly discriminates between men and women in that it treats women more favourably than men "on the ground of their sex", any other differential treatment of men and women which adopts the same gender-based criterion must equally involve discrimination "on the ground of sex".

Sidhu v   **[2000] IRLR 602 CA**
Aerospace Composite Technology Ltd

In order to find direct discrimination under s.1(1)(a), the complainant must show that he has been treated less favourably by the discriminator than the discriminator treats or would treat other persons in the same circumstances. However, in certain cases the comparison need not be demonstrated by evidence as to how a comparator was or would be treated, because the very action complained of is in itself less favourable treatment on sexual or racial grounds. If a person is harassed or abused because of his race, that conduct is race-specific and it is not necessary to show that a person of another race would be treated more favourably.

Sidhu v   **[2000] IRLR 602 CA**
Aerospace Composite Technology Ltd

A policy in relation to incidents of violence by one employee against another which only looked at the fact of violence or abusive language and disregarded provocation and other mitigating factors, such as that the accused employee had been provoked by a racial assault, was not a race-specific policy merely because it ignored the racial element in the attack.

Baldwin v   **[2007] IRLR 232 EAT**
Brighton & Hove City Council

The statutory wording provides that a person (A) discriminates against another person (B) if he treats (B) less favourably than he treats or would treat a relevant comparator on the prohibited grounds. It is not enough that (A) would treat (B) less favourably.

Commissioners of   **[2002] IRLR 776 EAT**
   Inland Revenue v
Morgan

There is no statutory or other offence consisting of a body being institutionally racist. While it would be possible to imagine a body whose habitual rules or practices were such that one could fairly say of the body that as an institution it was racist, the charge would be relevant only as a step in the reasoning toward a conclusion that the body was or was not guilty of some unlawful discrimination that fell within the Act.

Smith v   **[1996] IRLR 456 CA**
Safeway plc

There is an important distinction between discrimination between the sexes and discrimination against one or other of the sexes. Discrimination is not failing to treat men and women the same. If discrimination is to be established, it is necessary to show, not merely that the sexes are treated differently, but that the treatment accorded to one is less favourable than the treatment accorded to the other.

R (on the application of Elias) v   **[2006] IRLR 934 CA**
Secretary of State for Defence

Direct and indirect discrimination are two different statutory torts. Although, in a general sense, discrimination with a discriminatory purpose, regardless of the particular form it takes, can be perceived as treating a person less favourably "on racial grounds", in the present state of the law, the particular *form* of discrimination matters, even if there are present in the circumstances of the case a discriminatory purpose and discriminatory effects.

Jaffrey v   **[2002] IRLR 688 EAT**
Department of Environment, Transport
   and Regions

The facts of a case might give rise to claims both in respect of direct and indirect discrimination if different facts demonstrate the different types of discrimination, and the factual circumstances overlap but not precisely coincide.

Motive

R v   **[1989] IRLR 173 HL**
Birmingham City Council ex parte
   Equal Opportunities Commission

The intention or motive of the defendant to discriminate is not a necessary condition to liability. There is discrimination within the meaning of s.1(1)(a) of the Sex Discrimination Act if there is less favourable treatment on the ground of sex, in other words if the relevant woman or women would have received the same treatment as the men but for their sex. Were that not the case, it would be a good defence for an employer to show that he discriminated against a woman not because he intended to but (for example) because of customer preference, or to save money, or even to avoid controversy.

R (on the application of E) v   **[2010] IRLR 136 SC**
Governing Body of JFS

The grounds for discrimination are the factual criteria applied by the discriminator in reaching his decision rather than the motive for taking the decision. The motive for discriminating is not relevant.

R (on the application of European   **[2005] IRLR 115 HL**
   Roma Rights Centre) v
Immigration Officer at Prague Airport

If a person acts on racial grounds, the reason why he does so is irrelevant.

James v   **[1990] IRLR 288 HL**
Eastleigh Borough Council

The correct test under s.1(1)(a) is objective, not subjective. Whether or not the treatment is less favourable on the ground of sex is not saved from constituting unlawful discrimination by the fact that the defendant acted from a benign motive.

James v   **[1990] IRLR 288 HL**
Eastleigh Borough Council

Per Lord Goff: If it were necessary for the purpose of s.1(1)(a) to identify the requisite intention of the defendant, that intention is simply an intention to perform the relevant act of less favourable treatment. However, in the majority of cases, it is doubtful if it is necessary to focus upon the intention or motive of the defendant in this way and the simple "but for" test avoids, in most cases at least, complicated questions relating to concepts such as intention, motive, reason or purpose, and the danger of confusion arising from the misuse of those elusive terms.

James v   **[1989] IRLR 318 CA**
Eastleigh Borough Council
There is direct discrimination if the overt basis for affording less favourable treatment was sex or, if the overt reason does not in terms relate to sex, it is shown that the overt reason was not the true reason and the true reason is the desire to treat women less favourably than men.

Moyhing v   **[2006] IRLR 860 EAT**
Barts and London NHS Trust
Direct discrimination cannot be justified. The fact that there may be good and sound reasons for distinguishing between men and women is no defence.

Din v   **[1982] IRLR 281 EAT**
Carrington Viyella Ltd
If an act of racial discrimination gives rise to actual or potential industrial unrest, an employer will or may be liable for unlawful discrimination if he simply seeks to remove that unrest by getting rid of the person against whom racial discrimination has been shown.

Stereotypical assumptions

R (on the application of European   **[2005] IRLR 115 HL**
   Roma Rights Centre) v
Immigration Officer at Prague Airport
The object of the legislation is to ensure that each person is treated as an individual and not assumed to be like other members of the group, whether or not most members of the group do have such characteristics. A person may be acting on beliefs or assumptions about members of the sex or racial group involved which are often true and which if true would provide a good reason for the less favourable treatment in question, but what may be true of a group may not be true of a significant number of individuals within that group.

Horsey v   **[1982] IRLR 395 EAT**
Dyfed County Council
The words "on the ground of" sex, marital status or race in the statutory definitions of discrimination cover cases where the reason for the discrimination was a generalised assumption that people of a particular sex, marital status or race possess or lack certain characteristics. They do not only cover cases where the sole factor influencing the deci-

sion of the alleged discriminator is the sex, marital status or race of the complainant. Most discrimination flows from generalised assumptions and not from a single prejudice dependent solely upon the sex or colour of the complainant. Therefore, a decision to treat a complainant in a particular way for reasons which, as an essential ingredient, contain a generalised assumption about a woman's behaviour is a decision made "on the ground of" her sex.

Coleman v   **[1981] IRLR 398 CA**
Skyrail Oceanic Ltd
An assumption that men are more likely than women to be the primary supporters of their spouses and children is an assumption based on sex. Therefore, the dismissal of a woman based upon an assumption that husbands are breadwinners, and wives are not, can amount to discrimination under the Sex Discrimination Act.

Bradford Hospitals NHS Trust v   **[2003] IRLR 4 EAT**
Al-Shahib
Whilst it may sometimes be legitimate for a tribunal to take into account differences in behaviour which reflect racial and cultural differences, it is wrong for a tribunal to make findings based on the existence of such differences unless there is some evidential basis for them, such as expert evidence. For a tribunal simply to assume that a particular ethnic group has a specific characteristic is fundamentally wrong, even if the assumption is made for benign purposes.

Causation

Owen & Briggs v   **[1982] IRLR 502 CA**
James
That a racial consideration was an important factor in an employer's decision is sufficient to found a case of discrimination. It is not necessary that the racial factor be the sole reason for the employer's decision.

Nagarajan v   **[1994] IRLR 61 EAT**
Agnew
Where there are mixed motives for the doing of an act, not all of which constitute unlawful discrimination, there will be unlawful discrimination if the unlawful motive was of sufficient weight in the decision-making process to be treated as a cause of the act thus motivated. An important factor in the decision is well within that principle.

Lewis Woolf Griptight Ltd v   **[1997] IRLR 432 EAT**
Corfield
There is sex discrimination where the principal reason for dismissal is gender-neutral, but the means by which the employer sought to effect the termination of employment are gender-specific, such as reliance upon the statutory maternity leave provisions, and could not be relied upon

in the case of a man. Therefore, the claimant was discriminated against when the employers used the expiry of the four-week period after maternity leave as an excuse for terminating the employment.

Seide v   **[1980] IRLR 427 EAT**
Gillette Industries Ltd
In determining whether there has been unlawful discrimination, the question is whether the activating cause of what happened is that the employer has treated a person less favourably than others on racial grounds. Where there is more than one ground for an employer's action, it might be enough if a substantial and effective cause for the action is a breach of the statute. However, it is not sufficient merely to consider whether the fact that the person is of a particular racial group is any part of the background or is a *causa sine qua non* of what happened. Therefore, an employee who was transferred in order to preserve good working relationships had not been discriminated against on racial grounds, notwithstanding that he might not have been transferred had he not been Jewish, since his being Jewish was not the activating cause of his transfer.

Statutory comparison

---

(3) A comparison of the cases of persons of different sex or marital status under s.1(1) or 3(1) must be such that the relevant circumstances in the one case are the same, or not materially different, in the other.

SEX DISCRIMINATION ACT – s.5
➡ **EQUALITY ACT 2010 – s.23**

(4) A comparison of the case of a person of a particular racial group with that of a person not of that group under s.1(1) must be such that the relevant circumstances in the one case are the same, or not materially different, in the other.

RACE RELATIONS ACT – s.3
➡ **EQUALITY ACT 2010 – s.23**

Macdonald v   **[2003] IRLR 512 HL**
Advocate General for Scotland
Pearce v
Governing Body of Mayfield Secondary School
The "relevant circumstances" for the purpose of the statutory comparison are those which the alleged discriminator takes into account when deciding to treat the woman or the man as he does. If the relevant circumstances are to be "the same or not materially different", within the meaning of s.5(3), all the characteristics of the complainant which are relevant to the way his case was dealt with must be found also in the comparator. They do not have to be precisely the same, but they must not be materially different. That is the basic rule, if one is to compare like with like. Characteristics that have no bearing on the way the woman was treated can

be ignored, but those that do have a bearing on the way she was treated must be the same if one is to determine whether, but for her sex, she would have been treated differently.

Ahsan v   **[2008] IRLR 243 HL**
Watt
The treatment of a person who does not qualify as a statutory comparator (because the circumstances are in some material respect different) may nevertheless be evidence from which a tribunal may infer how a hypothetical statutory comparator would have been treated. This is an ordinary question of relevance, which depends upon the degree of the similarity of the circumstances of the person in question (the "evidential comparator") to those of the complainant and all the other evidence in the case.

Ahsan v   **[2008] IRLR 243 HL**
Watt
It is probably uncommon to find a real person who qualifies as a statutory comparator. In most cases, however, a tribunal should be able, by treating the putative comparator as an evidential comparator, and having due regard to the alleged differences in circumstances and other evidence, to form a view on how the employer would have treated a hypothetical person who was a true statutory comparator.

Madden v   **[2005] IRLR 46 CA**
Preferred Technical Group Cha Ltd
The hypothetical comparator does not have to be a clone of the claimant in every respect (including personality and personal characteristics) except of a different race. If that were right, every case of alleged race discrimination in which there was a hypothetical comparator and less favourable treatment would result in a finding in the claimant's favour.

Chief Constable of West Yorkshire   **[2001] IRLR 124 EAT**
    Police v
Vento
Where there is no evidence as to the treatment of an actual male comparator whose position is wholly akin to the claimant's, a tribunal has to construct a picture of how a hypothetical male comparator would have been treated in comparable surrounding circumstances. Inferences will frequently need to be drawn. One permissible way of judging a question such as that is to see how unidentical but not wholly dissimilar cases were treated in relation to other individual cases. It is not required that a minutely exact actual comparator has to be found. If that were the case then isolated cases of discrimination would almost invariably go uncompensated.

Bullock v   **[1992] IRLR 564 CA**
Alice Ottley School
The "relevant circumstances" are the circumstances which are relevant to the comparison. "Relevant" has to be judged by an objective standard.

Showboat Entertainment   **[1984] IRLR 7 EAT**
Centre Ltd v
Owens

In judging whether there has been discrimination, although like has to be compared with like, the comparison is between the treatment actually meted out and the treatment which would have been afforded to a man having all the same characteristics as the complainant except his race or his attitude to race. Only by excluding matters of race can it be discovered whether the differential treatment was on racial grounds. Therefore, in a case where an employee was dismissed for refusing to carry out an unlawful discriminatory instruction, the correct comparison was between the employee dismissed and another employee who did not refuse to obey the unlawful discriminatory instruction rather than between the employee and how the employers would have treated another employee who refused to obey the instruction.

Re EOC for Northern Ireland's   **[1989] IRLR 64 NIHC**
Application

To be relied upon, a material difference must be one which itself has not been created by discrimination on the ground of sex.

James v   **[1990] IRLR 288 HL**
Eastleigh Borough Council

Because pensionable age is itself discriminatory, it cannot be treated as a relevant circumstance in making the comparison.

Grieg v   **[1979] IRLR 158 EAT**
Community Industry

The relevant employment for the purposes of comparison under s.5(3) of the Sex Discrimination Act is the employment for which the claimant applied, not some hypothetical employment with totally different personnel concerned. Therefore, where a woman complains that she has been discriminated against in not getting a job where the other workers are men, the correct approach is to ask whether a man would have got the job, not what would have happened had all the other workers been women and a man had applied.

Dhatt v   **[1991] IRLR 130 CA**
McDonalds Hamburgers Ltd

The nationality of someone seeking work is a relevant circumstance within the meaning of s.3(4) because Parliament itself recognises and seeks to enforce by reference to nationality a general division between those who by reason of their nationality are free to work and those who require permission. Although nationality is itself discriminatory in racial terms, it is discrimination which has been sanctioned by statute.

B v   **[2007] IRLR 576 EAT**
A

The appropriate comparators in respect of a female personal assistant who had a consensual sexual relationship with her male employer and was dismissed when he became jealous of her relationship with another man was a homosexual male employer and a homosexual male employee. Since such an employee would have received exactly the same treatment – ie he would have been dismissed when his apparent infidelity was discovered, driven by feelings of jealousy – there was no discrimination on grounds of sex.

Evidence

Standard of proof

Igen Ltd v   **[2005] IRLR 258 CA**
Wong

The guidance issued by the EAT in *Barton v Investec Henderson Crosthwaite Securities Ltd* in respect of Sex Discrimination Act cases, which has been applied in relation to race and disability discrimination, would be approved in amended form, as set out below:

(1) Pursuant to section 63A of the SDA, it is for the claimant who complains of sex discrimination to prove on the balance of probabilities facts from which the tribunal could conclude, in the absence of an adequate explanation, that the respondent has committed an act of discrimination against the claimant which is unlawful by virtue of Part II or which by virtue of s.41 or s.42 of the SDA is to be treated as having been committed against the claimant. These are referred to below as "such facts".

(2) If the claimant does not prove such facts he or she will fail.

(3) It is important to bear in mind in deciding whether the claimant has proved such facts that it is unusual to find direct evidence of sex discrimination. Few employers would be prepared to admit such discrimination, even to themselves. In some cases the discrimination will not be an intention but merely based on the assumption that "he or she would not have fitted in".

(4) In deciding whether the claimant has proved such facts, it is important to remember that the outcome at this stage of the analysis by the tribunal will therefore usually depend on what inferences it is proper to draw from the primary facts found by the tribunal.

(5) It is important to note the word "could" in s.63A(2). At this stage the tribunal does not have to reach a definitive determination that such facts would lead it to the conclusion that there was an act of unlawful discrimination. At this stage a tribunal is looking at the primary facts before it to see what inferences of secondary fact could be drawn from them.

(6) In considering what inferences or conclusions can be drawn from the primary facts, the tribunal must assume that there is no adequate explanation for those facts.

(7) These inferences can include, in appropriate cases, any inferences that it is just and equitable to draw in accordance

with s.74(2)(b) of the SDA from an evasive or equivocal reply to a questionnaire or any other questions that fall within s.74(2) of the SDA.

(8) Likewise, the tribunal must decide whether any provision of any relevant code of practice is relevant and if so, take it into account in determining, such facts pursuant to s.56A(10) of the SDA. This means that inferences may also be drawn from any failure to comply with any relevant code of practice.

(9) Where the claimant has proved facts from which conclusions could be drawn that the respondent has treated the claimant less favourably on the ground of sex, then the burden of proof moves to the respondent.

(10) It is then for the respondent to prove that he did not commit, or as the case may be, is not to be treated as having committed, that act.

(11) To discharge that burden it is necessary for the respondent to prove, on the balance of probabilities, that the treatment was in no sense whatsoever on the grounds of sex, since "no discrimination whatsoever" is compatible with the Burden of Proof Directive.

(12) That requires a tribunal to assess not merely whether the respondent has proved an explanation for the facts from which such inferences can be drawn, but further that it is adequate to discharge the burden of proof on the balance of probabilities that sex was not a ground for the treatment in question.

(13) Since the facts necessary to prove an explanation would normally be in the possession of the respondent, a tribunal would normally expect cogent evidence to discharge that burden of proof. In particular, the tribunal will need to examine carefully explanations for failure to deal with the questionnaire procedure and/or code of practice.

Madarassy v   **[2007] IRLR 246 CA**
Nomura International plc
The burden of proof does not shift to the employer simply on the claimant establishing a difference in status (eg sex) and a difference in treatment. Those bare facts only indicate a possibility of discrimination. They are not, without more, sufficient material from which a tribunal "could conclude" that, on the balance of probabilities, the respondent had committed an unlawful act of discrimination. "Could conclude" in s.63A(2) must mean that "a reasonable tribunal could properly conclude" from all the evidence before it. This would include evidence adduced by the claimant in support of the allegations of sex discrimination, such as evidence of a difference in status, a difference in treatment and the reason for the differential treatment. It would also include evidence adduced by the respondent contesting the complaint. Subject only to the statutory "absence of an adequate explanation" at this stage, the tribunal needs to consider all the evidence relevant to the discrimination complaint, such as evidence as to whether the act complained of occurred at all, evidence as to the actual comparators relied on by the claimant to prove less favourable treatment, evidence as to whether the comparisons being made by the claimant were of like with like as required by s.5(3), and available evidence of the reasons for the differential treatment. The correct legal position was made plain by the guidance in *Igen v Wong*.

Madarassy v   **[2007] IRLR 246 CA**
Nomura International plc
Although s.63A(2) involves a two-stage analysis of the evidence, it does not expressly or impliedly prevent the tribunal at the first stage from hearing, accepting or drawing inferences from evidence adduced by the respondent disputing and rebutting the claimant's evidence of discrimination. The respondent may adduce evidence at the first stage to show that the acts which are alleged to be discriminatory never happened; or that, if they did, they were not less favourable treatment of the claimant; or that the comparators chosen by the claimant or the situations with which comparisons are made are not truly like the claimant or the situation of the claimant; or that, even if there has been less favourable treatment of the claimant, it was not on the ground of her sex or pregnancy. Such evidence from the respondent could, if accepted by the tribunal, be relevant as showing that, contrary to the claimant's allegations of discrimination, there is nothing in the evidence from which the tribunal could properly infer a prima facie case of discrimination on the proscribed ground. The approach of Elias J in *Laing v Manchester City Council* would be approved.

Laing v   **[2006] IRLR 748 EAT**
Manchester City Council
A tribunal should have regard to all facts at the first stage to see what proper inferences can be drawn. The onus lies on the claimant to show potentially less favourable treatment from which an inference of discrimination could properly be drawn. Typically, this will involve identifying an actual comparator treated differently or, in the absence of such a comparator, a hypothetical one who would have been treated more favourably. This involves a consideration of all material facts, as opposed to any explanation. The reference to "the claimant proving facts" in s.54A(2) is merely indicating that, at that stage, the burden rests on the claimant to satisfy the tribunal, after a consideration of all the facts, that a prima facie case exists sufficient to require an explanation. It does not mean that it is only the facts adduced by the claimant (plus supporting facts adduced by the respondent) that can be considered. Thus, if a manager acts rudely to a black employee, that will not necessarily raise a prima facie case if there is evidence that that conduct is manifest to all indiscriminately, regardless of race.

Brown v   **[2007] IRLR 259 CA**
London Borough of Croydon
It is not an error of law for a tribunal not to apply the two-stage approach to the burden of proof laid down in *Igen Ltd v Wong*. There are cases in which the claimant is not prejudiced by the tribunal omitting express consideration of the

first stage of the test, moving straight to the second stage of the test, the "reason why" question, and concluding that the respondent has discharged the burden on him under the second stage by proving that the treatment was not on the proscribed ground.

Amnesty International v   **[2009] IRLR 884 EAT**
Ahmed
There would be fewer appeals in discrimination cases if more tribunals made an explicit finding as to the reason for the claimant's treatment, thereby rendering the elaborations of the *Barton/Igen* guidelines otiose, and only resorted to the provisions of s.54A (or its cognates) where they felt unable to make positive findings on the evidence without its assistance.

Network Rail Infrastructure Ltd v   **[2006] IRLR 865 EAT**
Griffiths-Henry
There does not have to be positive evidence that the difference in treatment is race or sex in order to establish a prima facie case.

Dresdner Kleinwort Wasserstein   **[2005] IRLR 514 EAT**
  Ltd v
Adebayo
In view of the statutory "like for like' requirement and the need for the relevant circumstances in the claimant's case to be the same or not materially different in the case of the comparator, in order to establish a prima facie case, a claimant in a promotion case would have to show not only that he met the stated qualifications for promotion to the post, but that he was at least as well qualified as the successful candidate.

Network Rail Infrastructure Ltd v   **[2006] IRLR 865 EAT**
Griffiths-Henry
The suggestion in *Adebayo* that an employee would be able to establish a prima facie case if he were black, was not promoted and was at least as well qualified as the white comparator would be agreed with where there were only two candidates, but the case becomes weaker where there are a number of candidates and the black candidate is rejected with a number of equally well-qualified white candidates. There is then no distinction between all the unsuccessful candidates and the justification for inferring a prima facie case is significantly weaker.

Network Rail Infrastructure Ltd v   **[2006] IRLR 865 EAT**
Griffiths-Henry
A tribunal at the second stage is simply concerned with the reason why the employer acted as he did. The burden imposed on the employer will depend on the strength of the prima facie case. A black candidate who is better qualified than the only other candidate, who is white, and does not get the job imposes a greater burden at the second stage than would a black candidate rejected along with some others who were equally qualified.

Dresdner Kleinwort Wasserstein   **[2005] IRLR 514 EAT**
  Ltd v
Adebayo
The shifting of the burden to employers means that tribunals are entitled to expect employers to call evidence which is sufficient to discharge the burden of proving that the explanation advanced was non-discriminatory and that it was the real reason for what occurred. Equivocal or evasive answers to legitimate queries in statutory questionnaires, failures to follow recommendations in relevant codes of practice, or the failure to call as witnesses those who were involved in the events and decisions about which complaint is made will all properly assume a greater significance in future, in cases where the burden of proving that no discrimination has occurred is found to have passed to the employer.

Pothecary Witham Weld v   **[2010] IRLR 572 EAT**
Weld
In a case where a claimant has raised a prima facie case, it must in principle be enough to say "we were not persuaded that his explanation was right", rather than "we reject his explanation": that is what the burden of proof is about. In cases where any discriminatory motivation may well be subconscious – something notoriously difficult to prove or disprove – a tribunal may reasonably prefer to go no further than saying that the burden of proof has not been discharged.

Zafar v   **[1998] IRLR 36 HL**
Glasgow City Council
The conduct of a hypothetical reasonable employer is irrelevant to deciding whether a discrimination claimant has been treated by the alleged discriminator "less favourably" than that person treats or would have treated another. It cannot be inferred only from the fact that an employer has acted unreasonably towards one employee that he would have acted reasonably if he had been dealing with another in the same circumstances

Network Rail Infrastructure Ltd v   **[2006] IRLR 865 EAT**
Griffiths-Henry
It would be inappropriate to find discrimination simply because an explanation given by the employer for the difference in treatment is not one which the tribunal considers objectively to be justified or reasonable. Unfairness is not itself sufficient to establish discrimination.

Qureshi v   **[1991] IRLR 264 CA**
London Borough of Newham
Incompetence does not, without more, become discrimination merely because the person affected by it is from an ethnic minority.

Anya v   **[2001] IRLR 377 CA**
University of Oxford
Very little direct discrimination today is overt or even deliberate. The guidance from the case law tells tribunals to look for indicators from a time before or after the particular deci-

sion which may demonstrate that an ostensibly fair-minded decision was, or equally was not, affected by racial bias.

Nelson v   [2009] IRLR 549 NICA
Newry and Mourne District Council
The fact that a decision could not be found to be irrational or perverse must be very relevant in deciding whether there was evidence from which it could properly be inferred that the decision-making was motivated by an improper sexually discriminatory intent.

Rihal v   [2004] IRLR 642 CA
London Borough of Ealing
In determining whether there were racial grounds for less favourable treatment, a tribunal is obliged to look at all the material put before it which is relevant to determination of that issue, which may include evidence about the conduct of the alleged discriminator before or after the act about which complaint is made. The total picture has to be looked at. In constructing a picture of how a hypothetical comparator would have been treated in comparable circumstances, the tribunal may have to look beyond the immediate circumstances of the incident about which complaint is made. Moreover, where there are allegations of discrimination by an employer over a substantial period of time, it would be wrong for a tribunal to treat the individual incidents complained of in isolation from one another. That would be a fragmented approach and would overlook the relevance which the wider profile may have to the decisions to be reached on those individual complaints.

EB v   [2006] IRLR 471 CA
BA
Once the burden of proof has shifted, the consequences of the absence of documents from the employers could only be adverse to them because the failure deprived the employers of the opportunity to rebut the case made against it. Employers should not be permitted to escape the provisions of s.63A of the Sex Discrimination Act by leaving it to the employee to prove her case. If an employer takes the stance of "you prove it", claimants – particularly those with limited or no means – who challenge large corporations would be at a great disadvantage. That might render the reverse burden of proof provision of little or no use to a claimant.

West Midlands Passenger Transport   [1988] IRLR 186 CA
     Executive v
Singh
Statistical evidence may establish a discernible pattern in the treatment of a particular group: if that pattern demonstrates a regular failure of members of the group to obtain particular jobs and of underrepresentation in such jobs, it may give rise to an inference of discrimination against the group. Statistics obtained through monitoring of the workforce and of applications for recruitment and promotion are not conclusive in themselves, but if they show imbalances or disparities, they may indicate areas of discrimination.

West Midlands Passenger Transport   [1988] IRLR 186 CA
     Executive v
Singh
If a practice is being operated against a racial group then, in the absence of a satisfactory explanation in a particular case, it is reasonable to infer that the complainant, as a member of the group, has himself been treated less favourably on grounds of race. Evidence of discriminatory treatment against the group may be more persuasive of discrimination in a particular case than previous treatment of the complainant by the employer, which may be indicative of personal factors peculiar to the complainant and not necessarily racially motivated.

Rihal v   [2004] IRLR 642 CA
London Borough of Ealing
If an employer institutes an arrangement which is discriminatory, that arrangement does not cease to be so merely because the manager in charge changes. It is the employers against whom the complaint is made, not the individual manager.

Robson v   [1998] IRLR 186 EAT
Commissioners of Inland Revenue
Whether someone is related by marriage to someone from an ethnic minority is not probative of whether they discriminated against someone from a different racial group.

Oxford v   [1977] IRLR 225 EAT
Department of Health and
     Social Security
Although the formal burden of proof lies upon the claimant, it would only be in exceptional or frivolous cases that it would be right for an employment tribunal to find at the end of the claimant's case that there was no case to answer and that it was not necessary to hear what the respondents had to say about it.

Scope of evidence

West Midlands Passenger Transport   [1988] IRLR 186 CA
     Executive v
Singh
As evidence from employers that both white and non-white persons hold responsible positions has been accepted as demonstrating that the employers have a policy of non-discrimination and as providing probative evidence from which an employment tribunal can decide that a particular claimant had not been discriminated against, so evidence of a discriminatory attitude on the employers' part may also have probative effect.

Din v   [1982] IRLR 281 EAT
Carrington Viyella Ltd
Section 68(1) of the Race Relations Act prevents an act which occurred more than three months before the start of proceedings being treated as the cause of action giving

rise to a remedy under the Act. Section 68(1) does not say that no regard shall be had to any discriminatory acts done outside the period of three months. Though no damages or other relief can be obtained relying simply on acts done outside the period of three months, it does not follow that acts done within the three months' period which are related to acts done outside the three months' period are incapable of giving rise to a cause of action.

Chattopadhyay v   [1981] IRLR 487 EAT
The Headmaster of Holloway School
Evidence of events subsequent to an alleged act of discrimination is admissible where it is logically probative of a relevant fact.

Chattopadhyay v   [1981] IRLR 487 EAT
The Headmaster of Holloway School
If a person involved in an alleged act of discrimination had, before the act complained of, treated the complainant with hostility, that evidence of hostility would be admissible as showing circumstances consistent with a racialist attitude of that person, even though there might be another, innocent explanation for such hostility. There is no relevant distinction between hostility before the event and hostility after the event. Evidence of such hostility is admitted with a view to showing that the person involved was treating the complainant differently from other people, whether he was animated by racial considerations or not. In either case, it calls for an answer.

Chapman v   [1994] IRLR 124 CA
Simon
The jurisdiction of the employment tribunal is limited to complaints which have been made to it. If the act of which complaint is made is found to be not proven, it is not for the tribunal to find another act of discrimination of which complaint has not been made to give a remedy in respect of that other act.

Dimtsu v   [1991] IRLR 450 EAT
Westminster City Council
In determining a discrimination complaint, an employment tribunal does not have an inquisitorial role to investigate generally and see that the requirements of the Act have in all respects been observed. An employment tribunal's duty is to adjudicate upon the issues before it. A tribunal is not under a duty to investigate other possible complaints, even though they arise out of the same incident, unless it is asked to do so.

Zurich Insurance Co v   [1998] IRLR 118 EAT
Gulson
An employment tribunal was entitled to exercise its discretion not to allow the employers to cross-examine the claimant about her family outgoings, with a view to showing that she and her husband could stretch their income to pay for a full-time nanny so that she comply with a requirement to work on a rota basis.

Discovery and particulars

GENERAL PRINCIPLES

Nasse v   [1979] IRLR 465 HL
Science Research Council
Vyas v
Leyland Cars
In cases under the Sex Discrimination Act and the Race Relations Act, the necessary information and material to support or refute a claim will rarely be in the possession of the employee, but, on the contrary, is likely to be in the possession of the employer. Discrimination often involves an allegation that, although the unselected complainant is as well qualified as the person selected, or indeed better qualified, he was not chosen, an allegation which almost necessarily involves a careful comparison of qualifications and an inquiry into the selection process. The employer is likely to have information on these matters. There is a clear public interest, accepted and emphasised by Parliament in the Sex Discrimination and Race Relations Acts, that the fullest information should be before the tribunals.

Canadian Imperial Bank of   [2009] IRLR 740 CA
    Commerce v
Beck
The law on disclosure of documents is very clear, and of universal application. The test is whether or not an order for discovery is necessary for fairly disposing of the proceedings. Relevance is a factor, but is not, of itself, sufficient to warrant making an order. Confidentiality is not, of itself, sufficient to warrant the refusal of an order and does not render documents immune from disclosure.

West Midlands Passenger Transport   [1988] IRLR 186 CA
    Executive v
Singh
Statistics of the number of white and non-white persons who applied for similar posts with the employers over a period, categorised as to whether or not they had been appointed, are discoverable by an unsuccessful claimant for promotion since they are logically probative of whether the employers discriminated against him on racial grounds when they denied him promotion. The statistical material was relevant in that it might assist the complainant in establishing a positive case that the treatment of non-white employees was on racial grounds, which was an effective cause for their, and his, failure to obtain promotion and it might assist the complainant to rebut the employers' contention that they operated an equal opportunities policy and applied it in his case.

Perera v   [1980] IRLR 233 EAT
Civil Service Commission
Since it is rare for there to be direct evidence or a direct admission of racial discrimination, tribunals will have to probe the facts which are put forward initially by the person against whom the proceedings are brought to consider

whether there has been discrimination. Therefore, a claimant is entitled to have the opportunity of looking, in such form as is convenient and fair, at such material which is in the possession of the employer and which is necessary for the tribunal to consider the matter.

Rasul v   **[1978] IRLR 203 EAT**
Commission for Racial Equality

A complainant is entitled to discovery of documents from the respondents, which will enable him to make a comparative analysis between his own qualifications and history and that of his competitors for a job for which he applied unsuccessfully, in order that an employment tribunal can legitimately draw the inference that the reason for his non-success was that the respondents had discriminated against him on grounds of his race. It is not easy for a complainant in a discrimination case to give direct evidence to establish whether somebody has practised discrimination, since it is what happens in the decision-making process of the prospective employer that is, or is not, discrimination.

Commissioner of Police of   **[1993] IRLR 319 EAT**
**   the Metropolis v**
Locker

Discovery of statements made in the course of the grievance procedure dealing with the employee's allegations of discrimination in respect of her non-selection for a post was necessary for fairly disposing of her employment tribunal complaints, notwithstanding that the statements sought to be inspected were about events which may have preceded the discriminatory conduct complained of, since the allegations went significantly wider than the conduct of the interview when she was not selected. She relied upon a background of discriminatory treatment which would, if proved, clearly be admissible material from which inferences could be drawn of discrimination on racial grounds, and the grievance procedure may well have produced statements that would tend to prove such background facts.

West Midlands Passenger Transport   **[1988] IRLR 186 CA**
**   Executive v**
Singh

A tribunal may decide that a request for discovery is oppressive and not order discovery even where it is relevant if it is of the opinion that it is not necessary for disposing fairly of the proceedings or for saving costs. Discovery may be oppressive if it requires the provision of material not readily to hand, which can only be made available with difficulty and at great expense, or if it requires the party ordered to make discovery to embark on a course which will add unreasonably to the length and cost of the hearing.

Carrington v   **[1990] IRLR 6 EAT**
Helix Lighting Ltd

There are no powers under the Employment Tribunals Rules of Procedure to require an employer to prepare a schedule of evidence disclosing details of the ethnic composition of its workforce where this information is not available and can only be produced by carrying out a survey of the workforce. "Discovery" is limited to the production of documents in being.

CONFIDENTIAL DOCUMENTS

Nasse v   **[1979] IRLR 465 HL**
Science Research Council
Vyas v
Leyland Cars

There is no principle of law by which documents are protected from discovery by confidentiality in and of itself. If an employment tribunal is satisfied that discovery of a document is necessary in order to dispose fairly of proceedings or for saving costs, it must order the document to be disclosed, notwithstanding that the document is confidential.

Nasse v   **[1979] IRLR 465 HL**
Science Research Council
Vyas v
Leyland Cars

Where there is an objection by an employer to the disclosure of documents on the grounds of confidentiality, the employment tribunal should inspect the documents to decide whether disclosure is necessary for the fair disposal of the case or for saving costs. An employment tribunal should not order discovery without first inspecting the documents concerned. In exercising its discretion as to whether to order disclosure, the tribunal should have regard to the fact that documents are confidential and should consider whether the necessary information can be obtained by other means, not involving a breach of confidence. It should consider whether justice can be done by special measures such as "covering up" or substituting anonymous references for specific names.

British Railways Board v   **[1979] IRLR 45 EAT**
Natarajan

Before deciding whether an examination of confidential documents is necessary, an employment tribunal chairman should decide whether there is any prima facie prospect of the confidential material being relevant to an issue which arises in the litigation. If there is not, the examination of the documents should not take place. If it is reasonable to expect that there is a real likelihood of relevance emerging from the examination, it is a matter of convenience in each case as to whether the examination should take place at the interlocutory stage of discovery or immediately the matter arises at the trial.

The British Library v   **[1984] IRLR 306 EAT**
Palyza

In considering whether discovery sought is necessary for disposing fairly of the proceedings, a tribunal should confine its attention to matters which are, or might be, of assistance to the claimant. The tribunal is not required to order the disclosure against the employer's wishes of material which would or could help the employer's case. The "fair disposal of the proceedings" means a disposal which is fair to the claimant. The justification for ordering the disclosure of information which would otherwise remain confidential is that Parliament has seen fit to place upon the complainant of racial or sexual discrimination the burden of proving his or her case, notwithstanding that the bulk of the relevant evidence is likely to be in the possession of the respondent to the complaint. The procedure of discovery is designed to offset the probative disadvantages which the complainant would otherwise suffer. It is designed to do justice to the complainant, and there is no reason why it should seek to go further than that. The governing concept is fairness, not absolute justice, and it would be strange if one of the adversaries was compelled to adduce favourable evidence which he would rather withhold.

The British Library v Palyza
[1984] IRLR 306 EAT

The decision of an employment tribunal as to whether or not it is necessary for fairly disposing of the proceedings that confidential reports should be disclosed in cases of alleged discrimination is one which the EAT is free to review and to substitute its own view. The decision whether discovery should be ordered is of such importance as to make it highly desirable that its review by the appellate court should be unfettered.

Commissioner of Police of the Metropolis v Locker
[1993] IRLR 319 EAT

Whether public interest immunity exists depends upon whether the court is satisfied that the nature and status of the procedure in which the class of documents was generated is of a type to which public interest immunity should apply. On that basis, public interest immunity does not attach to statements made during the course of a police grievance procedure.

PARTICULARS

Carrington v Helix Lighting Ltd
[1990] IRLR 6 EAT

An employment tribunal does not have power in a case of alleged discrimination to require a schedule of evidence to be produced by an employer where there is no documentation upon which the schedule is to be based and where the production of the schedule is in the nature of creating evidence. Such information cannot be regarded as "particulars" as particulars are the basis whereby a party may ascertain the way the other side is putting their case so that they can prepare accordingly. Particulars are not evidence.

FORMS FOR QUESTIONING

(1) With a view to helping a person ("the person aggrieved") who considers he may have been discriminated against or subjected to harassment in contravention of this Act to decide whether to institute proceedings and, if he does so, to formulate and present his case in the most effective manner, the Secretary of State shall by order prescribe –

> *(a) forms by which the person aggrieved may question the respondent on his reasons for doing any relevant act, or on any other matter which is or may be relevant;*
> *(b) forms by which the respondent may if he so wishes reply to any questions.*

(2) Where the person aggrieved questions the respondent (whether in accordance with an order under subsection (1) or not) –

> *(a) the question, and any reply by the respondent (whether in accordance with such an order or not) shall, subject to the following provisions of this section, be admissible as evidence in the proceedings;*
> *(b) if it appears to the court or tribunal that the respondent deliberately, and without reasonable excuse omitted to reply within a reasonable period or that his reply is evasive or equivocal, the court or tribunal may draw any inference from that fact that it considers it just and equitable to draw, including an inference that he committed an unlawful act.*

SEX DISCRIMINATION ACT – s.74
RACE RELATIONS ACT – s.65

Carrington v Helix Lighting Ltd
[1990] IRLR 6 EAT

The statutory procedure by way of questionnaire is the way in which the legislature has made provision for a claimant to advance his or her case of discrimination. Tribunals are encouraged by the statutes to take a serious view of any unsatisfactory answering of questionnaires and have ample power to draw adverse inferences.

Dattani v Chief Constable of West Mercia Police
[2005] IRLR 327 EAT

Section 65 of the Race Relations Act, which allows a tribunal to draw an inference of discrimination from an evasive or equivocal reply to questions from a claimant, covers replies given in a form other than that prescribed in the statutory discrimination questionnaires, such as the employer's notice of appearance, and further and better particulars.

D'Silva v NATFHE
[2008] IRLR 412 EAT

There is a tendency for respondents' failures in answering a questionnaire, or otherwise in providing information or documents, to be relied on by claimants, and even sometimes by tribunals, as automatically raising a presumption of discrimination. An inference can be drawn from failures of this kind only in appropriate cases, and the drawing of inferences from such failures is not a tick-box exercise. It is necessary in each case to consider whether the failure in question is capable of constituting evidence supporting the inference that the respondent acted discriminatorily in the manner alleged; and if so whether in the light of any explanation supplied it does in fact justify that inference. Such failures are only relevant to the extent that they potentially shed light on the actual discrimination complained of and thus, necessarily, on the mental processes of the decision-taker. There will be many cases where it should be clear from the start, or soon becomes evident, that any alleged failure of this kind, however reprehensible, can have no bearing on the reason why the respondents did the act complained of.

Carrington v   **[1990] IRLR 6 EAT**
Helix Lighting Ltd
It is a sensible and necessary part of the procedure that after any initial questionnaire, a claimant should be able to seek leave, on notice, to administer a further questionnaire.

Oxford v   **[1977] IRLR 225 EAT**
Department of Health and
  Social Security
There is no obligation on an employer, in answer to a form for questioning under s.74 of the Sex Discrimination Act, to provide a complainant with the names and addresses of successful claimants for the position for which the complainant applied. Information as to the qualifications of successful claimants and other relevant information should generally be disclosed, with the identity of the individuals being concealed and their address withheld.

Sex discrimination

Pregnancy and maternity discrimination

(1) In any circumstances relevant for the purposes of a provision to which this subsection applies, a person discriminates against a woman if –

  (a) at a time in a protected period, and on the ground of the woman's pregnancy, the person treats her less favourably; or

  (b) on the ground that the woman is exercising or seeking to exercise, or has exercised or sought to exercise, a statutory right to maternity leave, the person treats her less favourably.

(2) In any circumstances relevant for the purposes of a provision to which this subsection applies, a person discriminates against a woman if, on the ground that s.72(1) of the Employment Rights Act 1996 (compulsory maternity leave) has to be complied with in respect of the woman, he treats her less favourably.

(3) For the purposes of subsection (1) –

  (a) in relation to a woman, a protected period begins each time she becomes pregnant, and the protected period associated with any particular pregnancy of hers ends in accordance with the following rules –

    (i) if she is entitled to ordinary but not additional maternity leave in connection with the pregnancy, the protected period ends at the end of her period of ordinary maternity leave connected with the pregnancy or, if earlier, when she returns to work after the end of her pregnancy;

    (ii) if she is entitled to ordinary and additional maternity leave in connection with the pregnancy, the protected period ends at the end of her period of additional maternity leave connected with the pregnancy or, if earlier, when she returns to work after the end of her pregnancy;

    (iii) if she is not entitled to ordinary maternity leave in respect of the pregnancy, the protected period ends at the end of the 2 weeks beginning with the end of the pregnancy;

  (b) where a person's treatment of a woman is on grounds of illness suffered by the woman as a consequence of a pregnancy of hers, that treatment is to be taken to be on the ground of the pregnancy;

  (c) a "statutory right to maternity leave" means a right conferred by s.71(1) or 73(1) of the Employment Rights Act 1996 (ordinary and additional maternity leave).

SEX DISCRIMINATION ACT 1975 (as amended) – s.3A
➡ EQUALITY ACT 2010 – s.18

(1) In any circumstances relevant for the purposes of a provision to which this subsection applies, a person discriminates against a woman if, on the ground that she is exercising or seeking to exercise, or has exercised or sought to exercise, a statutory right to maternity leave, he treats her less favourably than he would treat her if she were neither exercising nor seeking to exercise, and had neither exercised nor sought to exercise, such a right.

(2) In any circumstances relevant for the purposes of a provision to which this subsection applies, a person discriminates against a woman if, on the ground that s.72(1) of the Employment Rights Act 1996 (compulsory maternity leave) has to be complied with in respect of the woman, he treats her less favourably than he would treat her if that provision did not have to be complied with in respect of her.

SEX DISCRIMINATION ACT 1975 (as amended) – s.3B
➡ EQUALITY ACT 2010 – s.17

(1) Subject to subsection (2), s.6(1)(b) and (2) does not make it unlawful to deprive a woman who is on maternity leave of any benefit from the terms and conditions of her employment relating to remuneration.

(2) The reference in subsection (1) to benefit from the terms and conditions of a woman's employment relating to remuneration does not include a reference to –

(a) maternity-related remuneration (including maternity-related remuneration that is increase-related),

(b) remuneration (including increase-related remuneration) in respect of times when the woman is not on maternity leave, or

(c) remuneration by way of bonus in respect of times when a woman is on compulsory maternity leave.

(3) For the purposes of subsection (2), remuneration is increase-related so far as it falls to be calculated by reference to increases in remuneration that the woman would have received had she not been on maternity leave.

(4) In this section –

"maternity-related remuneration", in relation to a woman, means remuneration to which she is entitled as a result of being pregnant or being on maternity leave;

"on compulsory maternity leave" means absent from work in consequence of the prohibition in s.72(1) of the Employment Rights Act 1996;

"on maternity leave" means –

> *(a) on compulsory maternity leave,*
>
> *(b) absent from work in exercise of the right conferred by s.71(1) of the Employment Rights Act 1996 (ordinary maternity leave), or*
>
> *(c) absent from work in exercise of the right conferred by s.73(1) of that Act (additional maternity leave); and*

"remuneration" means benefits –

> *(a) that consist of the payment of money to an employee by way of wages or salary, and*
>
> *(b) that are not benefits whose provision is regulated by the employee's contract of employment.*

SEX DISCRIMINATION ACT 1975 (as amended) – s.6A
➥ **EQUALITY ACT 2010 – Sch. 9, para. 17**

Webb v   **[1993] IRLR 27 HL**
EMO Air Cargo (UK) Ltd

To dismiss a woman because she is pregnant or to refuse to employ a woman of child-bearing age because she may become pregnant is unlawful direct discrimination since child-bearing and the capacity for child-bearing are characteristics of the female sex. To apply these characteristics as the criterion for dismissal or refusal to employ is to apply a gender-based criterion.

Webb v   **[1995] IRLR 645 HL**
EMO Air Cargo (UK) Ltd (No.2)

To dismiss a woman because she was found to be pregnant, in circumstances in which she had been recruited for an unlimited term with a view, initially, to replacing another employee during the latter's maternity leave and would not be available for work at the time when the task for which she was recruited fell to be performed, is unlawful discrimination contrary to the Sex Discrimination Act.

Fletcher v   **[2005] IRLR 689 EAT**
Blackpool Fylde & Wyre Hospitals NHS Trust

A complaint of sex discrimination by a pregnant woman cannot be defended by saying that all employees are treated in the same way. Treating pregnant women or women on maternity leave during the "protected period" in the same way as other employees, in circumstances in which they are disadvantaged because of their pregnancy or maternity, is applying the same treatment to different situations and is therefore discrimination.

Fletcher v   **[2005] IRLR 689 EAT**
Blackpool Fylde & Wyre Hospitals NHS Trust

Women on maternity leave are in a special, protected position and cannot compare themselves to men and women at work. However, the decision in *Webb v EMO Air Cargo*

(UK) Ltd did not rule out a comparison between sickness and pregnancy in all circumstances. Whilst it is not necessary for the pregnant woman to compare her treatment with that of a sick man in order to succeed in her claim of discrimination, and whilst an employer dismissing a woman on grounds of pregnancy cannot defend her complaint of sex discrimination by stating that he would have treated a sick man in the same way, the purpose of the *Webb* principle is to protect pregnant women. It is not to prevent them from comparing their treatment with more favourable treatment afforded to sick men, where appropriate, in order to demonstrate that a different rule is being applied in comparable circumstances and that discrimination has occurred.

O'Neill v   **[1996] IRLR 372 EAT**
Governors of St Thomas More
    RCVA Upper School

The distinction between pregnancy per se and pregnancy in the circumstances of the case as motives is legally erroneous. The critical question is whether, on an objective consideration of all the surrounding circumstances, the dismissal or other treatment complained of is on the ground of pregnancy, or on some other ground. This must be determined by an objective test of causal connection. The event or factor alleged to be causative of the matter complained of need not be the only or even the main cause of the result complained of. It is enough if it is an effective cause. The concept of pregnancy per se is misleading, because it suggests pregnancy as the sole ground for dismissal. Pregnancy always has surrounding circumstances. The Sex Discrimination Act requires the tribunal to decide a case by having regard to whether the treatment complained of was on the ground of sex, not by having regard to the subjective motives of the alleged discriminator.

O'Neill v   **[1996] IRLR 372 EAT**
Governors of St Thomas More
    RCVA Upper School

A religious education teacher who was dismissed after it became known that she had become pregnant by a Roman Catholic priest was dismissed on grounds of pregnancy and, therefore, discriminated against on grounds of sex. The factors surrounding the pregnancy – the paternity of the child, the publicity of that fact and the consequent untenability of the appellant's position as a religious education teacher – were all causally related to the fact that she was pregnant. Her pregnancy precipitated and permeated the decision to dismiss her. Therefore, it was not possible to say that the ground for dismissal was anything other than pregnancy.

Abbey National plc v   **[1999] IRLR 222 EAT**
Formoso

Where a woman is prevented from defending herself at a disciplinary hearing due to her absence for a pregnancy-related reason, that is direct sex discrimination.

Iske v   [1997] IRLR 401 EAT
P & O European Ferries (Dover) Ltd

The employers' failure to offer a pregnant seafarer a transfer to available and suitable shore work when she was no longer able to work at sea due to pregnancy, because alternative work was not given to women after the 28th week of pregnancy, was less favourable treatment on the grounds of her sex where such work would have been offered to a woman who was less than 28 weeks' pregnant or a man who was unfit for seagoing work.

O'Neill v   [2010] IRLR 384 EAT
Buckinghamshire County Council

There is no general obligation to carry out a risk assessment on pregnant employees. Therefore, failure to carry out such a risk assessment is not discrimination per se. The obligation to carry out a risk assessment of a pregnant worker is only triggered where (a) the employee notifies the employer that she is pregnant in writing; (b) the work is of a kind which could involve a risk of harm or danger to the health and safety of a new expectant mother or her baby; (c) the risk arises from either processes or working conditions or physical biological chemical agents in the workplace at the time specified in the list in Pregnant Workers Directive 92/85/EEC.

Hoyland v   [2005] IRLR 438 EAT
ASDA Stores Ltd

A worker who takes maternity leave during a bonus year must be paid bonus in respect of the periods when she is at work and the two weeks of compulsory maternity leave. However, a proportionate reduction to reflect absence on ordinary maternity leave is permitted.

GUS Home Shopping Ltd v   [2001] IRLR 75 EAT
Green

An employer unlawfully discriminated against the claimants on grounds of sex when it treated them as disqualified from receiving payment under a loyalty bonus scheme because they were absent from work during the relevant period because of pregnancy-related illness or maternity leave.

British Telecommunications plc v   [1996] IRLR 601 EAT
Roberts

A request to jobshare after maternity leave is not covered by the special protection against discrimination accorded to women during pregnancy and maternity leave. The period protected by statute is the period of the maternity leave. Once a woman returns to work after her leave, the statutory protection finishes, and her work thereafter is to be considered in the same circumstances as if she were a man. She is not permanently entitled to rely on having had babies as a protecting feature. Therefore, the employers' failure to give reasonable consideration to the claimants' requests to job share on returning from maternity leave could not be regarded as automatically direct discrimination on grounds

of sex in accordance with the principles laid down by the European Court in the *Webb* decision.

Kulikaoskas v   [2010] EqLR 276 EAT
Macduff Shellfish

Neither EU law nor the Sex Discrimination Act prohibits an employer from affording less favourable treatment to a man on the ground of a woman's pregnancy. A claim of associative discrimination, where one person suffers less favourable treatment because of the pregnancy of another person, is not permitted.

Discrimination on grounds of gender reassignment

(1) A person ("A") discriminates against another person ("B") in any circumstances relevant for the purposes of –
> *(a) any provision of Part II,*
> *(b) s.35A or 35B, or*
> *(c) any other provision of Part III, so far as it applies to vocational training,*

if he treats B less favourably than he treats or would treat other persons, and does so on the ground that B intends to undergo, is undergoing or has undergone gender reassignment.

(2) Subsection (3) applies to arrangements made by any person in relation to another's absence from work or from vocational training.

(3) For the purposes of subsection (1), B is treated less favourably than others under such arrangements if, in the application of the arrangements to any absence due to B undergoing gender reassignment –
> *(a) he is treated less favourably than he would be if the absence was due to sickness or injury, or*
> *(b) he is treated less favourably than he would be if the absence was due to some other cause and, having regard to the circumstances of the case, it is reasonable for him to be treated no less favourably.*

(4) In subsections (2) and (3) "arrangements" includes terms, conditions or arrangements on which employment, a pupillage or tenancy or vocational training is offered.

(5) For the purposes of subsection (1), a provision mentioned in that subsection framed with reference to discrimination against women shall be treated as applying equally to the treatment of men with such modifications as are requisite.

SEX DISCRIMINATION ACT 1975 – s.2A
➡ **EQUALITY ACT 2010 – s.4, s.13, s.16**

(3) For the purposes of this Act, a person ("A") subjects another person ("B") to harassment if –
> *(a) A, on the ground that B intends to undergo, is undergoing or has undergone gender reassignment, engages in unwanted conduct that has the purpose or effect –*
> > *(i) of violating B's dignity, or*
> > *(ii) of creating an intimidating, hostile, degrading, humiliating or offensive environment for B, or*
> *(b) A, on the ground of B's rejection of or submission to unwanted conduct of a kind mentioned in paragraph (a), treats B less favourably than A would treat B had B not rejected, or submitted to, the conduct.*

(4) Conduct shall be regarded as having the effect mentioned in sub-paragraph (i) or (ii) of subsection (3)(a) only if, having regard to all the circumstances, including in particular the perception of B, it should reasonably be considered as having that effect.

SEX DISCRIMINATION ACT 1975 (as amended) – s.4A

➡ **EQUALITY ACT 2010 – s.26**

"Gender reassignment" means a process which is undertaken under medical supervision for the purpose of reassigning a person's sex by changing physiological or other characteristics of sex, and includes any part of such a process.

SEX DISCRIMINATION ACT 1975 – s.82

➡ **EQUALITY ACT 2010 – s.7**

A v   **[2004] IRLR 573 HL**
Chief Constable of West Yorkshire Police
EU law requires that a trans person must be recognised in her reassigned gender for the purposes of sex discrimination law. In sex discrimination cases, it is necessary to compare the claimant's treatment with that afforded to a member of the opposite sex. In gender reassignment cases, it is necessary to compare the claimant's treatment with that afforded to a member of the sex to which he or she used to belong. Thus, for the purposes of discrimination between men and women in the fields covered by the Equal Treatment Directive, a trans person is to be regarded as having the sexual identity of the gender to which he or she has been reassigned.

Croft v   **[2003] IRLR 592 CA**
Royal Mail Group plc
By virtue of the definition in s.82 of the Sex Discrimination Act as amended, the category of persons who are not to be discriminated against on grounds of gender reassignment includes persons at all stages of gender reassignment under medical supervision. However, acquiring the status of transsexual does not carry with it the right to choose which toilet to use. Conversely, it does not follow that, until the final stage is reached, an employee can necessarily be required, in relation to lavatories, to behave as if they were not undergoing gender reassignment. A judgment has to be made as to when a male to female transsexual employee becomes a woman and is entitled to the same facilities as other women. The moment at which a person at the "real life test" stage is entitled to use female toilets depends on all the circumstances. The employer must take into account the stage reached in treatment, including the employee's own assessment and presentation, although the employer is not bound by the employee's self-definition when making a judgment as to when the changes occurred. The employer is also entitled to take into account, though not to be governed by, the susceptibilities of other members of the workforce. Regard should also be had to the particular difficulties which arise with respect to toilet facilities, and the need for separate facilities for men and women. It is inherent in a situation in which two sets of facilities, male and female, are required and in which a category of persons changing from one sex to another is recognised, that there must be a

period during which the employer is entitled to make separate arrangements for those undergoing the change.

Sexual orientation discrimination

Macdonald v   **[2003] IRLR 512 HL**
Advocate General for Scotland
Pearce v
Governing Body of Mayfield Secondary School
In the context of s.1 of the Sex Discrimination Act, "sex" means "gender" and does not include sexual orientation.

Discrimination against married persons

3. (1) In any circumstances relevant for the purposes of any provision of Part 2, a person discriminates against a married person of either sex if –

(a) on the ground of his or her marital status he treats that person less favourably than he treats or would treat an unmarried person of the same sex, or

(b) he applies to that person a provision, criterion or practice which he applies or would apply equally to an unmarried person, but –

(i) which is such that it would be to the detriment of a considerably larger proportion of married persons than of unmarried persons of the same sex, and

(ii) which he cannot show to be justifiable irrespective of the marital status of the person to whom it is applied, and

(iii) which is to that person's detriment.

(2) For the purposes of subsection (1), a provision of Part 2 framed with reference to discrimination against women shall be treated as applying equally to the treatment of men, and for that purpose shall have effect with such modifications as are requisite."

SEX DISCRIMINATION ACT (as amended) – s.3

➡ **EQUALITY ACT 2010 – s.8, s.13**

Chief Constable of the Bedfordshire   **[2002] IRLR 239 EAT**
  Constabulary v
Graham
A police force's policy which restricted officers married to each other or who are in relationships with each other from working together would be more likely to affect women than men, since a higher proportion of female officers were in relationships with male officers than male officers with female officers.

Hurley v   **[1981] IRLR 208 EAT**
Mustoe
In general, a condition excluding all members of a class from employment cannot be justified on the ground that some members of that class are undesirable employees. Parliament has legislated that women with children are not to be treated as a class but as individuals. No employer is

bound to employ unreliable employees, whether men or women. But he must investigate each case and not simply apply a rule of convenience, or a prejudice, to exclude a whole class of women or married persons because some members of that class are not suitable employees. Therefore, a policy of not employing persons, of either sex, who had small children was indirectly discriminatory against married persons contrary to s.3(1)(b)(i) of the Sex Discrimination Act and could not be regarded as justifiable for the purposes of s.3(1)(b)(ii).

Race discrimination

Racial grounds

(1) In this Act, unless the context otherwise requires –
> *"racial grounds" means any of the following grounds, namely colour, race, nationality or ethnic or national origins;*
> *"racial group" means a group of persons defined by reference to colour, race, nationality or ethnic or national origins, and references to a person's racial group refer to any racial group into which he falls.*

(2) The fact that a racial group comprises two or more distinct racial groups does not prevent it from constituting a particular racial group for the purposes of this Act.

(3) In this Act –
> *(a) references to discrimination refer to any discrimination falling within s.1 or 2; and*
> *(b) references to racial discrimination refer to any discrimination falling within s.1;*
and related expressions shall be construed accordingly.

RACE RELATIONS ACT – s.3
➡ **EQUALITY ACT 2010 – s.9, s.25**

R (on the application of E) v   **[2010] IRLR 136 SC**
Governing Body of JFS
The definition of "racial grounds" includes "ethnic or national origins". Origins require one to focus on descent.

Mandla v   **[1983] IRLR 209 HL**
Lee
A group can be defined by reference to its "ethnic origins" within the meaning of s.3(1) if it constitutes a separate and distinct community by virtue of characteristics which are commonly associated with common racial origin. "Ethnic" is used in the Race Relations Act in a sense appreciably wider than strictly racial or biological.
Per Lord Fraser of Tullybelton: For a group to constitute an ethnic group for the purposes of the Race Relations Act, it must regard itself, and be regarded by others, as a distinct community by virtue of certain characteristics. It is essential that there is (1) a long shared history, of which the group is conscious as distinguishing it from other groups,

and the memory of which keeps it alive; (2) a cultural tradition of its own, including family and social customs and manners, often but not necessarily associated with religious observance. In addition, there are other relevant characteristics, one or more of which will commonly be found and will help to distinguish the group from the secondary community; (3) either a common geographical origin, or descent from a small number of common ancestors; (4) a common language, not necessarily peculiar to the group; (5) a common literature peculiar to the group; (6) a common religion different from that of the neighbouring groups or from the general community surrounding it; (7) a sense of being a minority or being an oppressed or a dominant group within a larger community.

CRE v   **[1989] IRLR 8 CA**
Dutton
Whether there is an identifiable group of persons who are defined by reference to ethnic origins is essentially a question of fact, to be determined on the evidence, applying the approach set out by Lord Fraser in *Mandla v Lee*.

CRE v   **[1989] IRLR 8 CA**
Dutton
If there remains a discernible minority of a religious, racial or ethnic group which adheres to the group it may still be a "racial group" within Lord Fraser's criteria, even though a substantial proportion of the group have become assimilated in the general public.

London Borough of Lambeth v   **[1990] IRLR 230 CA**
CRE
Section 3(1) provides that "racial group" can be defined by "colour" so that a racial group may be of more than one ethnic origin.

Mandla v   **[1983] IRLR 209 HL**
Lee
Sikhs are a group defined by "ethnic origins" for the purposes of s.3(1) of the Race Relations Act.

CRE v   **[1989] IRLR 8 CA**
Dutton
Gipsies, using the narrower meaning of the word "gipsies" as "a wandering race (by themselves called 'Romany'), of Hindu origin" rather than the larger, amorphous group of "travellers" or "nomads", are an identifiable group defined by reference to "ethnic origins" within the meaning of the definition of "racial group".

CRE v   **[1989] IRLR 8 CA**
Dutton
"Travellers" are not synonymous with "gipsies". Therefore, a notice in a pub stating "no travellers" did not indicate an intention by the licensee to discriminate on racial grounds, since the prohibited class included all those of a nomadic way of life and all nomads were treated equally whatever their race.

Dawkins v   **[1993] IRLR 284 CA**
Department of the Environment
Rastafarians are not a separate "racial group" within the meaning of s.3(1). Although they are a separate group with identifiable characteristics, they have not established some separate identity by reference to their ethnic origins. "Ethnic" has a racial flavour. Comparing Rastafarians with the rest of the Jamaican community in England or with the rest of the Afro-Caribbean community, there was nothing to set them aside as a separate ethnic group.

BBC Scotland v   **[2001] IRLR 150 CS**
Souster
Neither the English nor the Scots are an "ethnic group" within the meaning of the Race Relations Act because the distinctive racial element required for recognition as an ethnic group is lacking.

Seide v   **[1980] IRLR 427 EAT**
Gillette Industries Ltd
Although discrimination on the ground of religion is outside the provisions of the Race Relations Act, being "Jewish" can mean a member of a race or a particular ethnic origin as well as being a member of a particular religious faith, and can therefore fall within the scope of the Act.

BBC Scotland v   **[2001] IRLR 150 CS**
Souster
The phrase "national origins" in s.3(1) is not limited to "nationality" in the legal sense and thus to citizenship which an individual acquires at birth. An individual can become a member of a racial group defined by reference to "origins" through adherence, as for instance by marriage.

BBC Scotland v   **[2001] IRLR 150 CS**
Souster
There can be direct or indirect racial discrimination within Great Britain arising from the fact that a person is of Scots or English national origins.

Tejani v   **[1986] IRLR 502 CA**
**The Superintendent Registrar for
   the District of Peterborough**
"National origins" for the purpose of the Race Relations Act refers only to a particular place or country of origin in accordance with the decision of the House of Lords in *Ealing London Borough Council v Race Relations Board* that "national origins" means "national" in the sense of "race" and not "citizenship". Therefore, there was no discrimination on grounds of "national origins" where the complainant was treated less favourably on grounds that he had been born abroad, without any particular reference to any particular place or country of origin, notwithstanding that a person born in the UK would not have been treated in the same way.

R (on the application of Elias) v   **[2006] IRLR 934 CA**
Secretary of State for Defence
"Place of birth" is not identical to "national origins" and therefore not inextricably linked to a forbidden ground of discrimination.

BBC Scotland v   **[2001] IRLR 150 CS**
Souster
"Nationality" is not defined exclusively by reference to citizenship. Nationality can encompass a change in nationality, and can be referable to present nationality.

BBC Scotland v   **[2001] IRLR 150 CS**
Souster
A claimant can be discriminated against on grounds of his English nationality where that nationality has been acquired by adherence or adoption since his birth or because he has been perceived to have become a member of the racial group, the English. It will be for the claimant to prove that he is English, whether that be because his national origins are English or because he has acquired English nationality or that he is perceived to be English.

Dhatt v   **[1991] IRLR 130 CA**
McDonalds Hamburgers Ltd
An application form which distinguished between British citizens and EC nationals on the one hand and claimants who were not British citizens or EC nationals on the other hand did not discriminate on grounds of nationality.

Simon v   **[1987] IRLR 307 CA**
Brimham Associates
In determining whether an act was done on "racial grounds", which means by reason of the racial group to which the complainant belongs, although it cannot be conclusive that the alleged discriminator did not know of the racial origin of the complainant, the knowledge or lack of knowledge of the alleged discriminator must be material.

Vicarious discrimination

Redfearn v   **[2006] IRLR 623 CA**
Serco Ltd
Discrimination "on racial grounds" is not confined to less favourable treatment on the ground of the colour or race of the claimant. The racial characteristic of C, rather than that of B, the victim of the less favourable treatment, may be a racial ground of less favourable treatment of B by A, and therefore direct discrimination by A against B.

Showboat Entertainment Centre Ltd v   **[1984] IRLR 7 EAT**
Owens
Section 1(1)(a) of the Race Relations Act covers all cases of discrimination "on racial grounds" whether the racial char-

acteristics in question are those of the person treated less favourably or of some other person. Therefore, dismissal of an employee because he refused to carry out a racially discriminatory instruction to exclude blacks was "on racial grounds" within the meaning of s.1(1)(a), notwithstanding that the employee was white.

Redfearn v　　　　　　　　　**[2006] IRLR 623 CA**
Serco Ltd
The approach in *Showboat* is not confined to cases of an employer implementing a policy of race discrimination by giving a racially discriminatory instruction to an employee, who is then treated less favourably by being dismissed for not carrying it out. White persons would also be treated less favourably than other white persons on the ground of colour in the case of a white employer who dismisses a white employee for marrying a black person, or a white publican who refuses to admit or serve a white customer on the ground that he is accompanied by a black person.

Redfearn v　　　　　　　　　**[2006] IRLR 623 CA**
Serco Ltd
The expression "on racial grounds" does not cover every case in which the discriminator's less favourable act was significantly influenced by racial considerations, even if the race was that of a third party. That would mean that it could be an act of direct discrimination for an employer, who was trying to improve race relations in the workplace, to dismiss an employee, whom he discovered had committed an act of race discrimination, such as racist abuse, against a fellow employee or customer. That would turn the ratio of *Showboat* and the policy of the race relations legislation upside down.

Redfearn v　　　　　　　　　**[2006] IRLR 623 CA**
Serco Ltd
A bus driver was not discriminated against "on racial grounds" when the employers discovered his candidature as a British National Party councillor, and decided that he should be dismissed on health and safety grounds having regard to the significant number of passengers and employees who were of Asian origin. It was a non-sequitur to argue that the claimant was dismissed "on racial grounds" because the circumstances leading up to his dismissal included a relevant racial consideration, such as the race of fellow employees and customers and the policies of the BNP on racial matters. The claimant was no more dismissed "on racial grounds" than an employee who is dismissed for racially abusing his employer, a fellow employee or a valued customer.

Segregation

(2) It is hereby declared that, for the purposes of this Act, segregating a person from other persons on racial grounds is treating him less favourably than they are treated.
　　　　　　　　　　　　　RACE RELATIONS ACT – s.1
　　　　　　　　　➡ **EQUALITY ACT 2010 – s.13**

PEL Ltd v　　　　　　　　　**[1980] IRLR 142 EAT**
Modgill
Segregation for the purposes of s.1(2) of the Race Relations Act means the employer keeping apart one person from others on grounds of his race. "Congregating" does not amount to "segregating". Where the fact that all the workers are of a particular racial group arises by the acts of those working in the particular shop themselves, the failure by the employer to intervene and to insist on workers of other racial groups going into the shop, to introduce their friends, contrary to the wishes of the employees in the shop, does not constitute the act of segregating persons on racial grounds.

Sex and race discrimination by employers

(1) It is unlawful for a person, in relation to employment by him at an establishment in Great Britain, to discriminate against a woman –
　　　(a) in the arrangements he makes for the purpose of determining who should be offered that employment; or
　　　(b) in the terms on which he offers her that employment; or
　　　(c) by refusing or deliberately omitting to offer her that employment.
(2) It is unlawful for a person, in the case of a woman employed by him at an establishment in Great Britain, to discriminate against her –
　　　(a) in the way he affords her access to opportunities for promotion, transfer or training, or any other benefits, facilities or services, or by refusing or deliberately omitting to afford her access to them; or
　　　(b) by dismissing her, or subjecting her to any other detriment.
　　　　　　　　SEX DISCRIMINATION ACT – s.6
　　　　　　➡ **EQUALITY ACT 2010 – s.39**

(1) It is unlawful for a person, in relation to employment by him at an establishment in Great Britain, to discriminate against another –
　　　(a) in the arrangements he makes for the purpose of determining who should be offered that employment; or
　　　(b) in the terms on which he offers him that employment; or
　　　(c) by refusing or deliberately omitting to offer him that employment.

(2) It is unlawful for a person, in the case of a person employed by him at an establishment in Great Britain, to discriminate against that employee –
　　　(a) in the terms of employment which he affords him; or
　　　(b) in the way he affords him access to opportunities for promotion, transfer or training, or to any other benefits, facilities or services, or by refusing or deliberately omitting to afford him access to them; or
　　　(c) by dismissing him, or subjecting him to any other detriment.
　　　　　　　　RACE RELATIONS ACT – s.4
　　　　　　➡ **EQUALITY ACT 2010 – s.39**

(4A) In subsection (2)(c) reference to the dismissal of a person from employment includes, where the discrimination is on grounds of race or ethnic or national origins, reference –

(a) to the termination of that person's employment by the expiration of any period (including a period expiring by reference to an event or circumstance), not being a termination immediately after which the employment is renewed on the same terms; and

(b) to the termination of that person's employment by any act of his (including the giving of notice) in circumstances such that he is entitled to terminate it without notice by reason of the conduct of the employer.

RACE RELATIONS ACT 1976 (as amended) – s.4
➡ EQUALITY ACT 2010 – s.39

Selection arrangements

Nagarajan v   **[1999] IRLR 572 HL**
London Regional Transport
The reference to a "person" in s.4 of the Race Relations Act, which makes it unlawful for "a person, in relation to employment by him" to discriminate, is focused exclusively on the employer. On a complaint against an employer under s.4(1)(a), it does not matter that different employees were involved at different stages. The acts of both employees are treated as done by the respondent employer.

Nagarajan v   **[1999] IRLR 572 HL**
London Regional Transport
Interviewing and assessing candidates for a post can amount to making arrangements for the purpose of determining who should be offered that employment. *Brennan v J H Dewhurst Ltd* correctly held that the arrangements an employer makes encompasses more than setting up the arrangements for interviewing claimants, and also includes the manner in which the arrangements are operated.

Brennan v   **[1983] IRLR 357 EAT**
J H Dewhurst Ltd
Arrangements made for the purpose of determining who should be offered employment are unlawful within the meaning of s.6(1)(a) of the Sex Discrimination Act if they operate so as to discriminate against a woman, even though they were not made with the purpose of so discriminating.

Cardiff Women's Aid v   **[1994] IRLR 390 EAT**
Hartup
Placing a discriminatory advertisement is not an act of discrimination by an employer within the meaning of Part II in respect of which an individual can make a complaint. Only the statutory enforcement agencies can bring proceedings in respect of causing an advertisement to be published which indicates "an intention" by a person to do an act of discrimination.

Saunders v   **[1977] IRLR 362 EAT**
Richmond upon Thames
  Borough Council
The Sex Discrimination Act does not make it automatically unlawful to ask a woman a question at an interview which would not be asked of a man. Whether such questions do constitute discrimination in the "arrangements" made by an employer for filling a position within the meaning of s.6(1)(a) depends upon whether, by asking the question, the woman was treated less favourably on grounds of her sex than a man would be treated. This involves consideration of the circumstances in which, and the purposes for which, the questions were asked.

Hurley v   **[1981] IRLR 208 EAT**
Mustoe
A policy not to employ women with children which is not applied to men with children is discrimination against women on grounds of sex contrary to s.1(1)(a) of the Sex Discrimination Act.

Noble v   **[1980] IRLR 252 CA**
David Gold & Son (Holdings) Ltd
An employer who allocated light work to women and heavier work to men had not discriminated on grounds of sex where the division of work was based on practical experience of organising the work and not on the assumption that no woman was capable of doing the heavier work. The Sex Discrimination Act provides that employers, when offering jobs, must not assume that women are less capable of doing them than men, and vice versa. This does not mean that a particular claimant for a job, whether male or female, can do it. Much will depend upon the claimant's physical attributes. Whether a woman claimant for a job can physically do it is a matter of judgment for the employer, and he should base his judgment on his own assessment of the candidate, based upon her physique and his experience of what other women doing that kind of job have been able to do. What he must not do is assume that all women are incapable of doing a particular job.

Horsey v   **[1982] IRLR 395 EAT**
Dyfed County Council
The employers had unlawfully discriminated on grounds of sex against the complainant by refusing to second her from Wales to a training course in the London area where her husband was employed, because they assumed that she would remain in London when her course was completed and would not return to work with them in Wales.

Offer of employment

Anya v   **[2001] IRLR 377 CA**
University of Oxford
The choice between two comparably well-qualified candidates on the basis of how the panel viewed their personal and professional qualities is notoriously capable of being influenced, often not consciously, by idiosyncratic factors, especially where proper equal opportunity procedures have not been followed. If these are to any significant extent racial factors, it will in general be only from the surrounding

circumstances and the previous history, not from the act of discrimination itself, that they will emerge.

Adekeye v   **[1997] IRLR 105 CA**
Post Office (No.2)
Section 4(1) of the Race Relations Act, which refers to discrimination "in relation to employment" by the employer, prohibits discrimination against claimants and does not cover a situation where an employee has been dismissed and is applying to be reinstated on appeal. The sidenote to s.4 accurately reflects its substance: subsection (1) relates to claimants seeking the offer of a job. A dismissed employee seeking reinstatement by an appeal against dismissal cannot be regarded as seeking an offer of employment. On the appeal, the appellant is not seeking an offer which can be accepted or refused; the appellant is seeking the reversal of a decision to dismiss.

Promotion, transfer or training

West Midlands Passenger Transport   **[1988] IRLR 186 CA**
    Executive v
Singh
Since the suitability of candidates can rarely be measured objectively and often requires subjective judgments, evidence of a high percentage rate of failure to achieve promotion at particular levels by members of a particular racial group may indicate that the real reason for refusal is a conscious or unconscious racial attitude which involves stereotyped assumptions about members of that group.

Mecca Leisure Group plc v   **[1993] IRLR 531 EAT**
Chatprachong
The employers did not discriminate against an Asian-born employee on grounds of race by failing to provide him with English language training in order to prepare him for promotion where there was no evidence to suggest that the employers would have given special speech training to any member of staff not of Asian origin who had difficulties.

Iske v   **[1997] IRLR 401 EAT**
P & O European Ferries (Dover) Ltd
An employer cannot avoid the effect of s.6(2) by contracting out a job to which the employee could be transferred.

Access to benefits

Clymo v   **[1989] IRLR 241 EAT**
London Borough of Wandsworth
Section 6(2)(a) of the Sex Discrimination Act refers to the employer's acts or omissions in affording access to "facilities" which already exist. Therefore, the appellant could not complain that her employer's refusal to allow her to share her job was contrary to s.6(2)(a) since employment in the

appellant's job did not allow anyone to jobshare. It was just not available and therefore was not an existing facility.

Eke v   **[1981] IRLR 334 EAT**
Commissioners of Customs
   and Excise
A refusal to investigate complaints of unfair treatment, whether based on grounds of race or otherwise, may amount to a refusal of access to "any other benefits, facilities or services" within the meaning of s.4(2)(b) of the Race Relations Act. To be a breach of the Act, however, the refusal to investigate must be one which itself is "on racial grounds".

Wakeman v   **[1999] IRLR 424 CA**
Quick Corporation
Locally-recruited British managers were not discriminated against on racial grounds by being paid substantially less than managers seconded from Japan. The fact that locally-hired Japanese were paid on the same scale as other locally-hired nationals at their level indicated that locally-recruited staff were treated equally regardless of race, and that the secondees' pay depended on the place of their permanent employment rather than their racial origin.

Detrimental treatment

General principles

Shamoon v   **[2003] IRLR 285 HL**
Chief Constable of the Royal Ulster Constabulary
In order for a disadvantage to qualify as a "detriment", it must arise in the employment field in that the court or tribunal must find that by reason of the act or acts complained of a reasonable worker would or might take the view that he had thereby been disadvantaged in the circumstances in which he had thereafter to work.

Shamoon v   **[2003] IRLR 285 HL**
Chief Constable of the Royal
   Ulster Constabulary
An unjustified sense of grievance cannot amount to "detriment".

Jiad v   **[2003] IRLR 232 CA**
Byford
Enduring physical or psychological injury can (depending on the facts) be capable of constituting detriment in the sense that a reasonable worker would regard it as a disadvantage, even though transitory hurt feelings may not (depending on the facts) suffice.

The Home Office v   **[1984] IRLR 299 EAT**
Holmes
The "detriment" referred to in s.6(2)(b) of the Sex Discrimination Act does not have to be a detriment of a

different kind than that which must be shown under s.1(1)(b)(ii). It is entirely consistent with the scheme and language of the Act that the same disadvantage to a woman may be relied on to found the detriment of incapacity under s.1 as to qualify under the broad head of detriment under s.6.

Appearance

Schmidt v   **[1977] IRLR 360 EAT**
Austicks Bookshops Ltd
A rule prohibiting women from wearing trousers at work was not discriminatory where the employers treated both male and female staff alike in that there were rules restricting wearing apparel and governing appearance which applied to men and women, although the rules in the two cases were not the same given the difference of sexes. An employer is entitled to a large measure of discretion in controlling the image of his establishment, including the appearance of staff, especially when those staff, as a result of their duties, come into contact with the public.

Smith v   **[1996] IRLR 456 CA**
Safeway plc
An appearance code which applies a standard of what is conventional applies an even-handed approach between men and women, and not one which is discriminatory. The principle to be applied is that derived from *Schmidt v Austicks Bookshops Ltd*: Rules concerning appearance will not be discriminatory because their content is different for men and women if they enforce a common principle of smartness or conventionality, and taken as a whole and not garment by garment or item by item, neither gender is treated less favourably in enforcing that principle, for example, because of the impact on comfort or health.

Smith v   **[1996] IRLR 456 CA**
Safeway plc
A package approach to the effect of an appearance code necessarily follows once it is accepted that the code is not required to make provisions which apply identically to men and women. The requirement of one particular item of a code may have the effect that the code treats one sex less favourably than the other, but this has to be considered in the context of the code as a whole. This approach is to be applied both to dress and to more permanent characteristics such as hairstyle. That a restriction extends beyond the workplace is a factor to be taken into account in considering whether or not the rule is discriminatory and has been applied in a discriminatory fashion, but does not affect the test itself.

Smith v   **[1996] IRLR 456 CA**
Safeway plc
An appearance code can be challenged before an employment tribunal on the ground that it operates unfavourably towards the claimant on grounds of his or her sex, for example, because of the impact on comfort or health, or the degree of restriction imposed on the freedom to govern one's own appearance. A tribunal has to consider interrelated questions of whether the restriction, such as on the length of hair being worn by men, could properly be justified on the ground that it represents a requirement of conventional appearance, and whether the restriction, when considered in the context of the code as a whole, results in men being treated less favourably than women.

Department for Work and   **[2004] IRLR 348 EAT**
   Pensions v
Thompson
If members of one sex are required to wear clothing of a particular kind, and members of the other sex are not, the former are not necessarily treated less favourably than the latter. In a case where men are required to wear a collar and tie at work, the question is whether, in the context of an overarching requirement for staff to dress in a professional and businesslike way, the level of smartness which the employers required, applying contemporary standards of conventional dresswear, could only be achieved for men by requiring them to wear a collar and tie. If that could be achieved by men dressing otherwise than in a collar and tie, the lack of flexibility in the dress code would suggest that men were being treated less favourably than women because it would not have been necessary to restrict men's choice of what to wear in order to achieve the standard of smartness required.

Burrett v   **[1994] IRLR 7 EAT**
West Birmingham Health Authority
A female nurse who was required to wear a cap was not treated less favourably on grounds of sex than male nurses who were not required to wear a cap, even though she considered the requirement demeaning, where the requirement to wear a uniform applied equally to male and female nurses, and it was merely the form of uniform that differed for men and women.

Smith v   **[1996] IRLR 456 CA**
Safeway plc
An employment tribunal was entitled to find that it was not discriminatory for an employer to ban unconventionally long hair for men when such length of hair for a woman was not unconventional.

Other examples

Brumfitt v   **[2005] IRLR 4 EAT**
Ministry of Defence
A failure adequately to investigate a complaint of sex discrimination is not necessarily sex discrimination in itself.

Balgobin v   **[1987] IRLR 401 EAT**
London Borough of Tower Hamlets

Requiring women to continue to work with an alleged harasser after an employers' inquiry into their complaints of sexual harassment was inconclusive was not less favourable treatment on grounds of sex where it was accepted that if the victim had been a man to whom homosexual advances had been made it would have been dealt with in the same way, so that there was no evidence that the employers had treated the women less favourably than they would have treated a comparable man.

Jeremiah v   **[1979] IRLR 436 CA**
Ministry of Defence

Requiring a man to work in dirty conditions when women were not so required was a "detriment" to him within the meaning of s.6(2)(b) of the Sex Discrimination Act, notwithstanding that he was compensated for the working conditions by an additional payment. An employer cannot buy a right to discriminate by making an additional payment.

Automotive Products Ltd v   **[1977] IRLR 365 CA**
Peake

A complaint by a man under the Sex Discrimination Act objecting to a rule permitting women employees who ceased work at the same time as men to leave the factory premises five minutes earlier than men was subject to the maxim *de minimis non curat lex* and could not be upheld.

Moyhing v   **[2006] IRLR 860 EAT**
Barts and London NHS Trust

A male student nurse was subjected to a detriment when, in accordance with the respondents' policy, he was not permitted, without a chaperone, to carry out an ECG on a female patient in circumstances in which a female student nurse did not have to be chaperoned when carrying out such a procedure on a male patient, notwithstanding a finding that the claimant's objection to the policy was unjustified.

BL Cars Ltd v   **[1985] IRLR 193 EAT**
Brown

The issuing of a written instruction to check the identity of black employees and the setting up of a regime under which black employees would have to undergo special investigation before they could have access to their place of work was capable of amounting to a "detriment" to those employees contrary to s.4(2)(c) of the Race Relations Act. It could not be accepted that the "detriment" could only arise when the instruction issued was implemented.

Garry v   **[2001] IRLR 681 CA**
London Borough of Ealing

An employee was subjected to a "detriment" when, for reasons connected with her ethnic origin, an investigation by her employers into her activities was continued longer than an ordinary investigation would have been, even though she was unaware that the investigation was continuing.

Retirement

Bullock v   **[1992] IRLR 564 CA**
Alice Ottley School

There is nothing in the Sex Discrimination Act which prevents an employer having a variety of retiring ages for different jobs, provided that there is no direct or indirect discrimination based on gender.

INDIRECT DISCRIMINATION

(b) he applies to that other a requirement or condition which he applies or would apply equally to persons not of the same racial group as that other but –

(i) which is such that the proportion of persons of the same racial group as that other who can comply with it is considerably smaller than the proportion of persons not of that racial group who can comply with it, and

(ii) which he cannot show to be justifiable irrespective of the colour, race, nationality or ethnic or national origins of the person to whom it is applied, and

(iii) which is to the detriment of that other because he cannot comply with it.

RACE RELATIONS ACT – s.1(1)
➡ **EQUALITY ACT 2010 – s.19**

A person also discriminates against another if, in any circumstances relevant for the purposes of any provision referred to in subsection (1B), he applies to that other a provision, criterion or practice which he applies or would apply equally to persons not of the same race or ethnic or national origins as that other, but –

(a) which puts or would put persons of the same race or ethnic or national origins as that other at a particular disadvantage when compared with other persons,

(b) which puts or would put that other at that disadvantage, and

(c) which he cannot show to be a proportionate means of achieving a legitimate aim.

RACE RELATIONS ACT 1976 (as amended) – s.1(1A)
➡ **EQUALITY ACT 2010 – s.19**

(b) he applies to her a provision, criterion or practice which he applies or would apply equally to a man, but –

(i) which puts or would put women at a particular disadvantage when compared with men,

(ii) which puts her at that disadvantage, and

(iii) which he cannot show to be a proportionate means of achieving a legitimate aim.

SEX DISCRIMINATION ACT 1975 (as amended) – s.1(2)
➡ **EQUALITY ACT 2010 – s.19**

(3) A comparison of the cases of persons of different sex or marital status under s.1(1) or 3(1) must be such that the relevant circumstances in the one case are the same, or not materially different, in the other.

SEX DISCRIMINATION ACT – s.5
➡ **EQUALITY ACT 2010 – s.23**

(4) A comparison of the case of a person of a particular racial group with that of a person not of that group under s.1(1) or (1A) must be such that the relevant circumstances in the one case are the same, or not materially different, in the other.

RACE RELATIONS ACT – s.3
➡ **EQUALITY ACT 2010 – s.23**

General principles

R (on the application of E) v   **[2010] IRLR 136 SC**
Governing Body of JFS
Indirect discrimination looks beyond formal equality towards a more substantive equality of results.

James v   **[1990] IRLR 288 HL**
Eastleigh Borough Council
The provisions relating to indirect discrimination cannot sensibly apply in the case of a requirement or condition which is itself gender-based. The conditions for the application of s.1(1)(b) presuppose a requirement or condition which is of itself gender-neutral. Where the requirement or condition is gender-based, the question is whether or not there has been direct discrimination under s.1(1)(a).

R (on the application of E) v   **[2010] IRLR 136 SC**
Governing Body of JFS
Direct and indirect discrimination are mutually exclusive. You cannot have both at once.

R v   **[2000] IRLR 363 HL**
Secretary of State for Employment
    ex parte Seymour-Smith (No.2)
The approach adopted by the European Court is similar to that provided by the indirect discrimination provisions of the Sex Discrimination Act. A considerable disparity can be more readily established if the statistical evidence covers a long period and the figures show a persistent and relatively constant disparity. In such a case, a lesser statistical disparity may suffice to show that the disparity is considerable than if the statistics cover only a short period or if they present an uneven picture.

Clarke v   **[1982] IRLR 482 EAT**
Eley (IMI) Kynoch Ltd
The purpose of the legislature in introducing the concept of indirect discrimination was to seek to eliminate those practices which had a disproportionate impact on women and were not justifiable for other reasons. Although the policy lying behind the Act cannot be used to give the words any wider meaning than they naturally bear, it is a powerful argument against giving the words a narrower meaning thereby excluding cases which fall within the mischief with which the statute was meant to deal.

Provision, criterion or practice

British Airways plc v   **[2005] IRLR 862 EAT**
Starmer
A discretionary management decision not applying to others can be a "provision". There is no necessity for the provision actually to apply to others. What is required in order to test

whether the provision, criterion or practice is discriminatory is to extrapolate it to others.

Disproportionate impact

Pool for comparison

Allonby v   **[2001] IRLR 364 CA**
Accrington & Rossendale College
The identification of the pool for comparison is a matter of logic rather than of discretion or fact-finding. Once the requirement or condition has been defined, there is likely to be only one pool which serves to test its effect.

Rutherford v   **[2006] IRLR 551 HL**
Secretary of State for Trade and Industry (No.2)
Since the sections of the Employment Rights Act that provide that an employee who has reached age 65 does not have the right either not to be unfairly dismissed or to receive a redundancy payment apply to everyone over age 65 and can apply to nobody under that age, the Equal Treatment Directive's requirement that, to establish indirect discrimination, a higher proportion of the members of one sex must be disadvantaged than of the other was not satisfied. There were no proportions to compare. The rule applies to the same proportion of women over age 65 as it applies to men.

Ministry of Defence v   **[2010] IRLR 471 EAT**
DeBique
No universal principle of law dictates what the pool should be in any particular case. In reaching their decision as to the appropriate pool, an employment tribunal should consider the position in respect of different pools within the range of decisions open to them, but they are entitled to select from that range the pool which they consider will realistically and effectively test the particular allegation before them.

Somerset County Council v   **[2009] IRLR 870 CA**
Pike
The correct ratio of *Rutherford* is that those who have no interest in the advantage or disadvantage in question should not be brought into the equation.

British Medical Association v   **[2007] IRLR 800 CA**
Chaudhary
Where the appropriate pool comprised all members who wanted the advice and support of the BMA for race discrimination claims against specific regulatory bodies, and no member of the pool could comply with the condition imposed by the BMA that it would not support such a claim, there was no comparative disadvantage for any racial group and no indirect race discrimination.

Proportionate comparison

Rutherford v   **[2006] IRLR 551 HL**
Secretary of State for Trade and Industry (No.2)
The question in an indirect discrimination case is whether the apparently neutral criteria or rules put one group at a comparative disadvantage to the other. The Burden of Proof Directive refers to a "substantially higher proportion of the members of one sex" being disadvantaged. This is the language of comparison. The concept is normally applied to a rule or requirement that selects people for a particular advantage or disadvantage. The disparate impact complained of is that a group of people cannot have what they want because of the rule or requirement, whereas others can.

R v   **[2000] IRLR 363 HL**
Secretary of State for Employment
    ex parte Seymour-Smith (No.2)
The claimants had shown that at the time of their dismissal in 1991 the two-year qualifying period to bring an unfair dismissal complaint had a disparately adverse impact on women so as to amount to indirect discrimination contrary to Article 141 in circumstances in which, from 1985 up to and including 1991, the ratio of men and women who qualified was roughly 10:9. A persistent and constant disparity of that order in respect of the entire male and female labour forces was adequate to demonstrate that the extension of the qualifying period from one to two years had a considerably greater adverse impact on women than men.

Harvest Town Circle Ltd v   **[2001] IRLR 599 EAT**
Rutherford
The proper approach to statistics relating to disparate impact is as follows:

(i) There will be some cases where, on the statistics, a disparate impact is so obvious that a look at numbers alone or proportions alone, whether of the advantaged (qualifiers) or disadvantaged (non-qualifiers), will suffice beyond doubt to show that members of one sex are substantially or considerably disadvantaged in comparison with those of the other.

(ii) However, in less obvious cases it will be proper for an employment tribunal to use more than one form of comparison, no one of which is necessarily to be regarded as on its own decisive.

(iii) In such less obvious cases it will be proper for the employment tribunal to look not merely at proportions (as proportions alone can be misleading) but also at numbers, and to look at both disadvantaged and non-disadvantaged groups and even to the respective proportions in the disadvantaged groups expressed as a ratio of each other.

(iv) It will never be wrong for a tribunal to look at more than one form of comparison, if only to confirm that the case remains as obvious as it had first appeared. Moreover, if there is any doubt as to the obviousness of the case, the tendency should always be to look at a second or further form of comparison.

(v) As more cases of indirect discrimination are heard, a better feel, a more soundly based assessment of what is or is not properly to be regarded as a considerable or substantial disparity will develop.

(vi) No distinction is to be drawn between a considerable and a substantial disparity. That being so, it would be a mistake to conclude that anything that was merely not trivial or de minimis sufficed.

(vii) The employment tribunal, in such less obvious cases, after looking in detail at such figures as should have been laid before it, must then stand back and, assimilating all the figures then judge whether the apparently neutral provision, criterion or practice in issue has a disparate impact, be it on men or women, that could fairly be described as considerable or substantial.

British Airways plc v   **[2005] IRLR 862 EAT**
Starmer
A tribunal is entitled to take into account, where appropriate, a more general picture than is specifically displayed by statistics put in evidence.

Coker v   **[2002] IRLR 80 CA**
Lord Chancellor's Department
Making an appointment from within a circle of family, friends and personal acquaintances is seldom likely to constitute indirect discrimination since the requirement of personal knowledge will exclude the vast proportion of the pool, be they men, women, white or another racial group.

Whether particular disadvantage to complainant

Barclays Bank plc v   **[1995] IRLR 87 CA**
Kapur
An unjustified sense of grievance cannot amount to detriment.

Shackletons Garden Centre Ltd v   **[2010] EqLR 138 EAT**
Lowe
Although a requirement to work weekends on a rotational basis put women at a particular disadvantage compared with men because of their childcare commitments, there was insufficient evidence to support a finding that the claimant was put at an individual disadvantage by this because childcare arrangements would not be available.

Justifiable

Standard of proof

Hampson v   **[1989] IRLR 69 CA**
Department of Education and Science
Whether a requirement or condition is "justifiable" requires an objective balance to be struck between the discriminatory effect of the requirement or condition and the reasonable needs of the person who applies it. It is not sufficient for the employer to establish that he considered his reasons adequate.

Hardys & Hansons plc v   **[2005] IRLR 726 CA**
Lax
The test of justification requires the employer to show that a provision, criterion or practice is justified objectively notwithstanding its discriminatory effect. The principle of proportionality requires the tribunal to take into account the reasonable needs of the business, but it has to make its own judgment, upon a fair and detailed analysis of the working practices and business considerations involved, as to whether the proposal is reasonably necessary. That "necessary" is qualified by "reasonably" reflects the applicability of the principle of proportionality and does not permit a margin of discretion or range of reasonable responses.

R v   **[2000] IRLR 363 HL**
Secretary of State for Employment
    ex parte Seymour-Smith (No.2)
The onus is on the Member State to show (1) that the allegedly discriminatory rule reflects a legitimate aim of its social policy, (2) that this aim is unrelated to any discrimination based on sex, and (3) that the Member State could reasonably consider that the means chosen were suitable for attaining that aim. Governments must be able to govern and are to be afforded a broad measure of discretion. Generalised assumptions, lacking any factual foundation, are not good enough, but national courts, acting with hindsight, are not to impose an impracticable burden on governments which are proceeding in good faith.

R (on the application of Elias) v   **[2006] IRLR 934 CA**
Secretary of State for Defence
A three-stage test is applicable to determine whether criteria are proportionate to the aim to be achieved. First, is the objective sufficiently important to justify limiting a fundamental right? Secondly, is the measure rationally connected to the objective? Thirdly, are the means chosen no more than is necessary to accomplish the objective?

Allen v   **[2008] IRLR 690 CA**
GMB
If a legitimate objective is achievable only by disproportionate means, then it would not be susceptible to justification. To conclude otherwise would be to license disproportionality.

British Airways plc v   **[2005] IRLR 862 EAT**
Starmer

Whereas, in carrying out the critical evaluation, a tribunal is obliged to give respect to a business decision taken by the respondent at the time, that does not apply where the consideration relied on retrospectively did not form part of that decision at the time. In such a case, the test is entirely objective.

Whiffen v   **[2001] IRLR 468 CA**
Milham Ford Girls' School

It is not a sufficient justification of a condition that has operated in a discriminatory manner that the policy of which that condition is a part, or even the condition itself, may operate in a non-discriminatory manner in other cases. The fact that a policy on its face is gender-neutral and is not inherently sex discriminatory is the very fact that brings the indirect discrimination provisions into operation and that fact loses any conclusive nature once the policy is found to have a discriminatory effect.

R (on the application of Elias) v   **[2006] IRLR 934 CA**
Secretary of State for Defence

A stringent standard of scrutiny of the justification is appropriate where the discrimination, although indirect in form, is so closely related in substance to the direct form of discrimination on grounds of national origins, which can never be justified.

Rainey v   **[1987] IRLR 26 HL**
Greater Glasgow Health Board

Per Lord Keith: There is no material difference in principle between the need to demonstrate objectively justified grounds of difference for the purposes of s.1(3) of the Equal Pay Act and the need to justify a requirement or condition under s.1(1)(b)(ii) of the Sex Discrimination Act.

Allonby v   **[2001] IRLR 364 CA**
Accrington & Rossendale College

Once a finding of a condition having a disparate impact on women has been made, what is required of the tribunal at a minimum is a critical evaluation of whether the employers' reasons demonstrate a real need; if there was such a need, consideration of the seriousness of the disparate impact on women including the claimant; and an evaluation of whether the former were sufficient to outweigh the latter.

British Airways plc v   **[2005] IRLR 862 EAT**
Starmer

Justification involves a weighing exercise, in which the detriment to the claimant and the (hypothetical) detriment to others, is put on the scales. The test is objective. The decision of the employer and its business reasons will be respected, but they must not be uncritically accepted.

Hockenjos v   **[2005] IRLR 471 CA**
Secretary of State for Social Security

In considering whether an indirectly sex discriminatory rule

of entitlement had been objectively justified, it could not be accepted that the Secretary of State was entitled to succeed unless there was an alternative means of achieving the policy aim that was so obviously better that no reasonable Secretary of State could have avoided choosing it. That focused solely on the means of achieving the policy aim and did not allow for any balancing consideration to be given to the need not to frustrate a fundamental principle of Community law, the equal treatment of men and women. Proportionality had to be considered, and it was necessary to feed into the question of proportionality the importance of the principle of equality. Although the Government has a broad margin of discretion in respect of social policy, it is not possible or appropriate to defer to that margin of appreciation when the effect of doing so would be to frustrate the implementation of a fundamental principle of Community law. The Secretary of State could not ignore the discriminatory extent of the measure he was seeking to justify.

R (on the application of Elias) v   **[2005] IRLR 788 HC**
Secretary of State for Defence

Although it is not necessary as a matter of law for the alleged discriminator to have analysed the proportionality question at the time of adopting a rule or policy, where a defendant seeks to rely as the rationale for a particular rule or policy on something which he only identifies in the course of the litigation and which had not been in his mind at the time it was adopted, a court will look with some concern to see whether it really did constitute a legitimate aim.

Greater Manchester Police   **[1990] IRLR 372 EAT**
  Authority v
Lea

In order to carry out the objective balance between the discriminatory effect of a condition and the reasonable needs of the person who applies it, there has to be a nexus established between the function of the employer and the imposition of the condition. It is not enough for it to be shown that a condition was imposed in pursuance of an intrinsically laudable and otherwise reasonable policy if there is no relevant need of the employer in connection with the condition.

Cobb v   **[1989] IRLR 464 EAT**
Secretary of State for Employment
  and Manpower Services Commission

The respondent is under no obligation to prove that there was no other possible way of achieving his objective however expensive and administratively complicated.

Cobb v   **[1989] IRLR 464 EAT**
Secretary of State for Employment
  and Manpower Services Commission

If alternative criteria are thought to be reasonable, then those should be put forward by the complainant. If the tribunal finds that the respondent ought reasonably to have considered and adopted them, in carrying out the balancing exercise the tribunal might find that the defence is not proved.

Ojutiku v　　　　　　　　　　　**[1982] IRLR 418 CA**
Manpower Services Commission
There is no rule of law which requires an employer to call independent evidence to establish the justifiability of a requirement.

Cobb v　　　　　　　　　　　**[1989] IRLR 464 EAT**
Secretary of State for Employment
　　and Manpower Services Commission
The production of a mass of statistics, or of sociological or other expert evidence, is not necessary to find that a respondent has established his defence. A respondent is entitled to take a broad and rational view provided that it is based on logic, and is in the view of the tribunal a tenable view.

Panesar v　　　　　　　　　　　**[1980] IRLR 60 EAT**
The Nestlé Co Ltd
In order to show that a requirement or condition is justifiable, it is not enough merely for an employer to show that it was introduced as a matter of convenience.

Panesar v　　　　　　　　　　　**[1980] IRLR 60 EAT**
The Nestlé Co Ltd
In determining whether a requirement is justifiable, the employment tribunal must be satisfied that it was genuinely introduced for the reason which was put forward.

Panesar v　　　　　　　　　　　**[1980] IRLR 60 EAT**
The Nestlé Co Ltd
If a rule is applied to a particular individual in a particular case, it is for the employment tribunal to decide whether the employer has shown that the rule is justifiable in relation to the individual complaint. That the rule is not applied by most companies does not mean that the employer cannot establish that it is justifiable if, on its own merit, it is shown to be justifiable in the particular case.

Cross v　　　　　　　　　　　**[2005] IRLR 423 EAT**
British Airways plc
An employer seeking to justify a discriminatory provision, criterion or practice cannot rely solely on considerations of cost. It can, however, put cost into the balance, together with other justifications if there are any. It is a matter of obvious common sense and in accordance with the principle of proportionality that economic justification, such as the saving or non-expenditure of costs (which include the avoidance of loss) must be considered in the weighing exercise. Accordingly, the costs to the employer of changing its terms and conditions could be taken into account as a justification for an indirectly discriminatory provision, criterion or practice relating to retirement.

R (on the application of Elias) v　　　**[2005] IRLR 788 HC**
Secretary of State for Defence
Budgetary concerns do not in general justify discrimination and it cannot be a legitimate defence for a discriminator to say that they did not wish to discriminate and would not have done so with greater resources. However, making distinctions

for the purpose of deciding who should benefit from public funds is in principle perfectly sensible. Once that is accepted, it inevitably follows that questions of funding are material considerations. Therefore, having regard to these financial considerations does not render the objective unlawful.

R v　　　　　　　　　　　**[2000] IRLR 363 HL**
Secretary of State for Employment
　　ex parte Seymour-Smith (No.2)
If the Government introduces a measure which proves to have a disparately adverse impact, it is under a duty to take reasonable steps to monitor the working of the measure and review the position periodically. The requirements of Community law must be complied with at all relevant times. The retention of a measure having a disparately adverse impact may no longer be objectively justifiable.

Tribunal discretion

Mandla v　　　　　　　　　　　**[1983] IRLR 209 HL**
Lee
Whether a requirement or condition is "justifiable" is a question of fact for the tribunal to discover, and if there is evidence for which it can find the condition to be justifiable, its finding is not liable to be disturbed on appeal.

Raval v　　　　　　　　　　　**[1985] IRLR 370 EAT**
Department of Health and
　　Social Security
The issue of justifiability, being a question of fact, is one that has been left by Parliament to the employment tribunals. Instances are bound to be rare in which a finding on justifiability is capable of being disturbed on appeal. A tribunal's finding on whether or not a requirement is justifiable cannot be disturbed if the conclusion was capable of having been reached by any reasonable tribunal, notwithstanding that another tribunal might perfectly reasonably have taken a contrary view.

Specific examples

The Home Office v　　　　　　　**[1984] IRLR 299 EAT**
Holmes
An employment tribunal's conclusion that the employers had not shown that a requirement to work full time was justifiable could not be held to have been perverse. Whether such a requirement is justified or not is precisely the line of inquiry that Parliament intended to entrust to the employment tribunals. All such cases will turn upon their own particular facts.

Greater Glasgow Health Board v　　**[1987] IRLR 484 EAT**
Carey
An employment tribunal which concluded that an employer's requirement that a health visitor work a five-day week was not justifiable within the meaning of s.1(1)(b)(ii) of the Sex Discrimination Act had failed to have sufficient regard to the

administrative "efficiency" of the service as referred to by the House of Lords in *Rainey v Greater Glasgow Health Board*.

London Underground Ltd v   **[1997] IRLR 157 EAT**
Edwards (No.2)
The employment tribunal was entitled to find that the employers had not justified indirectly discriminatory rostering arrangements requiring employees to make an early start. There was good evidence that the employers could have made arrangements which would not have been damaging to their business plans but which would have accommodated the reasonable demands of their employees.

Shackletons Garden Centre Ltd v   **[2010] EqLR 138 EAT**
Lowe
An employment tribunal erred in failing to address whether a requirement to work weekends on a rotational basis, if it put the claimant at a disadvantage on gender discriminatory grounds, was nonetheless a proportionate means of achieving a legitimate aim. There was ample material to suggest that the employers were addressing a legitimate aim, namely the need to provide cover at weekends, and to play fair with all of their employees, each of whom was expected to work at weekends in accordance with the rota.

Bullock v   **[1992] IRLR 564 CA**
Alice Ottley School
In order to justify a later retirement age for a group which in fact though not by design consists wholly or largely of men it is necessary for the employer to show a real and genuine need for this later retirement age. In this case, the employment tribunal was entitled to accept evidence that a later retirement age for gardeners and the maintenance staff was objectively justified in that it was necessary because of the difficulty of recruiting such staff and the need to retain them as long as possible.

R v   **[2000] IRLR 363 HL**
Secretary of State for Employment
    ex parte Seymour-Smith (No.2)
The Secretary of State had discharged the burden of showing that he was reasonably entitled in 1985 to consider that the extension of the unfair dismissal qualifying period from one to two years was justified by objective factors unrelated to sex, and that the 1985 Order was still objectively justified in 1991.

R v   **[1987] IRLR 53 HC**
Secretary of State for Education
    ex parte Schaffter
Statutory eligibility requirements for education grants which distinguished between single and married lone parents and had a disproportionate impact upon women had not been shown to be objectively justified for the purposes of the Equal Treatment Directive where the argument relied upon by the Secretary of State did not give reasons for the distinction drawn but merely stated that the purpose of the Regulations was to benefit married lone parents. That did not amount to a justification. Therefore, the requirements infringed the principle of equal treatment for men and women as regards access to vocational training embodied in the Equal Treatment Directive.

Secretary of State for Trade and   **[2003] IRLR 858 EAT**
    Industry v
Rutherford and others (No.2)
The Secretary of State objectively justified the default limitation on the right to claim unfair dismissal or redundancy payments to those under age 65. The policy arguments advanced by the Secretary of State in respect of the upper age limit for unfair dismissal and redundancy payments were legitimate aims of the State's social policy and were not related to any discrimination based on sex.

Osborne Clarke Services v   **[2009] IRLR 341 EAT**
Purohit
A policy of not considering any application for solicitor training contracts from individuals requiring permission from the Border and Immigration Agency to work in the UK, which had a disproportionate impact on non-EEA nationals, had not been shown to be objectively justified where the employers had made no attempts to apply for a work permit. In the absence of any clear evidence as to the likelihood of failure, the employers' own conjecture that they could not apply or would not be successful was insufficient. The Code of Practice on racial equality and employment makes it clear that as far as possible selection should be based purely on merit, and that work permit issues should only come into consideration at the later stage of selection. It also makes it clear that as far as possible employers should make an application leaving it up to the immigration authorities to determine the outcome.

Allen v   **[2008] IRLR 690 CA**
GMB
An employment tribunal did not err in finding that the union had failed to justify its agreement with Middlesbrough Council over implementation of the local government single status scheme which disadvantaged women by prioritising pay protection and future pay rather than maximising claims for past unequal pay.

HARASSMENT AND SEXUAL HARASSMENT

(1) For the purposes of this Act, a person subjects a woman to harassment if –

> *(a) he engages in unwanted conduct that is related to her sex or that of another person and has the purpose or effect –*
>> *(i) of violating her dignity, or*
>> *(ii) of creating an intimidating, hostile, degrading, humiliating or offensive environment for her,*
>
> *(b) he engages in any form of unwanted verbal, non-verbal or physical conduct of a sexual nature that has the purpose or effect –*
>> *(i) of violating her dignity, or*
>> *(ii) of creating an intimidating, hostile, degrading, humiliating or offensive environment for her, or*
>
> *(c) on the ground of her rejection of or submission to unwanted conduct of a kind mentioned in paragraph (a) or (b), he treats her less favourably than he would treat her had she not rejected, or submitted to, the conduct.*

(2) Conduct shall be regarded as having the effect mentioned in sub-paragraph (i) or (ii) of subsection (1)(a) or (b) only if, having regard to all the circumstances, including in particular the perception of the woman, it should reasonably be considered as having that effect.

(5) Subsection (1) is to be read as applying equally to the harassment of men, and for that purpose shall have effect with such modifications as are requisite.

SEX DISCRIMINATION ACT 1975 (as amended) – s.4A
➡ EQUALITY ACT 2010 – s.26, s.11

(2A) It is unlawful for an employer, in relation to employment by him at an establishment in Great Britain, to subject to harassment –
> *(a) a woman whom he employs, or*
> *(b) a woman who has applied to him for employment.*

(2B) For the purposes of subsection (2A), the circumstances in which an employer is to be treated as subjecting a woman to harassment shall include those where –
> *(a) a third party subjects the woman to harassment in the course of her employment, and*
> *(b) the employer has failed to take such steps as would have been reasonably practicable to prevent the third party from doing so.*

(2C) Subsection (2B) does not apply unless the employer knows that the woman has been subject to harassment in the course of her employment on at least two other occasions by a third party.

(2D) In subsections (2B) and (2C), "third party" means a person other than –
> *(a) the employer, or*
> *(b) a person whom the employer employs,*

and for the purposes of those subsections it is immaterial whether the third party is the same or a different person on each occasion.

SEX DISCRIMINATION ACT 1975 (as amended) – s.6
➡ EQUALITY ACT 2010 – s.40

Richmond Pharmacology Ltd v Dhaliwal   **[2009] IRLR 336 EAT**

The necessary elements of liability for harassment are three-fold: (1) Did the respondent engage in unwanted conduct? (2) Did the conduct in question either (a) have the purpose or (b) the effect of either (i) violating the claimant's dignity or (ii) creating an adverse environment for her – the proscribed consequences. (3) Was the conduct on a prohibited ground? However, there is substantial overlap between the questions that arise in relation to each element. Whether conduct was "unwanted" will overlap with whether it creates an adverse environment for the claimant. Many or most acts that are found to create an adverse environment for an employee will also violate her dignity.

Richmond Pharmacology Ltd v Dhaliwal   **[2009] IRLR 336 EAT**

Reading across the case law in relation to harassment as a variety of discrimination prior to implementation of the EU Directives is likely to hinder more than it helps. Still less assistance is likely to be gained from the Protection from Harassment Act 1997 and the associated case law.

Reed and Bull Information Systems Ltd v Stedman   **[1999] IRLR 299 EAT**

The essential characteristic of sexual harassment is that it is words or conduct which are unwelcome to the recipient and it is for the recipient to decide for themselves what is acceptable to them and what they regard as offensive.

Reed and Bull Information Systems Ltd v Stedman   **[1999] IRLR 299 EAT**

Some conduct, if not expressly invited, could properly be described as unwelcome. A woman does not have to make it clear in advance that she does not want to be touched in a sexual manner. At the lower end of the scale, a woman may appear, objectively, to be unduly sensitive to what might otherwise be regarded as unexceptional behaviour. But because it is for each person to define their own levels of acceptance, the question would then be whether by words or conduct she had made it clear that she found such conduct unwelcome. Provided that any reasonable person would understand her to be rejecting the conduct of which she was complaining, continuation of the conduct would, generally, be regarded as harassment.

Insitu Cleaning Co Ltd v Heads   **[1995] IRLR 4 EAT**

Whether a single act of verbal sexual harassment is sufficient to found a complaint is a matter of fact and degree. That the EC Code of Practice refers to "unwanted conduct" does not mean that a single act can never amount to harassment in that it cannot be said to be "unwanted" until it is done and rejected. The word "unwanted" is essentially the same as "unwelcome" or "uninvited".

Wileman v   **[1988] IRLR 144 EAT**
Minilec Engineering Ltd

A person may be happy to accept the remarks of A or B in a sexual context, and wholly upset by similar remarks made by C. Therefore, the probative value in a sexual harassment case of the fact that the complainant posed for a newspaper in a flimsy costume was almost minimal since the fact that she was upset at remarks made by a director of the employers was not vitiated in any way or inconsistent with her being willing to pose for a newspaper.

Driskel v   **[2000] IRLR 151 EAT**
Peninsula Business Services Ltd

A tribunal should not lose sight of the significance of the sex of both the complainant and the alleged discriminator. Sexual badinage of a heterosexual male by another man cannot be completely equated with like badinage by him of a woman. Prima facie the treatment is not equal, since in the latter circumstance it is the sex of the alleged discriminator that potentially adds a material element absent as between two heterosexual men.

Insitu Cleaning Co Ltd v   **[1995] IRLR 4 EAT**
Heads

A remark by a man about a woman's breasts cannot sensibly be equated with a remark by a woman about a bald head or a beard. One is sexual, the other is not.

Moonsar v   **[2005] IRLR 9 EAT**
Fiveways Express Transport Ltd

The claimant was discriminated against on grounds of her sex when on three occasions male colleagues in the same room downloaded pornographic images on to a computer. Viewed objectively, this behaviour clearly had the potential effect of causing an affront to a female employee working in a close environment, and as such would be regarded as degrading or offensive to an employee as a woman. The fact that the claimant did not complain at the time did not afford a defence where the behaviour was so obvious.

Nixon v   **[2010] EqLR 284 EAT**
Ross Coates Solicitors

Subjecting a pregnant employee to gossip about the paternity of her unborn child was unwanted conduct meeting the definition of harassment on grounds of sex in that it created an intimidating, hostile, degrading or humiliating working environment for her.

Wileman v   **[1988] IRLR 144 EAT**
Minilec Engineering Ltd

Evidence of how a director was alleged to have harassed other women was correctly not admitted by an employment tribunal since sexual remarks made to a number of people have to be looked at in the context of each person. All the people to whom they are made may regard them as wholly inoffensive; everyone else may regard them as offensive. Each individual has the right, if the remarks are regarded as offensive, to treat them as an offence under the Sex Discrimination Act.

British Telecommunications plc v **[1997] IRLR 668 EAT**
Williams

An employment tribunal erred in finding that an interview by a male manager of a female employee was sexually intimidating because there was no woman present and the interview took place in a confined space. It is neither required by law nor desirable in practice that employers should see that male managers are chaperoned when dealing with female staff.

Richmond Pharmacology Ltd v **[2009] IRLR 336 EAT**
Dhaliwal

The broad thrust of the proviso in subsection (2) is that a respondent should not be held to be liable merely because his conduct has the effect of producing a proscribed consequence: it should be reasonable that that consequence has occurred. Whether it was reasonable for a claimant to have felt her dignity to have been violated is quintessentially a matter for the factual assessment of the tribunal, but one question that may be material is whether it should reasonably have been apparent whether the conduct was, or was not, intended to cause offence (or produce the proscribed consequences). If the perpetrator evidently did not intend to cause offence, it may not be reasonable for the claimant to have taken offence.

Richmond Pharmacology Ltd v **[2009] IRLR 336 EAT**
Dhaliwal

The inquiry into the perpetrator's grounds for acting as he did is logically distinct from any issue which may arise about whether he intended to produce the proscribed consequences: a perpetrator may intend to violate a claimant's dignity for reasons other than any of the proscribed reasons. However, in some cases, the ground for the treatment is inherently discriminatory and it is not necessary to consider the respondent's mental processes.

Snowball v   **[1987] IRLR 397 EAT**
Gardner Merchant Ltd

Evidence as to a complainant's attitude to matters of sexual behaviour was relevant and admissible for the purpose of determining the degree of injury to feelings that the complainant suffered as a result of sexual harassment. Compensation for sexual harassment must relate to the degree of detriment, and evidence as to whether she had talked freely to fellow employees about her attitude to sexual matters was relevant for determining whether the complainant was unlikely to be very upset by a degree of familiarity with a sexual connotation, so as to challenge the alleged detriment suffered and any hurt to feelings.

VICTIMISATION

(1) A person ("the discriminator") discriminates against another person ("the person victimised") in any circumstances relevant for the purposes of any provision of this Act if he treats the person victimised less favourably than in those circumstances he treats or would treat other persons, and does so by reason that the person victimised has –

> *(a) brought proceedings against the discriminator or any other person under this Act [or the Equal Pay Act 1970 – SDA], or*
>
> *(b) given evidence or information in connection with proceedings brought by any person against the discriminator or any other person under this Act [or the Equal Pay Act 1970 – SDA], or*
>
> *(c) otherwise done anything under or by reference to this Act [or the Equal Pay Act 1970 – SDA] in relation to the discriminator or any other person, or*
>
> *(d) alleged that the discriminator or any other person has committed an act which (whether or not the allegation so states) would amount to a contravention of this Act [or give rise to a claim under the Equal Pay Act 1970 – SDA],*

or by reason that the discriminator knows the person victimised intends to do any of those things, or suspects the person victimised has done, or intends to do, any of them.

(2) Subsection (1) does not apply to treatment of a person by reason of any allegation made by him if the allegation was false and not made in good faith.

SEX DISCRIMINATION ACT – s.4
RACE RELATIONS ACT – s.2
➡ EQUALITY ACT 2010 – s.27

General principles

Chief Constable of   **[2001] IRLR 830 HL**
  West Yorkshire Police v
Khan
Victimisation occurs when, in any circumstances relevant for the purposes of any provision of the Act, a person is treated less favourably than others because he has done one of the protected acts.

Aziz v   **[1988] IRLR 204 CA**
Trinity Street Taxis Ltd
The categories of acts set out in s.2(1)(a)-(d) of the Race Relations Act may fairly be described as "protected acts" and the clear legislative purpose of s.2(1) is to ensure, so far as possible, that victims of racial discrimination shall not be deterred from doing any of the acts set out in paras (a)-(d) by the fear that they may be further victimised in one way or another.

Cornelius v   **[1987] IRLR 141 CA**
University College of Swansea
The purpose of the "victimisation" provisions in s.4 of the Sex Discrimination Act is to protect those who seek to rely

on the Act or to promote its operation by word or deed. Discrimination under s.4 is not discrimination on the ground of sex but discrimination on the ground of conduct of the type described in that section. Thus the word "discriminate" as used in the Act bears both its meaning under s.1 and its meaning under s.4.

Nagarajan v   **[1994] IRLR 61 EAT**
Agnew
An infringement of the statutory provisions relating to victimisation can only constitute an unlawful act if there is a case established under one of the sections in Part II. There is no illegality involved in victimisation by itself without any repercussions. One cannot have an unlawful act if all there is is either discrimination under s.1 or discrimination by way of victimisation, unaccompanied by any event or action which fits into one of the sections in Part II.

Waters v   **[1997] IRLR 589 CA**
Commissioner of Police
  of the Metropolis
In the case of an act allegedly committed by an employee, s.4(1)(d) of the Sex Discrimination Act only applies where the act, if established, is one for which the employer would be vicariously liable and therefore treated as if the act of the employee had been done by the employer as well.

Standard of proof

Nagarajan v   **[1999] IRLR 572 HL**
London Regional Transport
Conscious motivation on the part of the discriminator is not a necessary ingredient of unlawful victimisation.

Chief Constable of West Yorkshire   **[2001] IRLR 830 HL**
  Police v
Khan
In order to determine whether there has been less favourable treatment, the statute calls for a simple comparison between the treatment afforded to the complainant who has done a protected act and the treatment which was or would be afforded to other employees who have not done the protected act.

St Helens Metropolitan   **[2007] IRLR 540 HL**
  Borough Council v
Derbyshire
Whether a particular act can be said to amount to victimisation must be judged primarily from the point of view of the alleged victim, whether or not they suffered any "detriment", rather than from the point of view of the alleged discriminator.

HM Prison Service v   **[2008] IRLR 940 EAT**
Ibimidun
Bringing discrimination proceedings to harass the employer is not a protected act. The victimisation provisions are designed to protect bona fide claims.

Nagarajan v   **[1999] IRLR 572 HL**
London Regional Transport
If racial grounds or protected acts had a significant influence on the outcome, discrimination is made out.

Chief Constable of West Yorkshire   **[2001] IRLR 830 HL**
   Police v
Khan
Whether a complainant has been victimised "by reason" that he has done a protected act is not to be determined by application of a "but for" test.

Villalba v   **[2006] IRLR 437 EAT**
Merrill Lynch & Co Inc
In finding that victimisation was "a very small factor, not a significant influence" in the decision to remove the claimant, the tribunal correctly applied the observations of Lord Nicholls in *Nagarajan v London Regional Transport* that discrimination is made out if the prohibited ground had a "significant influence" on the outcome. Although that wording was interpreted by the Court of Appeal in *Igen Ltd v Wong* as meaning an "influence which is more than trivial", if in relation to any particular decision a discriminatory influence is not a material influence or factor, then it is trivial.

Aziz v   **[1988] IRLR 204 CA**
Trinity Street Taxis Ltd
For the purpose of the requisite comparison, which requires a claimant seeking to establish that there has been discrimination by victimisation to show that the respondent "in any circumstances relevant for the purposes of any provision of this Act" treated him "less favourably than in those circumstances it treats or would treat other persons", the relevant circumstances do not include the fact that the complainant has done a protected act. The treatment applied by the alleged discriminator to the complainant has to be compared with the treatment which has applied or would apply to persons who have not done the relevant protected act. If the doing of a protected act itself constituted part of the relevant circumstances, a complainant would necessarily fail to establish discrimination if the alleged discriminator could show that he treated or would treat all other persons who did the like protected act with equal intolerance.

St Helens Metropolitan   **[2007] IRLR 540 HL**
   Borough Council v
Derbyshire
Although the victimisation provisions do not prevent an employer sending a letter pointing out to the employee the possible consequences of an equal pay claim succeeding, or with a view to settling the claim, in writing letters to the claimants warning them of the consequences of continuing their equal pay claims, which caused the claimants distress, the employers had contravened the victimisation provisions in the Sex Discrimination Act. The tribunal was entitled to find that the detrimental treatment suffered by the claimants was "by reason that" they were insisting on continuing with their equal pay claims.

Oyarce v   **[2008] IRLR 653 CA**
Cheshire County Council
The reversal of the burden of proof in the Race Relations Act only applies in cases where the complaint is of discrimination on grounds of race and does not extend to cases where the complaint is of victimisation.

Specific examples

Aziz v   **[1986] IRLR 435 EAT**
Trinity Street Taxis Ltd
Section 2(1)(b) of the Race Relations Act, which applies where the person victimised has "given evidence or information in connection with proceedings brought by any person against the discriminator or any other person under this Act", is intended to cover the situation where the person victimised is not a party but is a witness or provides information in connection with the proceedings.

Kirby v   **[1980] IRLR 229 EAT**
Manpower Services Commission
Although the giving of information prior to the commencement of proceedings may fall within s.2(1)(b) of the Race Relations Act, before an allegation of victimisation can be made it must be shown that the victimisation has occurred at a time when proceedings have actually been brought. If the proceedings had been brought, it does not matter whether the information was given before or after the commencement of proceedings so long as it is something which is relied upon by the discriminator as a reason for the victimisation.

Aziz v   **[1988] IRLR 204 CA**
Trinity Street Taxis Ltd
An act can properly be said to be done "by reference to" the Race Relations Act within the meaning of s.2(1)(c) – which applies where a person allegedly victimised has "otherwise done anything under or by reference to this Act in relation to the discriminator or any other person" – if it is done by reference to the race relations legislation in the broad sense, even though the doer does not focus his mind specifically on any provision of the Act. The phrase "by reference to" is a much wider one than "under" and should be read accordingly.

National Probation Service for   **[2006] IRLR 508 EAT**
   England and Wales (Cumbria Area) v
Kirby
Section 2(1)(c) of the Race Relations Act is a "catch-all" which is necessarily wider than the more restricted circumstances set out in s.2(1)(a), (b) and (d).

Kirby v   **[1980] IRLR 229 EAT**
Manpower Services Commission
Making a report of alleged discrimination is an act done "by reference to" the statute in relation to another person within

the meaning of s.2(1)(c). If a report is made which states that facts are available which ought to be investigated, and which indicates a possible breach of the Race Relations Act, the making of that report is an act done by reference to the statute in relation to the person against whom it is said discrimination might have occurred.

National Probation Service for   **[2006] IRLR 508 EAT**
  England and Wales (Cumbria Area) v
Kirby
Providing information during an interview by the employers in connection with an allegation of race discrimination against a manager raised in internal grievance procedures by one of the claimant's work colleagues amounted to a protected act within the scope of s.2(1)(c) because it was otherwise doing something by reference to the Act in relation to another person, the manager, for whose acts the employer was responsible.

Chief Constable of West Yorkshire   **[2001] IRLR 830 HL**
  Police v
Khan
It was not unlawful victimisation to refuse to provide a reference in respect of an employee because the employee had a pending discrimination claim against the employer and the employer needed to preserve its position in the outstanding proceedings. In such a case, the reference was not withheld "by reason that" the claimant had brought discrimination proceedings, but rather because the employer temporarily needed to preserve his position, in that the evidence established that once the litigation had concluded, the request for a reference would have been complied with.

Kirby v   **[1980] IRLR 229 EAT**
Manpower Services Commission
What has to be considered under s.2(1)(d) is whether the allegation, which must be assumed for this purpose to be true, does amount to an act which would be a contravention of the statute.

Waters v   **[1995] IRLR 531 EAT**
Commissioner of Police
  of the Metropolis
An employer cannot be liable for victimising an employee who alleged that she was sexually harassed by a work colleague, where the alleged harassment was not committed in the course of employment.

Bird v   **[2008] IRLR 232 CA**
Sylvester
A reasonable employee would not have concluded that a letter from her employer threatening an application for costs in respect of her tribunal claim offered any detriment beyond what was properly involved in the honest and reasonable conduct of the employer's case. The letter was a perfectly reasonable and proper act in the context of the case.

Rank Nemo (DMS) Ltd v   **[2009] IRLR 672 CA**
Coutinho
A former employee who was awarded compensation for race discrimination and unfair dismissal, and secured an order for payment in the county court, was not precluded from bringing a claim that the employer's failure to pay the judgment debt was an unlawful act of victimisation under the Race Relations Act. If it was established that the reason the award had not been paid was retaliation against the claimant for having brought discrimination proceedings against the employer, there could be a link to the previous employment relationship sufficient to support a claim for post-termination discrimination.

EMPLOYER LIABILITY

(1) Anything done by a person in the course of his employment shall be treated for the purposes of this Act [(except as regards offences thereunder) – RRA] as done by his employer as well as by him, whether or not it was done with the employer's knowledge or approval.

(2) Anything done by a person as agent for another person with the authority (whether express or implied, and whether precedent or subsequent) of that other person shall be treated for the purposes of this Act [(except as regards offences thereunder) – RRA] as done by that other person as well as by him.

(3) In proceedings brought under this Act against any person in respect of an act alleged to have been done by an employee of his it shall be a defence for that person to prove that he took such steps as were reasonably practicable to prevent the employee from doing that act, or from doing in the course of his employment acts of that description.

SEX DISCRIMINATION ACT – s.41
RACE RELATIONS ACT – s.32
➡ EQUALITY ACT 2010 – s.109

Jones v　　　　　　　　　　　　**[1997] IRLR 168 CA**
Tower Boot Co Ltd
In determining whether conduct complained of was done by a person "in the course of employment", for the purposes of s.32 of the Race Relations Act and the corresponding provisions in s.41 of the Sex Discrimination Act, the words "in the course of employment" should be interpreted in the sense in which they are employed in everyday speech and not restrictively by reference to the principles laid down by case law for establishing an employer's vicarious liability for the torts committed by an employee. The application of the phrase is a question of fact for each employment tribunal to resolve.

Liversidge v　　　　　　　　　　**[2002] IRLR 651 CA**
Chief Constable of Bedfordshire Police
Section 32(1) of the Race Relations Act is not a provision making the employer vicariously liable for the acts of the employee, but one deeming the employer also to have done the employee's acts. The employer may also be liable directly for the discrimination if what was done by the employee was sufficiently under the control of the employer that he could have prevented what was done.

Liversidge v　　　　　　　　　　**[2002] IRLR 651 CA**
Chief Constable of Bedfordshire Police
In the ordinary employment case, where employee A makes a remark racially abusive of employee B in the course of employment, the employer may be liable for an unlawful act under s.4(2)(c) of the Race Relations Act by virtue of s.32(1).

Kingston v　　　　　　　　　　　**[1982] IRLR 274 EAT**
British Railways Board
As a matter of law, an employer cannot say that it is not liable for the unlawful discriminatory behaviour of one

employee just because the detriment flowing from that unlawful conduct involves a step taken by another, innocent employee. In such circumstances, the detriment to the complainant would flow directly from the discriminatory conduct of an employee for whom the employer was responsible under s.32 of the Race Relations Act.

Waters v　　　　　　　　　　　　**[1997] IRLR 589 CA**
Commissioner of Police of the
　　Metropolis
No tribunal applying the *Tower Boot* test could find that an alleged sexual assault by a male police constable on a female police constable was committed in the "course of employment", where both parties were off duty at the time of the alleged offence, and the man was a visitor to the woman's room at a time and in circumstances which placed them in no different position from that which would have applied if they had been social acquaintances only, with no working connection.

Chief Constable of the　　　　　**[1999] IRLR 81 EAT**
　　Lincolnshire Police v
Stubbs
A police officer was acting in the "course of his employment" when he subjected a female colleague to inappropriate sexual behaviour, even though the incidents occurred at social events away from the police station. When there is a social gathering of work colleagues, a tribunal should consider whether or not the circumstances show that what was occurring was an extension of their employment. In the present case, both incidents were at social gatherings involving officers from work and the claimant could not be thought to have been socialising with the male police officer on either occasion. It would have been different had the discriminatory acts occurred during a chance meeting.

Defence

Jones v　　　　　　　　　　　　**[1997] IRLR 168 CA**
Tower Boot Co Ltd
The policy of the statutory provisions on employer liability is to deter racial and sexual harassment in the workplace through a widening of the net of responsibility beyond the guilty employees themselves, by making all employers additionally liable for such harassment, and then supplying them with the reasonable steps defence, which will exonerate the conscientious employer who has used his best endeavours to prevent such harassment, and will encourage all employers who have not yet undertaken such endeavours to take the steps necessary to make the same defence available in their own workplace.

Croft v　　　　　　　　　　　　**[2003] IRLR 592 CA**
Royal Mail Group plc
In considering whether an action which it is submitted the employers should have taken is reasonably practicable, it is permissible to take into account the extent of the difference, if any,

which the action is likely to make. The concept of reasonable practicability entitles the employer in this context to consider whether the time, effort and expense of the suggested measures are disproportionate to the result likely to be achieved.

Canniffe v   **[2000] IRLR 555 EAT**
East Riding of Yorkshire Council

An employer does not satisfy the defence to liability for acts of their employee merely by showing that there was nothing it could have done to stop the discrimination from occurring. The proper approach to determining whether an employer has satisfied the defence is first to identify whether the employer took any steps at all to prevent the employee from doing the act or acts complained of in the course of his employment; and secondly, having identified what steps, if any, they took, to consider whether there were any further acts that they could have taken which were reasonably practicable. Whether taking any such steps would have been successful in preventing the acts of discrimination in question is not determinative. An employer will not be exculpated if it has not taken reasonably practicable steps simply because, if it had taken those steps, they would not have prevented anything from occurring.

Balgobin v   **[1987] IRLR 401 EAT**
London Borough of Tower Hamlets

An employment tribunal was entitled to find that the employers had proved a defence under s.41(3) of the Sex Discrimination Act to acts of sexual harassment committed by their employee, by establishing that they "took such steps as were reasonably practicable to prevent the employee from doing" the acts complained of in circumstances in which the allegations had not been made known to management; that there was proper and adequate staff supervision; and that the employers had made known their policy of equal opportunities.

Direct liability

Macdonald v   **[2003] IRLR 512 HL**
Advocate General for Scotland
Pearce v
Governing Body of Mayfield Secondary School

Burton v De Vere Hotels Ltd was wrongly decided in that it treated an employer's inadvertent failure to take reasonable steps to protect employees from racial or sexual abuse by third parties as discrimination even though the failure had nothing to do with the sex or race of the employees. The employment tribunal's finding that the hotel manager's failure to protect the waitresses from the offensive content of the comedian's speech was not connected with their ethnic origin, and that, by implication, the employer would have treated white waitresses in the same way, negatived racial discrimination on the part of the employer. The approach of the EAT, that the tribunal should ask themselves whether the event in question was something which was sufficiently under the control of the employer that he could by the appli-

cation of "good employment practice" have prevented the harassment or reduced the effect of it was not based on anything which is to be found in the statute.

Chessington World of   **[1997] IRLR 556 EAT**
  Adventures Ltd v
Reed

The employers were directly liable for sex discrimination in circumstances in which it was clear that they were aware of a campaign of harassment by some of their employees directed towards the claimant, but took no adequate steps to prevent it, although it was plainly something over which they could exercise control.

Secondary liability

Lana v   **[2001] IRLR 501 EAT**
Positive Action Training in Housing
  (London) Ltd

Section 41(2) of the Sex Discrimination Act is not restricted to situations in which the contract gives the agent authority to discriminate. The proper construction of s.41(2) is that the "authority" referred to is the authority to do an act which is capable of being done in a discriminatory manner just as it is capable of being done in a lawful manner.

Lana v   **[2001] IRLR 501 EAT**
Positive Action Training in Housing
  (London) Ltd

The effect of the interaction of s.14 and s.41(2) is that where a person who agrees to provide or make arrangements for the provision of facilities for training discharges any obligation to make those arrangements by using another agency, he will be liable for any act of discrimination which falls within the scope of that agency. Accordingly, if it was within the authority of the agent to terminate the engagement of a claimant, and that act was done in circumstances in which it constituted discrimination, it falls within the scope of s.41(2). Thus, in such a case, the relevant question is why the agent terminated the engagement.

Nagarajan v   **[1994] IRLR 61 EAT**
Agnew

An employee is liable for the actions of a fellow employee only if there is a relationship of principal and agent between them. Simply by making a request to a fellow employee one employee does not make himself the principal of the another employee if that employee complies with the request.

OTHER UNLAWFUL ACTS

Aiding unlawful acts

(1) A person who knowingly aids another person to do an act made unlawful by this Act shall be treated for the purposes of this Act as himself doing an unlawful act of the like description.

(2) For the purposes of subsection (1) an employee or agent for whose act the employer or principal is liable under s.41 [s.32] (or would be so liable but for s.41(3)) [s.32(3)] shall be deemed to aid the doing of the act by the employer or principal.

SEX DISCRIMINATION ACT – s.42
RACE RELATIONS ACT – s.33
➥ **EQUALITY ACT 2010 – s.110, s. 112**

Anyanwu v   **[2001] IRLR 305 HL**
South Bank Students' Union
"Aids" is a familiar word in everyday use bearing no technical or special meaning in this context. A person aids another if he helps or assists, or co-operates or collaborates with him. He does so whether or not his help is substantial and productive, provided the help is not so insignificant as to be negligible. It does not matter who instigates or initiates the relationship, and it is not helpful to introduce "free agents" and "prime movers", which can only distract attention from the essentially simple test to be applied.

Hallam v   **[2001] IRLR 312 HL**
Cheltenham Borough Council
Section 33(1) of the Race Relations Act requires more than a general attitude of helpfulness and co-operation. It is aid to another to do the unlawful act in question which must be shown. Where a party gives information to another on which that other relies in doing an unlawfully discriminatory act, whether the first party will be liable under s.33(1) will almost always turn on the facts.

May & Baker Ltd v   **[2010] IRLR 394 EAT**
Okerago
The statutory definition is conditional upon a person aiding another person to do an unlawful act. A person cannot therefore aid another to do something which the second person has already done.

Allaway v   **[2007] IRLR 864 EAT**
Reilly
If a fellow employee does an act in the course of his employment that has the effect of discriminating against the claimant and that is a result that can be concluded to have been within his knowledge at the time he carried out the act in question, the requirements of the subsection are met. Discrimination does not have to be what he intended nor does it have to have been his motive. It is enough that, on the evidence, the conclusion can be drawn that

discrimination as the probable outcome was within the scope of his knowledge at the time. It would not need to be in the forefront of his mind nor would he need to have specifically addressed his mind to it.

Sinclair Roche & Temperley v   **[2004] IRLR 763 EAT**
Heard
The element of knowledge is additional to the element of aid. Whereas discrimination can be, and very often is, unconscious, aiding cannot be.

Gilbank v   **[2006] IRLR 538 CA**
Miles
In order to "aid" an act of unlawful discrimination, a person must have done more than merely create an environment in which discrimination can occur.

Yeboah v   **[2002] IRLR 634 CA**
Crofton
Even if an employer is not vicariously liable because it showed that it took such steps as were reasonably practicable to prevent its employee from doing the act in question within the meaning of s.32(3) of the Race Relations Act, an employee can be personally liable under s.33(1) for "knowingly" aiding the unlawful act by the employer. Under s.33(2), the employee for whose acts the employer is liable under s.32 or would be so liable but for s.32(3), is deemed to aid the doing of the act by the employer.

Gilbank v   **[2006] IRLR 538 CA**
Miles
Each employee is deemed to have aided the employer to do what she herself did, and so to be personally liable for it, but she is not deemed to have aided the employer to do what fellow employees did.

Gilbank v   **[2006] IRLR 538 CA**
Miles
A manager was jointly and severally liable to pay compensation for acts of sex discrimination against the claimant, notwithstanding that some of the acts of discrimination were carried out by other managers, in circumstances in which the manager could be regarded as having unlawfully aided the discriminatory acts within the meaning of s.42 of the Sex Discrimination Act by consciously encouraging the discrimination. An employer who knowingly fosters and encourages a sustained campaign of bullying and discrimination against a woman does an act that is unlawful by virtue of s.6(2). In accordance with s.41(1), the acts of an employee in fostering and encouraging such a campaign are to be treated as acts done by the employer as well as by the employee. As a result of s.42(2), the manager was deemed to have aided the employer in the doing of those acts. Therefore, in accordance with s.42(1), the manager was herself to be treated as having acted unlawfully in doing those acts.

Bird v   **[2008] IRLR 232 CA**
Sylvester

The execution by a solicitor of a client's instructions is not something that is properly to be treated as aiding an unlawful act, even if the instructions involved some decision by the principal that might offend the statutory discrimination provisions. Nor can a solicitor's role as an adviser render him an aider. It is very difficult to see how a solicitor who confines himself to giving objective legal advice in good faith as to the proper protection of his client's interests, and acts strictly upon his client's instructions, could be at risk of an adverse finding.

Shepherd v   **[2006] IRLR 190 EAT**
North Yorkshire County Council

An employer does not aid a failure by trade unions to represent their members properly merely by agreeing a particular result in collective bargaining. It is one thing to take advantage of a failure, another altogether to aid it. Merely because an employer and a union in collective bargaining have agreed an outcome which was detrimental to a union member, it does not follow that the employer thereby aided the union to fail to represent its member properly.

Instructions to discriminate

It is unlawful for a person –
> *(a) who has authority over another person; or*
> *(b) in accordance with whose wishes that other person is*
>> *accustomed to act,*

to instruct him to do any act which is unlawful by virtue of Part II or III [, s.76ZA or, where it renders an act unlawful on grounds of race or ethnic or national origins, s.76 – RRA], or procure or attempt to procure the doing by him of any such act.

> **SEX DISCRIMINATION ACT – s.39**
> **RACE RELATIONS ACT – s.30**
> ➡ **EQUALITY ACT 2010 – s.111**

Commission for Racial Equality v   **[1983] IRLR 315 EAT**
Imperial Society of Teachers of
   Dancing

The words "procure" and "attempt to procure" in s.30 of the Race Relations Act have a wide meaning and include the use of words which bring about or attempt to bring about a certain course of action. Therefore, an expression of preference for claimants from a particular racial group is "an attempt to procure" within the meaning of s.30.

Commission for Racial Equality v   **[1983] IRLR 315 EAT**
Imperial Society of Teachers of
   Dancing

Section 30 of the Race Relations Act requires that there should be some relationship between the person giving the instructions or doing the procuring and the other person and that the other person is a person who is accustomed to act in accordance with the wishes of the first person. Since "person", by reason of the Interpretation Act, includes "a body of persons incorporate or unincorporate", if there is evidence that the other person is accustomed to act in accordance with the wishes of the employer, it would not matter that the other person had never before spoken to the particular person giving the instructions. However, it is not possible to construe s.30 as meaning that it is sufficient to show that the other person is accustomed to act with another employer in accordance with the wishes of persons in the same position as the person giving the instructions.

Pressure to discriminate

(1) It is unlawful to induce, or attempt to induce, a person to do any act which contravenes Part II or III, s.76ZA or, where it renders an act unlawful on grounds of race or ethnic or national origins, s.76.

(2) An attempted inducement is not prevented from falling within subsection (1) because it is not made directly to the person in question, if it is made in such a way that he is likely to hear of it.

> **RACE RELATIONS ACT 1976 (as amended) – s.31**
> ➡ **EQUALITY ACT 2010 – s.111**

(1) It is unlawful to induce, or attempt to induce, a person to do any act which contravenes Part II or III by –
> *(a) providing or offering to provide him with any benefit; or*
> *(b) subjecting or threatening to subject him to any detriment.*

(2) An offer or threat is not prevented from falling within subsection (1) because it is not made directly to the person in question, if it is made in such a way that he is likely to hear of it.

> **SEX DISCRIMINATION ACT – s.40**
> ➡ **EQUALITY ACT 2010 – s.111**

Commission for Racial Equality v   **[1983] IRLR 315 EAT**
Imperial Society of Teachers of
   Dancing

The word "induce" in s.31 of the Race Relations Act covers a mere request to discriminate. It does not necessarily imply an offer of some benefit or the threat of some detriment. The ordinary meaning of the word "induce" is "to persuade or to prevail upon or to bring about" and there is no reason to construe the word narrowly or in a restricted sense. Therefore, a request by the respondents' secretary to a head of careers at a school that "she would rather the school did not send anyone coloured" to fill a job vacancy constituted an attempt to induce the head of careers not to send coloured claimants for interview in contravention of s.31.

DISCRIMINATION BY OTHERS THAN EMPLOYERS

Discrimination against contract workers

(1) This section applies to any work [at an establishment in Great Britain – SDA] for a person ('the principal') which is available for doing by individuals ('contract workers') who are employed not by the principal himself but by another person, who supplies them under a contract made with the principal.

(2) It is unlawful for the principal, in relation to work to which this section applies, to discriminate against [a woman who is – SDA] a contract worker –

(a) in the terms on which he allows her [him – RRA] to do that work, or

(b) by not allowing her [him – RRA] to do it or continue to do it, or

(c) in the way he affords her [him – RRA] access to any benefits, facilities or services or by refusing or deliberately omitting to afford her [him – RRA] access to them, or

(d) by subjecting her [him – RRA] to any other detriment.

SEX DISCRIMINATION ACT – s.9
RACE RELATIONS ACT – s.7
➡ **EQUALITY ACT 2010 – s.9**

Allonby v   **[2001] IRLR 364 CA**
Accrington & Rossendale College
The prohibition against discrimination against contract workers applies both between one contract worker and another and as between a contract worker and an employee so long as they are working for the same principal. Nothing in the section says that it is limited to discrimination between male and female contract workers supplied to a particular employer. It would be remarkable if it permitted an employer, by bringing in female workers on subcontract to work alongside a predominantly male employed workforce, to give them inferior conditions so long as they were all treated equally badly or (if differentially treated) were all of the same sex and so unable to complain.

Harrods Ltd v   **[1997] IRLR 583 CA**
Remick
The prohibition against discrimination against contract workers is not limited to cases where those doing the work are under the managerial power or control of the principal. Staff employed by concessionaires at Harrods department store were contract workers who worked "for" Harrods within the meaning of s.7 of the Race Relations Act and were therefore protected from being discriminated against by Harrods. It is implicit that the "work" to which s.7(1) is referring will not only be work for the employer, in that it is work done pursuant to the contract of employment, but will also be work done for

the principal. The fact that the claimants, as employees, also worked for their employer did not prevent the work which they did from being work "for" Harrods within the meaning of s.7.

Harrods Ltd v   **[1997] IRLR 583 CA**
Remick
The prohibition against discrimination against contract workers applies if there is a contractual obligation to supply individuals to do work that can properly be described as "work for" the principal. There is no requirement that the supply of workers should be the dominant purpose of the contract made between the principal and the employer.

Leeds City Council v   **[2010] IRLR 625 CA**
Woodhouse
Where the principal and the employer of the applicant are in the relationship of contractor and subcontractor, the mere fact that the applicant does work under the subcontract from which the principal will derive some benefit is not enough to bring the case within the contract worker provisions. If the principal can exercise an element of influence or control, that may be enough to bring the case within the provisions, but control and influence are not necessary elements.

Jones v   **[2004] IRLR 783 NICA**
Friends Provident Life Office
The statutory provisions relating to contract workers were designed to prevent an employer from escaping his responsibilities under anti-discrimination legislation by bringing in workers on sub-contract, and therefore should receive a broad construction which has the effect of providing the statutory protection to a wider range of workers. The purpose of the statutory provisions is to ensure that persons who are employed to perform work for someone other than their nominal employers receive the protection of the legislation forbidding discrimination by employers.

Jones v   **[2004] IRLR 783 NICA**
Friends Provident Life Office
It is implicit in the philosophy underlying the provision that the principal must be in a position to discriminate against the contract worker. The principal must therefore be in a position to influence or control the conditions under which the employee works. It is also inherent in the concept of supplying workers under a contract that it is contemplated by the employer and the principal that the former will provide the services of employees in the course of performance of the contract. It is necessary for both these conditions to be fulfilled to bring a case within the contract worker provisions. It is not sufficient, therefore, for a claimant to show that her employer had a contract with the principal to have certain work done for the latter and that the claimant did that work as an employee of the former.

BP Chemicals Ltd v   **[1995] IRLR 128 EAT**
Gillick
The prohibition on discrimination against a contract worker is not restricted to discrimination against a contract worker

who is actually working. It prohibits discrimination in the selection by the principal from among workers supplied under an agency arrangement. Therefore, a complaint could be brought by a contract worker that she had been discriminated against by a principal by not permitting her to return to work after absence due to maternity.

Patefield v [2000] IRLR 664 NICA
Belfast City Council
A council discriminated against a contract worker on grounds of sex when it replaced her with a permanent employee when she went on maternity leave, in circumstances in which there was a job available for a contract worker when she went off work for maternity reasons and she would have been kept in her post indefinitely if she had not gone off work at that time. By replacing her with a permanent employee when it knew that she wanted to return to her post after the birth of her child, the council subjected her to a detriment at that time by effectively removing the possibility of her returning to her post. In so acting, the council treated her less favourably than they would have treated a man, who would not have become unavailable for work because of pregnancy.

Discrimination by trade unions

(1) This section applies to an organisation of workers, an organisation of employers, or any other organisation whose members carry on a particular profession or trade for the purposes of which the organisation exists.

(2) It is unlawful for an organisation to which this section applies, in the case of a person [woman – SDA] who is not a member of the organisation, to discriminate against him [her – SDA] –
> *(a) in the terms on which it is prepared to admit him [her – SDA] to membership; or*
> *(b) by refusing, or deliberately omitting to accept, his [her – SDA] application for membership.*

(3) It is unlawful for an organisation to which this section applies, in the case of a person [woman – SDA] who is a member of the organisation, to discriminate against him [her – SDA] –
> *(a) in the way it affords him [her – SDA] access to any benefits, facilities or services, or by refusing or deliberately omitting to afford him [her – SDA] access to them; or*
> *(b) by depriving him [her – SDA] of membership, or varying the terms on which he [she – SDA] is a member; or*
> *(c) by subjecting him [her – SDA] to any other detriment.*
> > **SEX DISCRIMINATION ACT – s.12**
> > **RACE RELATIONS ACT – s.11**
> > ➡ **EQUALITY ACT 2010 – s.57**

Sadek v [2005] IRLR 57 CA
Medical Protection Society
A member of a profession can be a "worker" in terms of s.11(1) of the Race Relations Act. "Profession" is widely defined as including "any vocation or occupation", and there is no distinction between "workers" and "profession-

als". Accordingly, the Medical Protection Society, whose members are health care professionals, was an "organisation of workers".

Sadek v [2005] IRLR 57 CA
Medical Protection Society
The category in s.11(1) "any other organisation whose members carry on a particular profession … for the purposes of which the organisation exists" does not limit the category to organisations whose members are confined to a single profession.

FTATU v [1980] IRLR 142 EAT
Modgill
The task of an employment tribunal in a complaint of race discrimination against a union under s.11(3) of the Race Relations Act is to ask whether the complainants have shown that the union has treated them on racial grounds less favourably than the union treats or would treat other persons in the way it affords them access to benefits, facilities or services, or by refusing or deliberately omitting to afford them access to such benefits or by subjecting them to any other detriment. That a union did not give sufficient support to Asian members, or dealt with them inefficiently, was not evidence that there had been less favourable treatment by the union of this particular group of workers than the treatment afforded to any other group of workers. Nor was it evidence that such acts were attributable to racial discrimination.

Fire Brigades Union v [1998] IRLR 697 CS
Fraser
An employment tribunal erred in finding that a union discriminated against a member on grounds of sex by refusing to afford him access to representation or legal assistance for the purpose of disciplinary proceedings by his employer following a complaint of sexual harassment made against him by a woman member. Although the union might have treated those complaining of sexual harassment more favourably than alleged harassers, there was no material on which the tribunal could draw the inference that the decision not to provide representation was gender-related, rather than conduct-related. Therefore, the tribunal was not entitled to find that a woman accused of sexual harassment would have been treated differently.

National Federation of [1997] IRLR 340 EAT
Self-Employed and
Small Businesses Ltd v
Philpott
The expression "organisation of employers" has to be given its ordinary and natural meaning in the context in which it appears, having regard to the characteristics of the organisation in question. On that basis, the National Federation of Self-Employed and Small Businesses is an "organisation of employers", notwithstanding that not all of its members are employers, since it represents its members, who are predominantly employers, specific-ally as employers, as well as across a range of other matters.

Discrimination by qualifying bodies

(1) It is unlawful for an authority or body which can confer an authorisation or qualification which is needed for, or facilitates, engagement in a particular profession or trade to discriminate against a woman [person – RRA] –

> *(a) in the terms on which it is prepared to confer on her [him – RRA] that authorisation or qualification; or*
>
> *(b) by refusing or deliberately omitting to grant her [his – RRA] application for it; or*
>
> *(c) by withdrawing it from her [him – RRA] or varying the terms on which she [he – RRA] holds it.*

[(2) Where an authority or body is required by law to satisfy zit-self as to his good character before conferring on a person an authorisation or qualification which is needed for, or facilitates, his engagement in any profession or trade then, without prejudice to any other duty to which it is subject, that requirement shall be taken to impose on the authority or body a duty to have regard to any evidence tending to show that he, or any of his employees, or agents (whether past or present), has practised unlawful discrimination in, or in connection with, the carrying on of any profession or trade. – SDA]

(3) In this section –

> *(a) "authorisation or qualification" includes recognition, registration, enrolment, approval and certification;*
>
> *(b) "confer" includes renew or extend.*

SEX DISCRIMINATION ACT – s.13
RACE RELATIONS ACT – s.12
➡ **EQUALITY ACT 2010 – s.53, 54**

Ahsan v   **[2008] IRLR 243 HL**
Watt

An "authorisation or qualification" suggests some kind of objective standard which the qualifying body applies, an even-handed test which people may pass or fail.

British Judo Association v   **[1981] IRLR 484 EAT**
Petty

The prohibition on discrimination by qualifying bodies covers all cases where a qualification in fact facilitates a woman's employment, whether or not it is intended by the authority or body which confers the authorisation or qualification so to do.

British Judo Association v   **[1981] IRLR 484 EAT**
Petty

The prohibition on discrimination by qualifying bodies renders unlawful all discriminatory conditions attached to qualifications affecting employment. There is no requirement that the discriminatory term (as opposed to the qualification itself) has any impact on the employment prospects of the person discriminated against or that they must show proof of actual damage. A complainant must show simply that the qualification facilitates his or her job prospects and that attached to such qualification is a term which is discriminatory against the sex or race of the complainant.

Tattari v   **[1997] IRLR 586 CA**
Private Patients Plan

The prohibition on discrimination by qualifying bodies applies to a body which has the power or authority to confer on a person a professional qualification or other approval needed to enable them to practice a profession, exercise a calling or take part in some other activity. It does not refer to a body like PPP which is not authorised to or empowered to confer such qualification or permission but which stipulates that a particular qualification is required for the purpose of its commercial agreements. Therefore, the claimant could not bring a complaint that PPP's failure to include her on their list of specialists because it did not recognise her EC certificate of higher specialist training was racially discriminatory.

Ahsan v   **[2008] IRLR 243 HL**
Watt

A political party, such as the Labour Party, is not a "qualifying body" within the meaning of s.12 of the Race Relations Act because the main criteria for selection as a candidate are not objective.

Patterson v   **[2004] IRLR 153 CA**
Legal Services Commission

When the Legal Services Commission grants a franchise to a solicitor, it is conferring an authorisation on the franchisee to perform publicly funded legal services for its clients. The franchise "facilitates" engagement in the profession of solicitor, in that it makes it easier or less difficult to carry on the profession.

Appeals

(1) A complaint by any person ("the complainant") that another person ("the respondent") –

> *(a) has committed an act of discrimination against the complainant which is unlawful by virtue of Part II, or*
>
> *(b) is by virtue of s.41 or 42 [32 or 33 – RRA] to be treated as having committed such an act of discrimination against the complainant,*

may be presented to an employment tribunal.

(2) Subsection (1) does not apply to a complaint under s.13(1) [12(1) – RRA] of an act in respect of which an appeal, or proceedings in the nature of an appeal, may be brought under any enactment [or to a complaint to which s.75(8) applies – RRA].

SEX DISCRIMINATION ACT – s.63
RACE RELATIONS ACT – s.54
➡ **EQUALITY ACT 2010 – s.120**

Khan v   **[1994] IRLR 646 CA**
General Medical Council

The essence of what is meant by "proceedings in the nature of an appeal" is that the decision can be reversed by a differently constituted set of persons. The possibility of common membership of the original and appellate tribunals does not make the process any the less an appeal, though it might be a breach of natural justice if it were to happen.

Khan v   **[1994] IRLR 646 CA**
General Medical Council
The right to apply to a Review Board for a review of the General Medical Council's decision, conferred by s.29 of the Medical Act 1983, is a proceeding "in the nature of an appeal" within the meaning of s.54(2) of the Race Relations Act, since the proceedings had the necessary characteristics of a two-stage decision to be in the nature of an appeal.

INDIVIDUAL REMEDIES

(1) Where an employment tribunal finds that a complaint presented to it under [s.63 – SDA; s.54 – RRA] is well-founded the tribunal shall make such of the following as it considers just and equitable –

    (a) an order declaring the rights of the complainant and the respondent in relation to the act to which the complaint relates;

    (b) an order requiring the respondent to pay to the complainant compensation of an amount corresponding to any damages he could have been ordered by a county court or by a sheriff court to pay to the complainant if the complaint had fallen to be dealt with under [s.66 – SDA; s.57 – RRA];

    (c) a recommendation that the respondent take within a specified period action appearing to the tribunal to be practicable for the purpose of obviating or reducing the adverse effect on the complainant of any act of discrimination to which the complaint relates.

                    SEX DISCRIMINATION ACT – s.65
                    RACE RELATIONS ACT – s.56
            ➥ EQUALITY ACT 2010 – s.124

(1) A claim by any person ("the claimant") that another person ("the respondent") –

    (a) has committed an act of discrimination against the claimant which is unlawful by virtue of Part III, or

    (b) is by virtue of [s.41 – SDA; s.32 – RRA] or [s.42 – SDA; s.33 – RRA] to be treated as having committed such an act of discrimination against the claimant,

may be made the subject of civil proceedings in like manner as any other claim in tort or (in Scotland) in reparation for breach of statutory duty.

(3) As respects an unlawful act of discrimination falling within s.1(1)(b), no award of damages shall be made if the respondent proves that the requirement or condition in question was not applied with the intention of treating the claimant unfavourably on [racial grounds – RRA] [the ground of his sex – SDA].

(4) For the avoidance of doubt it is hereby declared that damages in respect of an unlawful act of discrimination may include compensation for injury to feelings whether or not they include compensation under any other head.

                    SEX DISCRIMINATION ACT – s.66
                    RACE RELATIONS ACT – s.57
            ➥ EQUALITY ACT 2010 – s.114

(1A) In applying s.66 for the purposes of subsection (1)(b), no account shall be taken of subsection (3) of that section.

(1B) As respects an unlawful act of discrimination falling within s.1(1)(b) or s.3(1)(b), if the respondent proves that the requirement or condition in question was not applied with the intention of treating the complainant unfavourably on the ground of his sex or marital status as the case may be, an order may be made under subsection (1)(b) only if the employment tribunal –

(a) makes such an order under subsection (1)(a) and such recommendation under subsection (1)[c] (if any) as it would have made if it had no power to make an order under subsection (1)(b);

and

(b) (where it makes an order under subsection (1)(a) or a recommendation under subsection (1)[c] or both) considers that it is just and equitable to make an order under subsection (1)(b) as well.

SEX DISCRIMINATION ACT – s.65
➥ **EQUALITY ACT 2010 – s.124**

Compensation

General principles

Ministry of Defence v   **[1998] IRLR 23 CA**
Wheeler
The general principle in assessing compensation is that, as far as possible, complainants should be placed in the same position as they would have been in but for the unlawful act.

Chagger v   **[2010] IRLR 47 CA**
Abbey National plc
The employment tribunal's task is to put the employee in the position he would have been in had there been no discrimination. That is not necessarily the same as asking what would have happened to the particular employment relationship had there been no discrimination. The reason is that the features of the labour market are not necessarily equivalent in the two cases. Where there has been a discriminatory dismissal, the employee is on the labour market at a time and in circumstances which are not of his own choosing. It does not follow therefore that his prospects of obtaining a new job are the same as they would have been had he not been dismissed. It is generally easier to obtain employment from a current job than from the status of being unemployed. It may also be that the labour market is more difficult in one case compared with another. In addition, the claimant may have been stigmatised by taking proceedings and that may have some effect on his chances of obtaining future employment.

Coleman v   **[1981] IRLR 398 CA**
Skyrail Oceanic Ltd
Compensation is to be awarded for foreseeable damage arising directly from an unlawful act of discrimination. It follows that a claimant can claim for any pecuniary loss properly attributable to an unlawful act of discrimination.

Sheriff v   **[1999] IRLR 481 CA**
Klyne Tugs (Lowestoft) Ltd
An employment tribunal has jurisdiction to award compen-

sation by way of damages for personal injury, including both physical and psychiatric injury, caused by the statutory tort of unlawful discrimination.

Essa v   **[2004] IRLR 313 CA**
Laing Ltd
A claimant who is the victim of direct discrimination in the form of racial abuse is entitled to be compensated for the loss which arises naturally and directly from the wrong. It is not necessary for the claimant to show that the particular type of loss was reasonably foreseeable.

Way v   **[2005] IRLR 603 EAT**
Crouch
An employment tribunal in a case of discrimination is entitled as a matter of law to make an award on a joint and several basis. However, if a tribunal considers it necessary to make a joint and several award rather than apportioning liability between the employer and individual employee, it should make clear its reason for doing so.

Thaine v   **[2010] EqLR 268 EAT**
London School of Economics
Where a tribunal finds that the loss that has been sustained by the claimant has more than one concurrent cause, one or more of which amounted to unlawful discrimination for which the employer is liable, and others which were not the legal responsibility of the employer, it is legally open to it to discount an award of compensation by such percentage as would reflect its apportionment of that responsibility.

Ministry of Defence v   **[1998] IRLR 23 CA**
Wheeler
The correct approach in calculating compensation to women dismissed on grounds of pregnancy is to take the sum they would have earned had they remained in the job, deduct from that the amount which they had, or should have, earned elsewhere, and then discount the net loss by a percentage to reflect the chance that they might have left the job in any event.

Abbey National plc v   **[1999] IRLR 222 EAT**
Formoso
The correct approach in awarding compensation for a discriminatory dismissal is to ask what were the chances, in percentage terms, that the employer would have dismissed the claimant had she not been pregnant and had a fair procedure been followed, rather than what a "reasonable employer" would have done. The "reasonable employer" approach is appropriate when considering the fairness of a dismissal, but not when assessing the loss flowing from a discriminatory dismissal.

Ministry of Defence v   **[1994] IRLR 509 EAT**
Cannock
There is no separate head of damage for loss of career prospects. The financial consequences of being deprived of the

opportunity of promotion should be compensated for under damages for loss of employment. The award for injury to feelings should include a sum for the injury to feelings sustained as a result of the loss of chosen career.

Chagger v   [2010] IRLR 47 CA
Abbey National plc
The original dismissing employer is liable for stigma loss. It is one of the difficulties facing an employee on the labour market. The mere fact that third-party employers are the immediate cause of the loss does not free the original wrongdoer from liability. The fact that the direct cause is their decision not to recruit does not of itself break the chain of causation.

Chagger v   [2010] IRLR 47 CA
Abbey National plc
It would be wrong for a tribunal to infer that the employee will in future suffer from widespread stigma simply from his assertion to that effect, or because he is suspicious that this might be the case. If he is unwilling to make good his suspicions by taking proceedings against the alleged wrongdoing employers, he cannot expect the tribunal to put much weight on what is little more than conjecture. However, where there is very extensive evidence of attempted mitigation failing to result in a job, a tribunal is entitled to conclude that, whatever the reason, the employee is unlikely to obtain future employment in the industry.

Bullimore v   [2010] EqLR 260 EAT
Pothecary Witham Weld Solicitors (No.2)
Where a claimant's former employer sent a reference concerning the claimant, which amounted to post-employment victimisation, the unlawful act of the recipient of the reference in withdrawing a job offer because of its contents did not break the chain of causation of loss. Accordingly, the former employer was still liable for any loss of earnings resulting from the post-employment victimisation. It would be most unsatisfactory if a claimant who lost the opportunity of employment as a result of such a reference were unable to recover substantial damages from the person giving it.

Alexander v   [1988] IRLR 190 CA
The Home Office
The mere fact that a defendant is guilty of discrimination is not in itself a factor affecting damages. Although in the substantial majority of discrimination cases the unlawful conduct will cause personal hurt, in the sense of injury to feelings, or of preventing the complainant from obtaining a better, more remunerative job, the court must feel it right to draw an inference that the discrimination will cause a plaintiff "hurt" of a particular kind.

Coleman v   [1981] IRLR 398 CA
Skyrail Oceanic Ltd
An appellate court is entitled to interfere with the assessment of compensation by an employment tribunal where the

tribunal has acted on a wrong principle of law or has misapprehended the facts, or for other reasons has made a wholly erroneous estimate of the damage suffered.

Orthet Ltd v   [2004] IRLR 857 EAT
Vince-Cain
In a case where the period of loss is likely to be more than two years, the correct method of calculating future pension loss is the "substantial loss approach" as suggested in the guidelines to employment tribunal chairmen on *Compensation for Loss of Pension Rights*.

Aggravated damages

Alexander v   [1988] IRLR 190 CA
The Home Office
Compensatory damages may, and in some instances should, include an element of aggravated damages where, for example, the defendant may have behaved in a high-handed, malicious, insulting or oppressive manner in committing the act of discrimination.

(1) Armitage, (2) Marsden and   [1997] IRLR 162 EAT
   (3) HM Prison Service v
Johnson
As a matter of principle, aggravated damages should be available to claimants for the statutory torts of race and sex discrimination. The torts may be sufficiently intentional as to enable the claimant to rely upon malice or the respondent's manner of committing the tort or other conduct as aggravating the injury to feelings.

Scott v   [2004] IRLR 713 CA
Commissioners of Inland Revenue
Aggravated damages are intended to deal with cases where the injury was inflicted by conduct which was high-handed, malicious, insulting or oppressive. Aggravated damages, therefore, should not be aggregated with and treated as part of the damages for injury to feelings.

Ministry of Defence v   [1995] IRLR 539 EAT
Meredith
In order for aggravated damages to be granted, there must be a causal connection between the exceptional or contumelious conduct or motive in committing the wrong and the intangible loss, such as injury to feelings, suffered by the plaintiff. Thus, in order for the plaintiff's feelings to have suffered an aggravated hurt, he or she must have had some knowledge or suspicion of the conduct or motive which caused that increase.

Zaiwalla & Co v   [2002] IRLR 697 EAT
Walia
There is no reason in law why aggravated damages should not be awarded by reference to conduct in the defence of proceedings in a discrimination case.

Governing Body of St Andrew's   **[2010] EqLR 156 EAT**
   Catholic Primary School v
Blundell

It was open to an employment tribunal to award aggravated damages in respect of the way the employers conducted a remedies hearing at the tribunal and, in particular, the bringing of a battery of evidence effectively to undermine the claimant's capability. This had the effect of causing further offence to the claimant, which aggravated her injury to feelings.

City of Bradford Metropolitan   **[1989] IRLR 442 EAT**
   Council v
Arora

In considering an award of aggravated damages for injury to feelings, an employment tribunal is entitled to take into account unsatisfactory answers to a questionnaire issued under s.74 of the Sex Discrimination Act or s.65 of the Race Relations Act. The answers to a questionnaire are part of the conduct of the proceedings and may in some cases merit consideration.

HM Prison Service v   **[2001] IRLR 425 EAT**
Salmon

An employment tribunal did not err in awarding aggravated damages to reflect its view that the manner in which the employers dealt with an incident in which offensive and sexually degrading comments were written about the claimant by one of her colleagues suggested that the employers perceived the entire incident as trivial and that the way the incident was dealt with communicated that perception to the claimant. The tribunal was entitled to find that conduct aggravated the injury to the claimant's feelings.

British Telecommunications plc v   **[2004] IRLR 327 CA**
Reid

A complainant having to undergo a totally unjustified disciplinary investigation into his own conduct could be an indignity which exacerbates his wounded feelings arising from the act of discrimination itself.

Ministry of Defence v   **[2010] IRLR 25 EAT**
Fletcher

It is open to an employment tribunal to award aggravated damages in respect of oppressive use of disciplinary procedures against a claimant and for failure properly to investigate and provide redress for her complaints of discrimination.

British Telecommunications plc v   **[2004] IRLR 327 CA**
Reid

Although there is no principle that an employer cannot promote an employee whilst disciplinary proceedings are hanging over his or her head, on the particular facts and circumstances of a particular case it can be a material factor demonstrating the high-handedness of the employer.

Exemplary damages

Ministry of Defence v   **[1995] IRLR 539 EAT**
Meredith

Exemplary damages are not available for breach of the Equal Treatment Directive.

Ministry of Defence v   **[2010] IRLR 25 EAT**
Fletcher

Exemplary damages are to be reserved for the very worst cases of oppressive use of power by public authorities. To merit an award of exemplary damages the conduct of the wrongdoer must be conscious and contumelious.

Psychiatric injury

HM Prison Service v   **[2001] IRLR 425 EAT**
Salmon

The assessment of damages for psychiatric injury caused by an act of unlawful discrimination is a matter of fact to be determined by the employment tribunal, which can only be overturned on appeal if the tribunal has made an error of principle or arrived at a figure which is so high or so low as to be perverse.

HM Prison Service v   **[2001] IRLR 425 EAT**
Salmon

In principle, injury to feelings and psychiatric injury are distinct. In practice, however, the two types of injury are not always easily separable, giving rise to a risk of double recovery. In a given case, it may be impossible to say with any certainty or precision when the distress and humiliation that may be inflicted on the victim of discrimination becomes a recognised psychiatric illness such as depression. Injury to feelings can cover a very wide range. At the lower end are comparatively minor instances of upset or distress, typically caused by one-off acts or episodes of discrimination. At the upper end, the victim is likely to be suffering from serious and prolonged feelings of humiliation, low self-esteem and depression; and in these cases it may be fairly arbitrary whether the symptoms are put before the tribunal as a psychiatric illness, supported by a formal diagnosis and/or expert evidence.

Injury to feelings

(1) Armitage, (2) Marsden and   **[1997] IRLR 162 EAT**
   (3) HM Prison Service v
Johnson

The relevant principles for assessing awards for injury to feelings for unlawful discrimination can be summarised as follows:

(i) Awards for injury to feelings are compensatory. They should be just to both parties. They should compensate fully without punishing the tortfeasor. Feelings of indignation at the tortfeasor's conduct should not be allowed to inflate the award.

(ii) Awards should not be too low as that would diminish respect for the policy of the anti-discrimination legislation. Society has condemned discrimination and awards must ensure that it is seen to be wrong. On the other hand, awards should be restrained, as excessive awards could be seen as the way to untaxed riches.

(iii) Awards should bear some broad general similarity to the range of awards in personal injury cases. This should be done by reference to the whole range of such awards, rather than to any particular type of award.

(iv) In exercising their discretion in assessing a sum, tribunals should remind themselves of the value in everyday life of the sum they have in mind. This may be done by reference to purchasing power or by reference to earnings.

(v) Tribunals should bear in mind the need for public respect for the level of awards made.

Vento v [2003] IRLR 102 CA
Chief Constable of West Yorkshire Police (No.2)

Observed: Three broad bands of compensation for injury to feelings, as distinct from compensation for psychiatric or similar personal injury, can be identified:

1. The top band should normally be between £15,000 and £25,000. Sums in this range should be awarded in the most serious cases, such as where there has been a lengthy campaign of discriminatory harassment on the ground of sex or race. Only in the most exceptional case should an award of compensation for injury to feelings exceed £25,000.

2. The middle band of between £5,000 and £15,000 should be used for serious cases, which do not merit an award in the highest band.

3. Awards of between £500 and £5,000 are appropriate for less serious cases, such as where the act of discrimination is an isolated or one off occurrence. In general, awards of less than £500 are to be avoided altogether, as they risk being regarded as so low as not to be a proper recognition of injury to feelings.

Vento v [2003] IRLR 102 CA
Chief Constable of West Yorkshire Police (No.2)

Subjective feelings of upset, frustration, worry, anxiety, mental distress, fear, grief, anguish, humiliation, stress, depression etc and the degree of their intensity are incapable of objective proof or of measurement in monetary terms. Translating hurt feelings into hard currency is bound to be an artificial exercise. Nevertheless, employment tribunals have to do the best they can on the available material to make a sensible assessment. In carrying out this exercise, they should have in mind the summary of the general principles on compensation for non-pecuniary loss by Smith J in *Armitage v Johnson*.

R (on the application of Elias) v [2006] IRLR 934 CA
Secretary of State for Defence

Quantifying injury to feelings is more a broad brush exercise of estimation than of calculation, comparison with precedents or cold logic. A trial judge's assessment of damages for injury to feelings will only be interfered with on appeal if the award is so much out of line as to amount to an error of law, because the trial judge has misdirected himself in principle or reached a decision which was for some other reason, such as an erroneous evaluation of the facts, plainly wrong. The court is not entitled to interfere simply on the ground that it would have awarded a higher amount, if it had been trying the case.

Ministry of Defence v [1994] IRLR 509 EAT
Cannock

An award for injury to feelings is not automatically to be made whenever unlawful discrimination is proved or admitted. Injury must be proved, though it will often be easy to prove in the sense that no tribunal will take much persuasion that the anger, distress and affront caused by the act of discrimination has injured the claimant's feelings.

Murray v [1992] IRLR 257 EAT
Powertech (Scotland) Ltd

A claim for hurt feelings is so fundamental to a sex discrimination case that it is almost inevitable. All that is required is that the matter of hurt feelings be simply stated. It is then for the employment tribunal to consider what degree of hurt feelings had been sustained and to make an award accordingly.

Coleman v [1981] IRLR 398 CA
Skyrail Oceanic Ltd

Injury to feelings unrelated to sex discrimination is not properly attributable to an unlawful act of sex discrimination and therefore must be disregarded in the assessment of compensation.

Taylor v [2010] IRLR 499 EAT
XLN Telecom Ltd

Compensation for discrimination is governed by the same principles as a claim in tort and in tort a claimant recovers for the injury caused by the wrongful act. Accordingly, the claimant should be able to recover for his injury irrespective of what he knew or did not know about the motivation of the employers in reaching the decision to dismiss him. The decision of the Court of Appeal in *Coleman v Skyrail Oceanic Ltd* should not be taken as precluding a tribunal from making an award for any injury to feelings and psychiatric injury attributable to the act complained of, irrespective of the claimant's knowledge of the employer's discriminatory motivation.

Alexander v [1988] IRLR 190 CA
The Home Office

The injury to feelings for which compensation is sought must have resulted from knowledge of the discrimination. If the plaintiff knows of the discrimination and that he has thereby been held up to "hatred, ridicule or contempt", then the injury to his feelings will be an important element in the damages.

Moyhing v   **[2006] IRLR 860 EAT**
Barts and London NHS Trust

Harbouring a legitimate and principled sense of grievance is not to be confused with suffering an injury to feelings.

ICTS (UK) Ltd v   **[2000] IRLR 643 EAT**
Tchoula

A global approach to assessing compensation for injury to feelings is preferable to making separate awards in respect of each of three acts of discrimination, since it would be unrealistic to seek to ascribe to each act of discrimination a proportion of the overall injury to feelings suffered.

Al Jumard v   **[2008] IRLR 345 EAT**
Clywd Leisure Ltd

Where more than one form of discrimination arises out of the same facts, such as race and disability discrimination, it can be artificial and unreal to ask to what extent each discrete head of discrimination has contributed to the injured feelings, and there will be no error of law where the tribunal fails to do that. However, where certain acts of discrimination fall only into one category or another, then the injury to feelings should be considered separately with respect to those acts. Each is a separate wrong for which damages should be provided.

O'Donoghue v   **[2001] IRLR 615 CA**
Redcar & Cleveland Borough Council

That a claimant would notionally have been fairly dismissed within a relatively short period is properly to be taken into account as a cut-off point in respect of any claim based on future loss of earnings in respect of a discriminatory dismissal but is not grounds for discounting an award for injury to feelings.

Alexander v   **[1988] IRLR 190 CA**
The Home Office

Damages for injury to feelings, humiliation and insult in respect of unlawful discrimination should not be minimal since this would tend to trivialise or diminish respect for the public policy to which the statute gives effect. On the other hand, awards should be restrained. To award sums which are generally felt to be excessive would do almost as much harm to the policy, and the results which it seeks to achieve, as nominal awards.

Vento v   **[2003] IRLR 102 CA**
Chief Constable of West Yorkshire Police (No.2)

An award of £74,000 for non-pecuniary loss, made up of £50,000 for injury to feelings, £15,000 aggravated damages and £9,000 for psychiatric injury, was so excessive as to constitute an error of law in that it was seriously out of line with the majority of awards made and approved on appeal in reported EAT cases, with the guidelines compiled for the Judicial Studies Board and with cases reported in the personal injury field where general damages have been awarded for pain, suffering, disability and loss of amenity. The fair, reasonable and just award for non-pecuniary loss was a total of

£32,000, made up as to £18,000 for injury to feelings, £5,000 aggravated damages and £9,000 for psychiatric damage.

Voith Turbo Ltd v   **[2005] IRLR 228 EAT**
Stowe

Compensation for injury to feelings caused by dismissal found to be on grounds of race was correctly assessed in accordance with the middle band set out by the Court of Appeal in *Vento (No.2)*, rather than the lowest band applicable to a one-off occurrence. Dismissal on grounds of race discrimination is a very serious incident and cannot be described as one-off or isolated.

Orlando v   **[1996] IRLR 262 EAT**
Didcot Power Station
   Sports & Social Club

In assessing injury to feelings, the willingness of the employer to admit that it has acted in breach of the discrimination legislation may help to reduce the hurt which is felt, in that it can spare the complainant the indignity and further hurt of having to rehearse the nature of her treatment.

Snowball v   **[1987] IRLR 397 EAT**
Gardner Merchant Ltd

Compensation for sexual harassment must relate to the degree of detriment suffered and, in that context, there has to be an assessment of the injury to the woman's feelings, which must be looked at both objectively, with reference to what any ordinary reasonable female employee would feel, and subjectively, with reference to her as an individual.

Wileman v   **[1988] IRLR 144 EAT**
Minilec Engineering Ltd

In awarding compensation for injury to feelings resulting from sexual harassment, an employment tribunal is entitled to take into account the fact that on occasions the complainant wore clothes at work which were scanty and provocative as an element in deciding whether the harassment to which she was subjected constituted a detriment.

Wileman v   **[1988] IRLR 144 EAT**
Minilec Engineering Ltd

In determining the detriment caused by sexual harassment for the purpose of awarding compensation for injury to feelings, employment tribunals have to be very careful to ensure that the situation is not one in which no complaint has been made and the matter was borne with increasing irritation and distress because the claimant was frightened of her boss or frightened of losing her job.

Orlando v   **[1996] IRLR 262 EAT**
Didcot Power Station
   Sports & Social Club

The nature of lost employment, including the fact that the position was part time, is relevant in making an award for injury to feelings. A person who unlawfully loses an evening job may be expected to be less hurt and humiliated by the discriminatory treatment than a person who loses their entire professional career.

Ministry of Defence v Cannock   [1994] IRLR 509 EAT

There is sufficient overlap between compensation for injury to feelings and loss of congenial employment due to discrimination for employment tribunals to confine themselves to making an award for injury to feelings, where such has been proved, which will include compensation for the hurt caused by the loss of a chosen career which gave job satisfaction.

HM Prison Service v Salmon   [2001] IRLR 425 EAT

There is nothing wrong in principle in a tribunal treating "stress and depression" as part of the injury to be compensated for under the heading "injury to feelings", provided it clearly identifies the main elements in the victim's condition which the award is intended to reflect (including any psychiatric injury) and the findings in relation to them. But where separate awards are made, tribunals must be alert to the risk that what is essentially the same suffering may be being compensated twice under different heads.

Orthet Ltd v Vince-Cain   [2004] IRLR 857 EAT

An award of compensation for injury to feelings should be made without regard to the tax implications of the award, and therefore should not be grossed-up.

Unintentional indirect discrimination

Orphanos v Queen Mary College   [1985] IRLR 349 HL

Whereas s.1(1)(b)(ii) of the Race Relations Act is looking at the objective possibility of justifying the discrimination without reference to racial grounds, s.57(3) is looking at the subjective intention of the discriminator. Therefore, where indirect discrimination is unintentional and not intended to discriminate on any racial ground, compensation will not be awarded.

J H Walker Ltd v Hussain   [1996] IRLR 11 EAT

"Intention", for the purpose of s.57(3), is concerned with the state of mind of the respondent in relation to the consequences of his acts. He intended those consequences to follow from his acts if he knew when he did them that those consequences would follow and if he wanted those consequences to follow. Accordingly, a requirement or condition resulting in indirect discrimination is applied with the "intention of treating the claimant unfavourably on racial grounds" if, at the time the relevant act is done, the person (a) wants to bring about the state of affairs which constitutes the pro-

hibited result of unfavourable treatment on racial grounds; and (b) knows that that prohibited result will follow from his acts. Section 57(3) is not concerned with the motivation of a respondent, ie the reason why he did what he did.

British Medical Association v Chaudhary   [2007] IRLR 800 CA

For the respondent to intend to treat the claimant unfavourably on racial grounds, he would have to have actual knowledge or conscious realisation that the condition he had imposed would have disparate impact on one racial group and that he positively wished to have that effect. It is doubtful that constructive knowledge of the discriminatory consequences would be sufficient to satisfy the first limb of the test in *Hussain*.

J H Walker Ltd v Hussain   [1996] IRLR 11 EAT

A tribunal may infer that a person wanted to produce certain consequences from the fact that he acted knowing what those consequences would be. For example, if an employer continued to apply an indirectly discriminatory requirement or condition after it had been declared unlawful, it would not be difficult for a tribunal to infer that he intended to treat an employee unfavourably on racial grounds, even though his reason or motive for persisting in the action was business efficiency.

British Medical Association v Chaudhary   [2007] IRLR 800 CA

The burden on the respondent to show that he did not intend to treat the claimant less favourably on racial grounds is a lesser hurdle for him to cross than simply to show that he had not treated the claimant less favourably on racial grounds. One may act on racial grounds subconsciously but one cannot intend to discriminate subconsciously.

Mitigation

Ministry of Defence v Hunt   [1996] IRLR 139 EAT

The burden of proving a failure to mitigate loss is on the person who asserts it. If a tribunal is to be invited to consider whether or not there has been a failure to mitigate or, if there has been such a failure, the quantification of any reduction in the value of the claim, it must be provided with the evidence with which to perform its task, either arising from cross-examination or from evidence called. It is not for the employment tribunal, as an industrial jury, to fill an evidential vacuum itself.

Ministry of Defence v Hunt   [1996] IRLR 139 EAT

In a case where an employment tribunal has assessed a percentage chance of completing a certain number of years service and has also found some failure to mitigate on the part of the claimant, in the final calculation of compensation the tribunal should deduct the failure to mitigate figure before, rather than after, applying the percentage chance figure.

Interest

4. *(1) In this regulation and regulations 5 and 6, "day of calculation" means the day on which the amount of interest is calculated by the tribunal;*

(2) In reg. 6, "mid-point date" means the day which falls halfway through the period mentioned in para. 3 or, where the number of days in that period is even, the first day of the second half of the period.

(3) The period referred to in para. 2 is the period beginning on the date, in the case of an award under the 1970 Act, of the contravention and, in other cases, of the act of discrimination complained of, and ending on the day of calculation.

5. *No interest shall be included in respect of any sum awarded for a loss or matter which will occur after the day of calculation or in respect of any time before the contravention or act of discrimination complained of.*

6. *(1) Subject to the following paragraphs of this regulation –*

> *(a) in the case of any sum for injury to feelings, interest shall be for the period beginning on the date of the contravention or act of discrimination complained of and ending on the day of calculation;*
> *(b) in the case of all other sums of damages or compensation in the award (other than any sum referred to in reg. 5) and all arrears of remuneration, interest shall be for the period beginning on the mid-point date and ending on the day of calculation.*

(2) Where any payment has been made before the day of calculation to the complainant by or on behalf of the respondent in respect of the subject matter of the award, interest in respect of that part of the award covered by the payment shall be calculated as if the references in para. 1, and in the definition of "mid-point date" in reg. 4, to the day of calculation were to the date on which the payment was made.

(3) Where the tribunal considers that in the circumstances, whether relating to the case as a whole or to a particular sum in an award, serious injustice would be caused if interest were to be awarded in respect of paras. 1 or 2, it may –

> *(a) calculate interest, or as the case may be interest on the particular sum, for such different period, or*
> *(b) calculate interest for such different periods in respect of various sums in the award,*

as it considers appropriate in the circumstances, having regard to the provisions of these Regulations.

EMPLOYMENT TRIBUNALS (INTEREST ON AWARDS IN DISCRIMINATION CASES) REGULATIONS 1996

Ministry of Defence v   **[1994] IRLR 509 EAT**
Cannock

An employment tribunal is entitled to exercise its powers to depart from the normal procedure of awarding interest from the mid-point date between the act of discrimination and the date of the employment tribunal hearing and to award interest over a different and longer period by reason of the fact that the whole of the loss was incurred many years ago. The statutory provisions expressly cater for the exceptional case and what is exceptional is a matter for the employment tribunal.

Derby Specialist Fabrication Ltd v **[2001] IRLR 69 EAT**
Burton

It is clear that Parliament intended that, unlike interest on other awards where the midpoint was to be taken, interest on an award for injury to feelings should normally be from the date of the discriminatory act. That must be taken to allow for the fact that injury to feelings is not a one-off event but something which will often persist over a period of time.

Ministry of Defence v   **[1994] IRLR 509 EAT**
Cannock

An employment tribunal is not entitled to award interest in respect of pension losses. [Regulation 5 of the Interest on Awards in Discrimination Cases Regulations] precludes interest "in respect of a sum awarded for a loss or matter which will occur after the day of calculation".

Action recommendation

Chief Constable of West   **[2002] IRLR 177 EAT**
 Yorkshire Police v
Vento (No.2)

The statutory provisions on action recommendations give the employment tribunal an extremely wide discretion.

Ministry of Defence v   **[1978] IRLR 402 EAT**
Jeremiah

Employment tribunals have no power under s.65 of the Sex Discrimination Act to order an employer to discontinue a discriminatory practice. The tribunal's powers are limited to making a recommendation, an order declaratory of the rights of the complainant, and an order requiring the respondent to pay compensation.

Irvine v   **[1981] IRLR 281 CA**
Prestcold Ltd

An employment tribunal's power to make a recommendation for the taking of action under s.65(1)(c) of the Sex Discrimination Act does not include the power to make a recommendation as to payment of remuneration. Monetary compensation for loss of remuneration is fully provided for by s.65(1)(b).

Noone v   **[1988] IRLR 530 CA**
North West Thames Regional Health
 Authority (No.2)

An employment tribunal exceeded its powers under s.56(1)(c) of the Race Relations Act to make a recommendation that an employer take action for the purpose of obviating or reducing the adverse effect on a complainant of any act of discrimination to which a complaint relates by recommending that a hospital authority seek the authority of the Secretary of State to dispense with its statutory obligations governing the appointment of consultants by not advertising its next vacancy for a consultant's post similar to that for which the complainant unsuccessfully applied. Such a recommendation would set at nought the statutory procedure for making consultant appointments set out for the benefit of the NHS, the public and the professions concerned.

British Gas plc v   **[1991] IRLR 101 EAT**
Sharma

An employment tribunal does not have the power to make a recommendation that the employers promote a successful complainant to the next suitable vacancy. The Act does not allow positive discrimination, and to promote a complainant without considering other claimants who might have superior qualifications for the vacancy could amount to direct discrimination against those other claimants on grounds of race.

Governing Body of St Andrew's   **[2010] EqLR 156 EAT**
  Catholic Primary School v
Blundell

An employment tribunal erred in making a recommendation that the employers should send a letter to all parents and teachers that included statements attributed to the head teacher with which she did not agree.

Chief Constable of West   **[2002] IRLR 177 EAT**
  Yorkshire Police v
Vento (No.2)

An employment tribunal did not err in making a recommendation that the Deputy Chief Constable should interview named police officers and discuss with them relevant parts of the decisions of the employment tribunal and the EAT on liability for sex discrimination.

Other statutory redress

R v   **[1991] IRLR 425 HC**
Army Board of the Defence Council
  ex parte Anderson

The Army Board, in exercising its statutory function of dealing with a complaint of racial discrimination, is obliged to give full effect to the substantive provisions of the Race Relations Act. It is thus necessary for the Board to give specific consideration to the relevant provisions of the Act, to consider whether there had been unlawful discrimination within the terms of the Act, and to give proper consideration to whether compensation or other redress should be granted. Moreover, as the forum of last resort dealing with an individual's fundamental statutory rights, the Army Board must by its procedures achieve a high standard of fairness.

R v   **[1991] IRLR 431 HC**
Department of Health
  ex parte Gandhi

In hearing an appeal under the National Health Service Act against a decision by a Medical Practices Committee not to appoint a doctor to a vacancy, where it is alleged that the decision was on racial grounds, the Secretary of State is not under a duty to pronounce separately on the complaint of racial discrimination, or grant any specific redress in respect of it. However, although the Secretary of State is not required to determine a race discrimination complaint discretely, he is required to consider it in determining the appeal and in doing so must apply the provisions of the Race Relations Act. Moreover, the procedures followed by the Secretary of State in exercising his appellate function must be fair to the appellant.

2. EQUAL PAY

SCOPE OF EC LAW

*Each Member State shall during the first stage ensure and sub-
sequently maintain the application of the principle that men and
women should receive equal pay for equal work.*

*For the purpose of this Article, "pay" means the ordinary basic
or minimum wage or salary and any other consideration, whether
in cash or in kind, which the worker receives, directly or indirectly,
in respect of his employment from his employer.*

Equal pay without discrimination based on sex means:
> *(a) that pay for the same work at piece rates shall be calcu-
> lated on the basis of the same unit of measurement;*
> *(b) that pay for work at time rates shall be the same for the
> same job.*

EC TREATY – Article 141

*For the same work or for work to which equal value is attributed,
direct and indirect discrimination on grounds of sex with regard to all
aspects and conditions of remuneration shall be eliminated. In particular, where a job classification system is used for determining pay,
it shall be based on the same criteria for both men and women and so
drawn up as to exclude any discrimination on grounds of sex.*

EQUAL TREATMENT DIRECTIVE 2006/54 – Article 4

*Member States shall introduce into their national legal systems
such measures as are necessary to ensure real and effective compensation or reparation as the Member States so determine for
the loss and damage sustained by a person injured as a result of
discrimination on grounds of sex, in a way which is dissuasive
and proportionate to the damage suffered. Such compensation
or reparation may not be restricted by the fixing of a prior upper
limit, except in cases where the employer can prove that the only
damage suffered by an applicant as a result of discrimination
within the meaning of this Directive is the refusal to take his/her
job application into consideration.*

EQUAL TREATMENT DIRECTIVE 2006/54 – Article 18

Remedies under EC law

Worringham v   **[1981] IRLR 178 ECJ**
Lloyds Bank Ltd
Article 141 applies directly in Member States, so as to confer enforceable Community rights upon individuals, to
all forms of discrimination which may be identified solely with the aid of the criteria of equal work and equal pay
referred to by that Article, without national or Community measures being required to define them with greater
precision in order to permit of their application. In such a
situation the court is in a position to establish all the
facts enabling it to decide whether a woman receives less pay
than a man engaged in the same work, or work of equal value.

Allonby v   **[2004] IRLR 224 ECJ**
Accrington & Rossendale College
The term "worker" used in Article 141 has a Community
meaning and cannot be defined by reference to the legislation
of Member States. A "worker" for the purposes of Article 141

is a person who, for a certain period of time, performs services
for and under the direction of another person for which they
receive remuneration. The term "worker" does not include
independent providers of services who are not in a relationship
of subordination with the person who receives the services.
However, provided that a person is a "worker" within the
meaning of Article 141, the nature of their legal relationship
with the other party to the employment relationship is of no
consequence in regard to the application of that Article.

Gerster v   **[1997] IRLR 699 ECJ**
Freistaat Bayern
Article 141 applies to employment relationships arising in
the public service.

Worringham v   **[1981] IRLR 178 ECJ**
Lloyds Bank Ltd
National courts have a duty to ensure the protection of the
rights which Article 141 vests in individuals.

Barber v   **[1996] IRLR 209 CA**
Staffordshire County Council
Article 141 can be relied upon by a claimant to disapply barri-
ers to a claim which are incompatible with Community law.

Smith v   **[1994] IRLR 602 ECJ**
Avdel Systems Ltd
Application of the principle of equal treatment between men
and women in relation to pay by employers must be immediate and full. Achievement of equality cannot be made progressive on a basis that still maintains discrimination, even
if only temporarily.

Claim in time

Biggs v   **[1996] IRLR 203 CA**
Somerset County Council
UK domestic law time limits apply to a claim relying on
Article 141 of the Treaty, unless it can be shown that they
are less favourable than those relating to similar actions of
a domestic nature or are such as to make it impossible in
practice to exercise the rights under Article 141.

Magorrian v   **[1998] IRLR 86 ECJ**
**Eastern Health and Social
  Services Board**
EC law precludes the application, to a claim based on Article
141, of a national rule, such as that in the Occupational Pensions Regulations, which limits the entitlement of a claimant
to join an occupational pension scheme to a period which
starts to run from two years prior to the date proceedings were
commenced. The rule was such as to render any action by individuals relying on Community law impossible in practice, in
that its application in the present case would deprive the claimants of the additional benefits under the scheme to which they

were entitled, since those benefits could be calculated only by reference to periods of service completed by them as from two years prior to commencement of proceedings.

Barber v   [1996] IRLR 209 CA
Staffordshire County Council
Article 141 does not confer any right to a redundancy payment or to unfair dismissal compensation. Community law does not create rights of action which have an existence apart from domestic law.

Setiya v   [1995] IRLR 348 EAT
East Yorkshire Health Authority
It would not be just to grant an employee, whose unfair dismissal complaint was dismissed by an employment tribunal in 1992 on grounds that he worked less than eight hours per week, an extension of time for appealing to the EAT against the tribunal's decision, in light of the decision of the House of Lords in 1994 that the hours per week qualification contravened EC law. To be granted an extension of time, it is not sufficient for the appellant simply to point to a subsequent decision of a higher court to the effect that the decision sought to be appealed against was wrongly decided.

Same work

Brunnhofer v   [2001] IRLR 571 ECJ
Bank der österreichischen Postsparkasse
In order to determine whether employees perform the same work or work to which equal value can be attributed, it is necessary to ascertain whether, taking account of a number of factors such as the nature of the activities actually entrusted to each of the employees, the training requirements for carrying them out and the working conditions, those persons are in fact performing the same or comparable work.

Angestelltenbetriebsrat der Wiener   [1999] IRLR 804 ECJ
Gebietskrankenkasse v
Wiener Gebietskrankenkasse
Two groups of employees who have different professional qualifications cannot be regarded as employed on "the same work" for the purpose of Article 141, even where the same activities are performed over a considerable length of time, if the different groups cannot be considered to be in a comparable situation. Professional training is not merely one of the factors that may be an objective justification for giving different pay for doing the same work; it is also one of the possible criteria for determining whether or not the same work is being performed.

Brunnhofer v   [2001] IRLR 571 ECJ
Bank der österreichischen Postsparkasse
The fact that the employees concerned are classified in the same job category under a collective agreement is not in itself sufficient for concluding that they perform the same work or work of equal value. The general indications provided in a collective agreement are only one indication amongst others and

must, as a matter of evidence, be corroborated by precise and concrete factors based on the activities actually performed by the employees concerned.

Burden of proof

Brunnhofer v   [2001] IRLR 571 ECJ
Bank der österreichischen Postsparkasse
The burden is normally on the employee to establish that the conditions giving rise to a presumption that there is unequal pay are fulfilled by proving by evidence that the pay she receives is less than that of her chosen comparator, and that she does the same work or work of equal value, comparable to that performed by him.

Brunnhofer v   [2001] IRLR 571 ECJ
Bank der österreichischen Postsparkasse
In comparing the pay of men and women in order to determine whether the principle of equal pay is being complied with, genuine transparency, permitting an effective review, is assured only if each aspect of remuneration is compared, rather than any general overall assessment of all the consideration paid to the workers.

Jämställdhetsombudsmannen v   [2000] IRLR 421 ECJ
Örebro Läns Landsting
Where the work of two groups can be regarded as of equal value, the national court must verify whether there is a substantially higher proportion of women than men in the disadvantaged group. If so, Article 141 requires the employer to justify the difference by showing that there are objective reasons for the difference in pay which are unrelated to any discrimination on grounds of sex.

Handels- og Kontorfunktionærernes   [1989] IRLR 532 ECJ
Forbund i Danmark v
Dansk Arbejdsgiverforening
(acting for Danfoss)
Pursuant to [Article 18 of the Equal Treatment Directive], Member States, in accordance with their national circumstances and their legal systems, must take the measures necessary in order to guarantee the application of the principle of equal pay and to ensure the existence of effective means to see to it that this principle is observed. The concern for effectiveness which therefore underlies the Directive must lead to an interpretation requiring adjustments to national rules relating to the burden of proof in specific situations where such adjustments are essential for the effective implementation of the principle of equality.

Handels- og Kontorfunktionaerernes   [1989] IRLR 532 ECJ
Forbund i Danmark v
Dansk Arbejdsgiverforening
(acting for Danfoss)
The EC [Equal Treatment Directive] must be interpreted as meaning that when an undertaking applies a pay system

which is characterised by a total lack of transparency, the burden of proof is on the employer to show that his pay practice is not discriminatory where a female worker establishes, by comparison with a relatively large number of employees, that the average pay of female workers is lower than that of male workers.

Specialarbejderforbundet   **[1995] IRLR 648 ECJ**
   i Danmark v
Dansk Industri, acting for
   Royal Copenhagen
The mere finding that in a piecework pay scheme the average pay of a group of workers consisting predominantly of women carrying out one type of work is appreciably lower than the average pay of a group of workers consisting predominantly of men carrying out another type of work to which equal value is attributed does not suffice to establish that there is discrimination with regard to pay, since that difference may be due to differences in individual output of the workers constituting the two groups. However, in a piecework pay system where individual pay includes a variable element depending on each worker's output and it is not possible to identify the factors which determined the rates or units of measurement used to calculate the variable element in the pay, the burden of proving that the differences found are not due to sex discrimination may shift to the employer in order to avoid depriving the workers concerned of any effective means of enforcing the principle of equal pay.

Specialarbejderforbundet   **[1995] IRLR 648 ECJ**
   i Danmark v
Dansk Industri, acting for
   Royal Copenhagen
Where a comparison between workers of different sexes for work to which equal value is attributed involves the average pay of two groups paid by the piece, the national court must satisfy itself that the two groups each encompass all the workers who, taking account of factors such as the nature of the work, the training requirements and the working conditions, can be considered to be in a comparable situation. A comparison is not relevant where it involves groups formed in an arbitrary manner so that one comprises predominantly women and the other predominantly men with a view to carrying out successive comparisons. The comparison must also cover a relatively large number of workers in order to ensure that the differences found are not due to purely fortuitous or short-term factors or to differences in the individual output of the workers concerned.

Meaning of "pay"

Garland v   **[1982] IRLR 111 ECJ**
British Rail Engineering Ltd
"Pay", for the purposes of Article 141, comprises any consideration, whether in cash or in kind, whether immediate or future, that the worker receives, albeit indirectly, in respect of his employment from his employer.

Barber v   **[1990] IRLR 240 ECJ**
Guardian Royal Exchange
   Assurance Group
Although many advantages granted by an employer also reflect considerations of social policy, the fact that a benefit is in the nature of pay cannot be called in question where the worker is entitled to receive it from his employer by reason of the existence of the employment relationship. Therefore, a redundancy payment made by an employer cannot cease to constitute a form of pay on the sole ground that, rather than deriving from the contract of employment, it is a statutory or ex gratia payment.

Barber v   **[1990] IRLR 240 ECJ**
Guardian Royal Exchange
   Assurance Group
Since Article 141 applies to discrimination arising directly from legislative provisions, benefits provided for by law may come within the concept of "pay".

Hill v   **[1998] IRLR 466 ECJ**
Revenue Commissioners
A system for classifying workers converting from jobsharing to full-time employment comes within the concept of "pay" for the purposes of Article 141, since it determines the progression of pay due to those workers.

Lewen v   **[2000] IRLR 67 ECJ**
Denda
A Christmas bonus constitutes "pay" within the meaning of Article 141, even if it is paid voluntarily by the employer as an exceptional allowance.

Jämställdhetsombudsmannen v   **[2000] IRLR 421 ECJ**
Örebro Läns Landsting
Differences in normal working time relate to working conditions and therefore fall under the Equal Treatment Directive rather than Article 141. The fact that the fixing of certain working conditions may have pecuniary consequences is not sufficient to bring such conditions within the scope of Article 141. However, any differences that might exist in the hours worked by two groups whose pay is being compared may constitute objective reasons unrelated to any discrimination on grounds of sex such as to justify a difference in pay.

Lommers v   **[2002] IRLR 430 ECJ**
Minister van Landbouw, Natuurbeheer en Visserij
A scheme under which an employer makes nursery places available to employees is to be regarded as a "working condition" within the meaning of the Equal Treatment Directive rather than as "pay" within the meaning of Article 141, notwithstanding that the cost of the nursery places was partly borne by the employer.

Gerster v   **[1997] IRLR 699 ECJ**
Freistaat Bayern
Rules concerning access to career advancement do not fall within the scope of Article 141, even though they are indirectly linked to pay. Such a rule is primarily designed to lay down conditions

for inclusion on a list of persons eligible for promotion and only indirectly affects the level of pay to which the person concerned is entitled upon completion of the promotions procedure.

Legislation

Rinner-Kühn v   **[1989] IRLR 493 ECJ**
FWW Spezial-Gebäudereinigung GmbH
A legislative provision which results in practice in discrimination between male and female workers is, in principle, to be regarded as contrary to the objective pursued by Article 141. It would only be otherwise if the different treatment between the two categories of workers was justified by objective factors unrelated to any discrimination on grounds of sex.

Rinner-Kühn v   **[1989] IRLR 493 ECJ**
FWW Spezial-Gebäudereinigung GmbH
The mere fact that a legislative provision affects a considerably greater number of female than of male workers cannot be regarded as an infringement of Article 141 if a Member State can establish before the national court that the means selected correspond to an objective necessary for its social policy and are appropriate and necessary to the attainment of that objective.

Allonby v   **[2004] IRLR 224 ECJ**
Accrington & Rossendale College
Where State legislation is at issue, the applicability of Article 141 to an undertaking is not subject to a condition that the worker concerned can be compared with a worker of the other sex who is or has been employed by the same employer and has received higher pay for equal work or work of equal value. A woman may rely on statistics to show that a clause in State legislation is contrary to Article 141 because it discriminates against female workers, and may invoke Article 141 against the employer concerned.

KB v   **[2004] IRLR 240 ECJ**
National Health Service Pensions Agency
Legislation which, in breach of the European Convention on Human Rights, prevents transsexuals from fulfilling a marriage requirement which must be met for one of them to be able to have the benefit of a survivor's pension, must be regarded as being in principle incompatible with the requirements of Article 141 of the EC Treaty.

Collective agreements

Kowalska v   **[1990] IRLR 447 ECJ**
Freie und Hansestadt Hamburg
Article 141 is sufficiently precise to be relied upon by an individual before a national court in order to have any national provision, including a collective agreement, contrary to Article 141 set aside.

Kowalska v   **[1990] IRLR 447 ECJ**
Freie und Hansestadt Hamburg
Article 141 precludes the application of a provision of a collective agreement under which part-time workers are excluded from a benefit where a considerably smaller percentage of men than of women work part time, unless the employer shows that the provision is justified by objective factors unrelated to any discrimination on grounds of sex. It is for the national court to determine whether and to what extent a provision of a collective agreement which in practice affects more women than men is justified on objective grounds unrelated to any discrimination based on sex.

Kowalska v   **[1990] IRLR 447 ECJ**
Freie und Hansestadt Hamburg
Where there is indirect discrimination in a provision of a collective agreement, the members of the group which is disadvantaged because of that discrimination must be treated in the same way and have the same system applied to them as the other workers, in proportion to their hours of work.

Nimz v   **[1991] IRLR 222 ECJ**
Freie und Hansestadt Hamburg
Where there is indirect discrimination in a provision of a collective agreement, the national court is required to disapply that provision, without requesting or awaiting its prior removal by collective negotiation or any other procedure. It would be incompatible with the nature of Community law for a judge to refuse to do all that is necessary, at the time when Community law is applied, to set aside any provisions of a collective agreement which might prevent Community standards from attaining their full effect.

Overtime

Stadt Lengerich v   **[1995] IRLR 216 ECJ**
Helmig
It is compatible with Article 141 and with the [Equal Treatment Directive] for a collective agreement to provide for the payment of overtime supplements only for hours worked in excess of the normal working hours for full-time employees fixed by the agreement and to exclude any overtime supplement for part-time employees for hours worked in excess of their individual working hours if those hours do not exceed the number determined by the agreement. There was no unequal treatment as between part-time and full-time employees, since the overall pay was the same for the same number of hours worked, and therefore no discrimination incompatible with Article 141 and the Directive.

Elsner-Lakeburg v   **[2005] IRLR 209 ECJ**
Land Nordrhein-Westfalen
Legislation which provides that both part-time and full-time teachers do not receive any remuneration for additional

hours worked when the additional work does not exceed three hours per calendar month is contrary to Article 141 and the [Equal Treatment Directive] if it affects considerably more women than men, and if there is no objective unrelated to sex which justifies that different treatment or if it is not necessary to achieve the objective pursued. Part-time workers are entitled to have the same scheme applied to them as that applied to other workers, on a basis proportional to their working time. In this case, three additional hours was in fact a greater burden for part-time teachers than it was for full-time teachers since a full-time teacher must work an additional 3% extra in order to be paid for additional hours, whereas a part-time teacher must work 5% extra. Since the number of additional teaching hours giving entitlement to pay was not reduced for part-time teachers in a manner proportionate to their working hours, they received different treatment compared with full-time teachers as regards pay for additional teaching hours.

Sick pay

Rinner-Kühn v   **[1989] IRLR 493 ECJ**
FWW Spezial-Gebäudereinigung GmbH
The continued payment of wages to a worker in the event of illness falls within the definition of "pay" within the meaning of Article 141.

Rinner-Kühn v   **[1989] IRLR 493 ECJ**
FWW Spezial-Gebäudereinigung GmbH
Article 141 of the EC Treaty precludes national legislation which permits employers to exclude employees whose normal working hours do not exceed 10 hours a week or 45 hours a month from the continued payment of wages in the event of illness, where that measure affects a considerably greater number of women than men, unless the Member State shows that that legislation is justified by objective factors unrelated to any discrimination on grounds of sex.

Rinner-Kühn v   **[1989] IRLR 493 ECJ**
FWW Spezial-Gebäudereinigung GmbH
A submission that workers who work less than 10 hours a week or 45 hours a month are not integrated in and connected with the undertaking in a way comparable to that of other workers only represented generalised statements concerning categories of workers and could not be regarded as objective criteria unrelated to any discrimination on grounds of sex.

Pregnancy

North Western Health Board v   **[2005] IRLR 895 ECJ**
McKenna
A sick leave scheme which treats female workers suffering from a pregnancy-related illness in the same way as other workers suffering from an illness that is unrelated to pregnancy is "pay" within the scope of Article 141 EC.

HK (acting on behalf of   **[1999] IRLR 55 ECJ**
   Hoj Pedersen) v
Fællesforeningen for Danmarks Brugsforeninger
   (acting on behalf of Kvickly Skive)
It is contrary to Article 141 and the [Equal Treatment Directive] to deprive a woman of her full pay when she is unfit for work before the beginning of her maternity leave as a result of a pregnancy-related condition, when a worker is in principle entitled to receive full pay in the event of incapacity for work on grounds of illness.

North Western Health Board v   **[2005] IRLR 895 ECJ**
McKenna
A rule of a sick leave scheme which provides for a reduction in pay where the absence exceeds a certain duration as regards both female workers absent prior to maternity leave by reason of an illness related to their pregnancy and male workers absent by reason of any other illness does not constitute discrimination on grounds of sex contrary to Article 141 and the [Equal Treatment Directive], so long as the amount of payment made is not so low as to undermine the objective of protecting pregnant workers.

North Western Health Board v   **[2005] IRLR 895 ECJ**
McKenna
It is not contrary to Article 141 and the [Equal Treatment Directive] for a sick leave scheme to treat all illnesses in an identical manner for the purpose of determining the maximum total number of days of paid sick leave to which a worker is entitled during a given period, and not to take any account of the special nature of pregnancy-related illnesses. However, the offsetting of absences during pregnancy on grounds of a pregnancy-related illness against a maximum total number of days of paid sick leave to which a worker is entitled over a specified period cannot have the effect that, during the absence affected by that offsetting after the maternity leave, the female worker receives pay that is below the minimum amount to which she was entitled over the course of the illness which arose during her pregnancy. Special provisions must be implemented in order to prevent such an effect.

Maternity pay

Gillespie v   **[1996] IRLR 214 ECJ**
Northern Health and Social Services Board
The principle of equal pay does not require that women should continue to receive full pay during maternity leave. Women taking maternity leave are in a special position, which requires them to be afforded special protection, but which is not comparable with that of a man or a woman actually at work. Although the benefit paid by an employer to a woman on maternity leave constitutes "pay" within the

meaning of Article 141 and the [Equal Treatment Directive], discrimination involves the application of different rules to comparable situations or the application of the same rule to different situations. Therefore, neither Article 141 or the Directive requires that women should continue to receive full pay during maternity leave.

Todd v   **[1997] IRLR 410 NICA**
Eastern Health and Social Services Board
Gillespie v
Northern Health and Social Services Board (No.2)
A healthy pregnancy did not come within the contractual provisions relating to sickness and disability. Pregnancy cannot be compared with sickness.

Clark v   **[1996] IRLR 578 CA**
Secretary of State for Employment
Special provisions which are made for women who are absent from work because of pregnancy or confinement are a separate code. The code provides pregnant women with special protection, but when in receipt of payments under the code their position cannot be "compared" with that of a man or with that of a woman in work.

Gillespie v   **[1996] IRLR 214 ECJ**
Northern Health and Social Services Board
A woman on maternity leave must receive a pay rise awarded before or during maternity leave.

Alabaster v   **[2004] IRLR 486 ECJ**
Woolwich plc
The principle of non-discrimination requires that a woman who still has a contract of employment or employment relationship during maternity leave must, like any other worker, benefit from any pay rise which is awarded between the beginning of the reference period and the end of maternity leave. To deny such an increase to a woman on maternity leave would discriminate against her since, had she not been pregnant, she would have received the pay rise. Therefore, a woman who receives a pay increase before the start of her maternity leave is entitled, in accordance with Article 141 of the EC Treaty and the judgment in *Gillespie v Northern Health and Social Services Board*, to have the increase taken into consideration in the calculation of the earnings-related element of her statutory maternity pay, even though the pay rise was not back-dated to the relevant reference period for calculating her entitlement under the Statutory Maternity Pay (General) Regulations.

Alabaster v   **[2005] IRLR 576 CA**
Barclays Bank plc (No.2)
In accordance with Article 141 and the judgment of the European Court of Justice, the claimant was entitled to have a pay increase which she received before the start of her maternity leave taken into consideration in the calculation of the earnings-related element of her statutory maternity pay, even though the pay rise was not backdated to the relevant refer-

ence period for calculating her entitlement under the Statutory Maternity Pay (General) Regulations. In order to give effect in national law to the rights of a woman on maternity leave in a way which complies with the requirements of EC law, it was appropriate to disapply those parts of s.1 of the Equal Pay Act which impose a requirement for a male comparator. In that way, the claimant could succeed in her claim for sex discrimination without the need for such a comparator.

Gillespie v   **[1996] IRLR 214 ECJ**
Northern Health and Social Services Board
It is for national legislature to set the amount of maternity pay, provided the amount is not so low as to undermine the purpose of maternity leave, namely the protection of women before and after giving birth. In order to assess the adequacy of the amount payable, the national court must take account of other forms of social protection afforded by national law in the case of justified absence from work, as well as the length of maternity leave.

Abdoulaye v   **[1999] IRLR 811 ECJ**
Régie Nationale des Usines Renault
The principle of equal pay presupposes that male and female workers whom it covers are in comparable situations. Women on maternity leave are in a different situation than men since there are occupational disadvantages, inherent in maternity leave, which arise as a result of being away from work. Therefore, it is not contrary to Article 141 to make a lump-sum payment to female workers who take maternity leave, and not to men who become fathers, notwithstanding women on maternity leave receive full pay, where the lump-sum payment is designed to offset the occupational disadvantages which arise for those workers as a result of their being away from work.

Todd v   **[1997] IRLR 410 NICA**
Eastern Health and Social Services Board
Gillespie v
Northern Health and Social Services Board (No.2)
Contractual maternity pay which was at a higher level than statutory sickness benefit could not be held to be inadequate, or such as to undermine the purpose of maternity leave, so as to fall within the proviso to the ruling of the European Court in the *Gillespie* case.

Parental leave

Lewen v   **[2000] IRLR 67 ECJ**
Denda
Article 141 of the EC Treaty precludes an employer from entirely excluding women on parental leave from the benefit of a Christmas bonus without taking account of the work done in the year in which the bonus is paid or of periods of maternity leave during which they were prohibited from working, where that bonus is awarded retroactively as pay

for work performed in the course of that year. If the Christmas bonus is retroactive pay for work performed, refusal to award a bonus, even one reduced proportionately, to workers on parental leave who worked during the year in which the bonus was granted, on the sole ground that their contract of employment is suspended when the bonus is granted, places them at a disadvantage as compared with those whose contract is not suspended at the time of the award. Such a refusal constitutes discrimination within the meaning of Article 141, since female workers are far more likely to be on parental leave when the bonus is awarded than male workers.

Time off

Arbeiterwohlfahrt der Stadt   **[1992] IRLR 423 ECJ**
  Berlin eV v
Bötel
Compensation in the form of paid leave or overtime pay for participation in training courses given by an employer to staff committee members in accordance with statutory provisions falls within the concept of "pay" within the meaning of Article 141 of the EC Treaty and the [Equal Treatment Directive]. Although such compensation does not arise from the contract of employment, it is nevertheless paid by the employer by virtue of legislative provisions and by reason of the existence of an employment relationship with an employee.

Kuratorium für Dialyse und   **[1996] IRLR 637 ECJ**
  Nierentransplantation e V v
Lewark
National legislation which causes indirect discrimination against women by limiting to their individual working hours the compensation which staff council members employed on a part-time basis receive from their employer for attending training courses held during full-time working hours but which exceed their individual part-time working hours, when staff council members employed full-time receive compensation for attendance at the same courses on the basis of their full-time working hours, can be justified by objective factors unrelated to any discrimination based on sex. The mere fact that a legislative provision affects far more women workers than men cannot be regarded as a breach of Article 141 if the Member State is able to show that the measures chosen reflect a legitimate aim of its social policy, are appropriate to achieve that aim and are necessary in order to do so.

Arbeiterwohlfahrt der Stadt   **[1992] IRLR 423 ECJ**
  Berlin eV v
Bötel
Article 141 and the [Equal Treatment Directive] preclude national legislation which applies to a considerably greater number of women than men limiting to their individual working hours the compensation which members of staff committees employed part-time should receive from their employer

in the form of paid leave or overtime pay, in respect of their participation in training courses providing the knowledge and skills required for the running of staff committees and which are organised during the full-time working hours applicable in the undertaking but exceeding their own working hours as part-time employees, whereas the members of staff committees participating in the same courses who are full-time employees are paid compensation up to the limit of the full-time working hours. It remains open to the Member State to establish that the said legislation is justified by objective factors unrelated to any discrimination on grounds of sex.

Davies v   **[1999] IRLR 769 EAT**
Neath Port Talbot County Borough Council
Part-time workers have a right under Article 141 to be paid on the same basis as their full-time counterparts when attending union-run training courses away from work.

Pension schemes

Scope of Article 141

Barber v   **[1990] IRLR 240 ECJ**
Guardian Royal Exchange
  Assurance Group
A pension paid under a contracted-out private occupational scheme constitutes consideration paid by the employer to the worker in respect of his employment and consequently falls within the scope of the definition of "pay" in Article 141.

Bestuur van het Algemeen   **[1995] IRLR 103 ECJ**
  Burgerlijk Pensioenfonds v
Beune
In order to determine whether the benefits provided by a pension scheme are within the scope of Article 141, the only possible decisive criterion is whether the pension is paid to the worker by reason of the employment relationship between him and his former employer.

Barber v   **[1990] IRLR 240 ECJ**
Guardian Royal Exchange
  Assurance Group
It is contrary to Article 141 to impose an age condition which differs according to sex in respect of pensions paid under a contracted-out scheme, even if the difference between the pensionable age for men and that for women is based on the one provided for by the national statutory scheme.

Coloroll Pension Trustees Ltd v   **[1994] IRLR 586 ECJ**
Russell
The principles laid down in the *Barber* judgment, and the limitation of its effects in time, concern not only contracted-out occupational schemes but also non-contracted-out occupational schemes.

Bestuur van het Algemeen   **[1995] IRLR 103 ECJ**
  Burgerlijk Pensioenfonds v
Beune

A civil service pension scheme, which essentially relates to the employment of the person concerned, forms part of the pay received by that person and comes within the scope of Article 141. If the pension paid by the public employer concerns only a particular category of workers, if it is directly related to the period of service, and if its amount is calculated by reference to the civil servant's last salary, it is entirely comparable to the pension paid by a private employer to its former employees.

Bestuur van het Algemeen   **[1995] IRLR 103 ECJ**
  Burgerlijk Pensioenfonds v
Beune

Article 141 precludes national legislation which applies different rules for calculating the occupational pension of married men and married women. Married men placed at a disadvantage by the discrimination are entitled to be treated in the same way and have the same scheme applied to them as is applied to married women.

Ten Oever v   **[1993] IRLR 601 ECJ**
Stichting Bedrijfspensioenfonds voor
  het Glazenwassers- en Schoonmaakbedrijf

A survivor's pension provided by an occupational pension scheme, whose rules were agreed between both sides of the industry concerned and which was funded by the industry's employees and employers to the exclusion of any financial contribution from the public purse, falls within the concept of "pay" within the meaning of Article 141 of the EC Treaty, notwithstanding that, by definition, a survivor's pension is not paid to the employee.

Coloroll Pension Trustees Ltd v   **[1994] IRLR 586 ECJ**
Russell

Article 141 may be relied upon by an employee's dependants.

Coloroll Pension Trustees Ltd v   **[1994] IRLR 586 ECJ**
Russell

Article 141 may be relied upon against the trustees of an occupational pension scheme. Since the trustees are required to pay benefits which are "pay" within the meaning of Article 141, they are bound, in so doing, to do everything within the scope of their powers to ensure compliance with the principle of equal treatment.

Coloroll Pension Trustees Ltd v   **[1994] IRLR 586 ECJ**
Russell

Employers and trustees cannot rely on the rules of their pension scheme, or those contained in the trust deed, in order to evade their obligation under Article 141 to ensure equal treatment in the matter of pay. In so far as the rules of national law prohibit them from acting beyond the scope of their powers or in disregard of the provisions of the trust deed, employers and trustees are bound to use all the means available under domestic law to ensure compliance with the principle of equal

treatment, such as recourse to the national courts to amend the provisions of the pension scheme or of the trust deed.

Worringham v   **[1981] IRLR 178 ECJ**
Lloyds Bank Ltd

A contribution to a retirement benefits scheme which is paid by an employer in the name of male employees only, by means of an addition to gross salary, is discrimination in the form of unequal pay for men and women contrary to Article 141, even though the salary of men after deduction of the contributions is comparable with that of women who do not pay contributions, since the amount of the gross salary determined the amount of certain benefits and social advantages to which workers of both sexes are entitled.

Barber v   **[1990] IRLR 240 ECJ**
Guardian Royal Exchange
  Assurance Group

It is contrary to Article 141 for a man made compulsorily redundant to be entitled to claim only a deferred pension payable at the normal pension age, when a woman in the same position is entitled to an immediate retirement pension as a result of the application of an age condition that varies according to sex in the same way as is provided for by the national statutory pension scheme.

Neath v   **[1994] IRLR 91 ECJ**
Hugh Steeper Ltd

The use of actuarial factors differing according to sex in funded defined-benefit occupational pension schemes to take account of the fact that women live on average longer than men does not fall within the scope of Article 141. Therefore, inequality of employers' contributions to funded defined-benefit pension schemes, which is due to the use of actuarial factors differing according to sex, is not prohibited by Article 141. Unlike periodic payment of pensions, the funding arrangement chosen to secure the adequacy of the funds necessary to cover the cost of the pensions promised is outside the concept of "pay" in Article 141 as it not a consequence of the employer's commitment to pay employees defined benefits or to grant them specific advantages and therefore does not come within the corresponding expectations of the employees as to the benefits which will be paid by the employer or the advantages with which they will be provided.

Coloroll Pension Trustees Ltd v   **[1994] IRLR 586 ECJ**
Russell

Transfer benefits and capital-sum benefits, whose value depends on the funding arrangements chosen, do not constitute "pay". Consequently, Article 141 does not cover an inequality where a reduced pension is paid when the employer opts for early retirement or in the amount of a reversionary pension payable to a dependant in return for the surrender of part of the annual pension.

Coloroll Pension Trustees Ltd v   **[1994] IRLR 586 ECJ**
Russell

Article 141 does not cover additional benefits stemming

from additional voluntary contributions by employees, where the pension scheme does no more than provide the membership with the necessary arrangements for management.

Smith v   **[1994] IRLR 602 ECJ**
Avdel Systems Ltd
Article 141 does not preclude an employer from raising the retirement age for women to that for men in order to comply with the *Barber* judgment. Article 141 does not preclude measures which achieve equal treatment by reducing the advantages of the persons previously favoured. It merely requires that men and women should receive the same pay for the same work without imposing any specific level of pay. However, once discrimination in pay has been found to exist, so long as measures for bringing about equal treatment have not been adopted by the scheme, the only proper way of complying with Article 141 is to grant the persons in the disadvantaged class the same advantages as those enjoyed by the persons in the favoured class. In the present case, that meant that, as regards the period between the date of the Barber judgment and the date on which the scheme adopted measures to achieve equality, the pension rights of men must be calculated on the basis of the same retirement age as that for women.

Smith v   **[1994] IRLR 602 ECJ**
Avdel Systems Ltd
Where the retirement age for women is raised to that of men in order to remove discrimination in relation to occupational pensions, Article 141 does not allow transitional measures designed to limit the adverse consequences for women as regards benefits payable in respect of future periods of service.

Van Den Akker v   **[1994] IRLR 616 ECJ**
Stichting Shell Pensioenfonds
Article 141 does not allow an occupational pension scheme to maintain in force after the date of the *Barber* judgment a condition as to retirement age differing according to sex, even where that difference is due to giving female employees an option before the *Barber* judgment to maintain a retirement age lower than that for men.

Smith v   **[1994] IRLR 602 ECJ**
Avdel Systems Ltd
Article 141 precludes an occupational pension scheme, even where there are objectively justifiable considerations relating to the needs of the undertaking or of the scheme concerned, from retrospectively raising the retirement age for women in relation to periods of service between the date of the *Barber* judgment and the date of entry into force of the measures designed to achieve equal treatment.

Coloroll Pension Trustees Ltd v   **[1994] IRLR 586 ECJ**
Russell
The national court is bound to ensure correct implementation of Article 141 and, in order to do so, may make use of all means available to it under domestic law, such

as by ordering the employer to pay additional sums into the scheme, ordering that any sum payable by virtue of Article 141 must be paid out of surplus funds or out of the scheme's assets. Any problems arising because the funds held by the trustee are insufficient or the employer cannot provide sufficient funds to equalise benefits must be resolved on the basis of national law in accordance with the principle of equal pay.

Coloroll Pension Trustees Ltd v   **[1994] IRLR 586 ECJ**
Russell
The rights accruing to a worker from Article 141 cannot be affected by the fact that he changes his job and has to join a new pension scheme, with his acquired pension rights being transferred to the new scheme. A worker entering retirement is entitled to expect the scheme of which he is then a member to pay him a pension calculated in accordance with the principle of equal treatment, and to increase benefits accordingly, even where the capital transferred is inadequate due to the discriminatory treatment under the first scheme. However, in accordance with the *Barber* judgment, neither the scheme which transferred rights nor the scheme which accepted them is required to take the financial steps necessary to bring about equality in relation to periods of service prior to 17 May 1990.

Bilka-Kaufhaus GmbH v   **[1986] IRLR 317 ECJ**
Weber von Hartz
Article 141 is restricted to pay discrimination and therefore does not have the effect of requiring an employer to organise an occupational pension scheme in such a manner as to take into account the particular difficulties faced by persons with family responsibilities in meeting the conditions for entitlement to such a pension.

Coloroll Pension Trustees Ltd v   **[1994] IRLR 586 ECJ**
Russell
Article 141 is not applicable to pension schemes which at all times have had members of only one sex.

Moroni v   **[1994] IRLR 130 ECJ**
Firma Collo GmbH
The provisions of EC Occupational Social Security Directive 86/378 cannot limit the scope of Article 141.

Temporal limitation

Barber v   **[1990] IRLR 240 ECJ**
Guardian Royal Exchange
  Assurance Group
The direct effect of Article 141 may not be relied upon in order to claim entitlement to a pension with effect from a date prior to that of the judgment in this case (17 May 1990), except in the case of those who have before that date initiated legal proceedings or raised an equivalent claim under the applicable national law.

Ten Oever v   **[1993] IRLR 601 ECJ**
Stichting Bedrijfspensioenfonds voor
  het Glazenwassers- en Schoonmaakbedrijf

The direct effect of Article 141 may be relied upon, for the purpose of claiming equal treatment in the matter of occupational pensions, only in relation to benefits payable in respect of periods of employment subsequent to 17 May 1990, the date of the *Barber* decision, subject to the exception in favour of those who before that date initiated legal proceedings or raised an equivalent claim under the applicable national law.

Coloroll Pension Trustees Ltd v   **[1994] IRLR 586 ECJ**
Russell

Where a benefit is not linked to the actual length of service, such as a lump-sum payment in the event of the employee's death during employment, the limitation of the effects in time of the *Barber* judgment applies only where the operative event occurred before 17 May 1990. After that date, such benefits must be granted in accordance with the principle of equal treatment without distinguishing between periods of service prior to and subsequent to the *Barber* judgment.

Vroege v   **[1994] IRLR 651 ECJ**
NCIV Instituut voor
  Volkshuisvesting BV

The temporal limitation of the *Barber* judgment concerns only those kinds of discrimination which employers and occupational pension schemes could reasonably have considered to be permissible owing to the transitional derogations provided by Community law in respect of equal treatment with regard to the determination of pensionable age.

Quirk v   **[2002] IRLR 353 CA**
Burton Hospitals NHS Trust

The decisions of the European Court of Justice reveal a difference in the treatment of "access cases" relating to the right to join or to be fully admitted to a pension scheme and its benefits, and claims relating to the calculation of the level of benefits under a pension scheme. The Court of Justice has applied the temporal limitation to level of benefit cases but not to access cases.

Quirk v   **[2002] IRLR 353 CA**
Burton Hospitals NHS Trust

The provision in the NHS Pension Scheme Regulations allowing a woman retiring before age 60 to receive benefits calculated by reference to all of her pensionable service, whereas the pension payable to men before age 60 is calculated only by reference to service from 17 May 1990, the date of the *Barber* decision, did not discriminate against a man contrary to Article 141 since the claim was caught by the temporal limitation contained in the European Court's decision in the *Barber* case and in the *Barber* Protocol to the EC Treaty, in that it was a complaint about the level of benefit payable, rather than a complaint relating to access to benefits under a pension scheme. The essence of the complaint was not that the claimant was denied the right to be a member of the pension scheme, but that, unlike the case of a female nurse, the calculation of pension benefits

on his retirement at age 55 would not take account of his years of pensionable service prior to 17 May 1990.

Howard v   **[1995] IRLR 570 EAT**
Ministry of Defence

The exclusion from the temporal limitation imposed by the European Court on the *Barber* decision for those who had made a claim "equivalent" to legal proceedings in national law, is restricted to where a dispute has been raised before an independent third party with power to determine the dispute conclusively, such as an administrative or arbitration tribunal, and does not extend to a person who only asserts a claim.

Admission

Bilka-Kaufhaus GmbH v   **[1986] IRLR 317 ECJ**
Weber von Hartz

The conditions for admission to an occupational pension scheme, where the benefits paid to employees constitute consideration received by the worker from the employer in respect of employment, fall within the scope of the definition of "pay" in Article 141 of the EC Treaty; such a scheme does not constitute a social security scheme governed directly by statute, which would be outside the scope of Article 141.

Vroege v   **[1994] IRLR 651 ECJ**
NCIV Instituut voor
  Volkshuisvesting BV

Article 141 of the EC Treaty covers the right to join an occupational pension scheme, as well as entitlement to benefits paid by an occupational pension scheme. Therefore, an occupational pension scheme which excludes part-time workers will contravene Article 141 if the exclusion affects a much greater number of women than men, unless the employer shows that it may be explained by objectively justified factors unrelated to any discrimination on grounds of sex.

Trustees of Uppingham School   **[2002] IRLR 792 CA**
  Retirement Benefit Scheme for
  Non-Teaching Staff v
Shillcock

Exclusion of the claimant part-time employee from membership of the appellant's occupational pension scheme on grounds that she earned less than the lower earnings limit for Class I national insurance contributions was not indirectly discriminatory on grounds of sex against women contrary to Article 141. Subtracting the lower earnings limit from the earnings of every employee for the purpose of assessing pensionable salary involved a consistent, and not a discriminatory, approach to all categories of employee.

Allonby v   **[2004] IRLR 224 ECJ**
Accrington & Rossendale College

A requirement of being employed under a contract of employment as a precondition for membership of a pension scheme for teachers, set up by State legislation, must be disapplied unless it is objectively justified, where it is shown that among the teachers who are "workers" within the meaning of Article 141 there is a much higher percentage of women than of men who fulfil all the conditions for membership of the scheme except that of being employed under a contract of employment as defined by national law.

Preston v   **[2004] IRLR 96 EAT**
Wolverhampton Healthcare
  NHS Trust (No.3)
There is a breach of the Equal Pay Act where pension scheme membership is compulsory for full-time staff but part-time staff are excluded, regardless of whether an employee joined the scheme when it became open to them. However, there is no breach of the Equal Pay Act where pension scheme membership is compulsory for full-time staff and optional for part-time staff.

Schröder v   **[2000] IRLR 353 ECJ**
Deutsche Telekom AG
Where the exclusion of part-time workers from an occupational pension scheme has been found to constitute indirect discrimination prohibited by Article 141, the only limitation in time on the possibility of relying on the direct effect of Article 141 in relation to membership of the scheme and the subsequent payment of a pension is that resulting from *Defrenne (No.2)*, that periods of service of such workers are to be taken into account only from 8 April 1976 onwards. The limitation in time of the *Barber* decision and the *Barber* Protocol concerns only those kinds of discrimination which employers and pension schemes could reasonably have considered to be permissible under Community law. Since it has been clear since the judgment in *Bilka* that any discrimination, based on sex, in the right to join an occupational pension scheme infringes Article 41, there was no reason to suppose that those concerned could have been mistaken as to the applicability of Article 41 to the right to join an occupational scheme.

Vroege v   **[1994] IRLR 651 ECJ**
NCIV Instituut voor
  Volkshuisvesting BV
The *Barber* Protocol to Article 141, which provides that benefits under occupational social security schemes shall not be considered as remuneration if and in so far as they are attributable to periods of employment prior to 17 May 1990, does not affect the right to join an occupational pension scheme. The Protocol is applicable to benefits paid under an occupational pension scheme, since that is all that is mentioned in the Protocol. Neither the Protocol, nor the *Barber* judgment, dealt with, or made any provision for, the conditions of membership of occupational schemes, which continues to be governed by the *Bilka* judgment.

Dietz v   **[1996] IRLR 692 ECJ**
Stichting Thuiszorg Rotterdam
The *Barber* Protocol to the Treaty on European Union does not affect the right to payment of a retirement pension where the worker was excluded from membership of an occupational pension scheme in breach of Article 141.

Fisscher v   **[1994] IRLR 662 ECJ**
Voorhuis Hengelo BV
National rules relating to time limits for bringing actions under national law may be relied on against workers who assert their right under Community law to join an occupational pension scheme, provided that they are not less favourable for that type of action than for similar actions of a domestic nature and that they do not render the exercise of rights conferred by Community law impossible in practice.

Fisscher v   **[1994] IRLR 662 ECJ**
Voorhuis Hengelo BV
The fact that a worker can claim retroactively to join an occupational pension scheme does not allow the worker to avoid paying the contributions relating to the period of membership concerned. The worker cannot claim more favourable treatment, particularly in financial terms, than if the worker had been duly accepted as a member.

Bridging pensions

Birds Eye Walls Ltd v   **[1994] IRLR 29 ECJ**
Roberts
It is not contrary to Article 141 for an employer to reduce the amount of a bridging pension to take account of the amount of the State pension which the employee will receive, even though, in the case of men and women aged between 60 and 65, the result is that a female ex-employee receives a smaller bridging pension than that paid to her male counterpart.

Birds Eye Walls Ltd v   **[1994] IRLR 29 ECJ**
Roberts
It is not contrary to Article 141 for an employer, when calculating a bridging pension, to take account of the full State pension which a married woman would have received if she had not opted in favour of paying contributions at a reduced rate. Nor is it contrary to Article 141 for an employer to take account of the widow's pension which may be drawn by the woman concerned.

Notice payment

Clark v   **[1995] IRLR 421 EAT**
Secretary of State for Employment
Sums payable by an employer to an employee for failing to give notice to which the employee is entitled are "pay" within the meaning of Article 141, because such payment is in respect of the employee's employment.

Clark v   **[1996] IRLR 578 CA**
Secretary of State for Employment
The exclusion of women absent from work because of pregnancy from the categories specified in para.2 of Schedule 3 to the Employment Protection (Consolidation) Act, which determines the liability of an employer for the statutory

minimum notice period, did not amount to discrimination on the ground of sex contrary to Article 141. Discrimination on grounds of sex means either that different rules are applied to men and women in comparable situations or that the same rule is applied to men and women in different situations. Women taking maternity leave, however, are in a special position, since men are never in a "comparable situation".

Redundancy payment

Barber v   **[1990] IRLR 240 ECJ**
Guardian Royal Exchange
  Assurance Group
Benefits paid by an employer to a worker in connection with the latter's compulsory redundancy fall within the scope of Article 141 of the EC Treaty, whether they are paid under a contract of employment, by virtue of legislative provisions or on a voluntary basis.

McKechnie v   **[1991] IRLR 283 EAT**
UBM Building Supplies (Southern) Ltd
The decision of the European Court in *Barber v Guardian Royal Exchange Assurance Group Ltd* removed any possible doubt that both a statutory redundancy payment and an ex-gratia payment based on the statutory payment provided by a collective agreement are properly to be regarded as coming within the definition of "pay" in Article 141.

Commission of the European   **[1993] IRLR 404 ECJ**
  Communities v
Kingdom of Belgium
Payments in addition to unemployment benefit provided under Belgian law to men who are made redundant between ages 60 and 65 constitute "pay" within the scope of Article 141 of the EC Treaty, rather than a social security benefit falling outside Article 141, since the payment is the responsibility of the last employer of the employee dismissed, is due by reason of the employment relationship which existed, and has its origins in an agreement between the social partners.

Rankin v   **[1993] IRLR 69 EAT**
British Coal Corporation
The general policy in legislation, concerned not only with redundancy but with similar statutory claims such as equal pay and racial and sexual discrimination provisions, suggests that a period for bringing claims directly under Article 141 in the region of three to six months could not properly be stigmatised as unreasonable, given that the starting date for the running of the period is also reasonable.

Rankin v   **[1993] IRLR 69 EAT**
British Coal Corporation
Balancing the requirements of certainty and the protection of rights under the Treaty, a claim in respect of a discriminatory statutory redundancy payment brought within a reasonable period of

time after the coming into force of the amending legislation which removed the discrimination should be regarded as timeous.

Severance pay

Barry v   **[1999] IRLR 581 HL**
Midland Bank plc
A security of employment agreement, whereby severance pay was calculated on the basis of the employee's current pay at the date of termination, was not indirectly discriminatory against women contrary to Article 141, even though the scheme made no allowance for employees whose hours of work fluctuated, thereby disadvantaging part-time workers by not taking into account any full-time service they may have had. The scheme did not have a discriminatory effect and thus did not infringe the principle of equal pay for equal work, since the same rules applied to women and men, to both full-time and part-time workers.

Unfair dismissal compensation

R v   **[1999] IRLR 253 ECJ**
Secretary of State for Employment
  ex parte Seymour-Smith
An award of unfair dismissal compensation constitutes "pay" within the meaning of Article 141, since it is paid to the employee by reason of his employment, which would have continued but for the unfair dismissal.

R v   **[1999] IRLR 253 ECJ**
Secretary of State for Employment
  ex parte Seymour-Smith
The conditions determining whether an unfairly dismissed employee is entitled to compensation fall within the scope of Article 141 rather than the Equal Treatment Directive, since the condition concerns access to a form of pay. However, where a dismissed employee seeks reinstatement or re-engagement, the conditions laid down by national law concern working conditions or the right to take up employment and would therefore fall under the Equal Treatment Directive.

Travel facilities

Garland v   **[1982] IRLR 111 ECJ**
British Rail Engineering Ltd
Travel facilities accorded to employees after retirement are "pay" within the meaning of Article 141, so that an employer who provided special travel facilities for former male employees to enjoy after their retirement discriminated within the meaning of Article 141 against former female employees who did not receive the same facilities.

PRELIMINARY ISSUES

Definition of "employed"

(6) Subject to the following subsections, for purposes of this section –

> *(a) "employed" means employed under a contract of service or of apprenticeship or a contract personally to execute any work or labour, and related expressions shall be construed accordingly;*

EQUAL PAY ACT – s.1
➡ **EQUALITY ACT 2010 – s.83**

Quinnen v   **[1984] IRLR 227 EAT**
Hovells
The definition of "employed" in s.1(6)(a) of the Equal Pay Act covering employment under "a contract personally to execute any work or labour" is a wide and flexible concept and was intended to enlarge upon the ordinary connotation of "employment" so as to include persons outside the master-servant relationship. It covers a self-employed person engaged by the respondent on activity amounting to work or labour, who was engaged personally and was discharging such functions under terms which were contractual.

Claim in time

(1) Any claim in respect of the contravention of a term modified or included by virtue of an equality clause, including a claim for arrears of remuneration or damages in respect of the contravention, may be presented by way of a complaint to an industrial tribunal.

EQUAL PAY ACT – s.2
➡ **EQUALITY ACT 2010 – s.127**

2(1) The following provisions –

> *(a) paragraph (2) of regulation 3, and*
> *(b) regulation 4,*

apply for the purpose of determining whether an employment tribunal may make a determination in proceedings instituted on or after the commencement date (subject to para. (2) below).

(2) Those provisions do not so apply if the last day on which the woman was employed in the employment falls more than six months before the commencement date.

(3) If those provisions do so apply so as to enable an employment tribunal to make a determination in proceedings in a stable employment case (within the meaning given by virtue of reg. 4), the determination may not relate to any non-qualifying contract of employment forming part of the stable employment relationship.

(4) For the purposes of para. (3) above a contract of employment is a non-qualifying contract of employment if it ended more than six months before the commencement date.

(5) The following provisions –

> *(a) paragraph (3) of regulation 3,*
> *(b) regulation 5,*
> *(c) paragraph (4) of regulation 6, and*
> *(d) regulation 8,*

apply in relation to proceedings instituted on or after the commencement date.

(6) The following provisions –

> *(a) para. (3) of regulation 6, and*
> *(b) regulation 7,*

apply for the purpose of determining whether an employment tribunal may make a determination on a complaint presented to it on or after the commencement date (subject to para. (7) below).

(7) Those provisions do not so apply if the last day of the woman's period of service falls more than nine months before the commencement date.

EQUAL PAY ACT 1970 (AMENDMENT)
REGULATIONS 2003 – reg. 2
➡ **EQUALITY ACT 2010 – s.129**

(4) No determination may be made by an employment tribunal in the following proceedings –

> *(a) on a complaint under subsection (1) above,*
> *(b) on an application under subsection (1A) above, or*
> *(c) on a reference under subsection (2) above,*

unless the proceedings are instituted on or before the qualifying date (determined in accordance with section 2ZA below).

EQUAL PAY ACT (as amended) – s.2
➡ **EQUALITY ACT 2010 – s.129**

(1) This section applies for the purpose of determining the qualifying date, in relation to proceedings in respect of a woman's employment, for the purposes of section 2(4) above.

(2) In this section –

"concealment case" means a case where –

> *(a) the employer deliberately concealed from the woman any fact (referred to in this section as a "qualifying fact") –*
> > *(i) which is relevant to the contravention to which the proceedings relate, and*
> > *(ii) without knowledge of which the woman could not reasonably have been expected to institute the proceedings, and*
>
> *(b) the woman did not discover the qualifying fact (or could not with reasonable diligence have discovered it) until after –*
> > *(i) the last day on which she was employed in the employment, or*
> > *(ii) the day on which the stable employment relationship between her and the employer ended,*
>
> *(as the case may be);*

"disability case" means a case where the woman was under a disability at any time during the six months after –

> *(a) the last day on which she was employed in the employment,*
> *(b) the day on which the stable employment relationship between her and the employer ended, or*
> *(c) the day on which she discovered (or could with reasonable diligence have discovered) the qualifying fact deliberately concealed from her by the employer (if that day falls after the day referred to in paragraph (a) or (b) above, as the case may be),*

"stable employment case" means a case where the proceedings relate to a period during which a stable employment relationship subsists between the woman and the employer, notwithstanding that the period includes any time after the ending of a contract of employment when no further contract of employment is in force;

"standard case" means a case which is not –

(a) a stable employment case,

(b) a concealment case,

(c) a disability case, or

(d) both a concealment and a disability case.

(3) In a standard case, the qualifying date is the date falling six months after the last day on which the woman was employed in the employment.

(4) In a case which is a stable employment case (but not also a concealment or a disability case or both), the qualifying date is the date falling six months after the day on which the stable employment relationship ended.

(5) In a case which is a concealment case (but not also a disability case), the qualifying date is the date falling six months after the day on which the woman discovered the qualifying fact in question (or could with reasonable diligence have discovered it).

(6) In a case which is a disability case (but not also a concealment case), the qualifying date is the date falling six months after the day on which the woman ceased to be under a disability.

(7) In a case which is both a concealment and a disability case, the qualifying date is the later of the dates referred to in subsections (5) and (6) above."

EQUAL PAY ACT (as amended) – s.2ZA

➡ EQUALITY ACT 2010 – s.129, s.130

Preston v   [2000] IRLR 506 ECJ
Wolverhampton Healthcare NHS Trust

Community law does not preclude a national procedural rule, such as that contained in s.2(4) of the Equal Pay Act, which requires that a claim for membership of an occupational pension scheme must be brought within six months of the end of the employment to which the claim relates, provided that that limitation period is not less favourable for actions based on Community law than for those based on domestic law. The setting of reasonable limitation periods for bringing proceedings satisfies the Community law principle of effectiveness, inasmuch as it constitutes an application of the fundamental principle of legal certainty, even if expiry of the limitation period results in the dismissal of the claimant's action.

Preston v   [2001] IRLR 237 HL
Wolverhampton Healthcare
NHS Trust (No.2)

The limitation under s.2(4) requiring a claim to be brought within six months of the end of the employment to which the claim relates, is not less favourable than the time limit of six years for bringing a claim for breach of contract. Therefore, s.2(4) does not breach the principle of equivalence.

Secretary of State for Health v   [2007] IRLR 665 EAT
Rance

The time limit under the Equal Pay Act is one of jurisdiction. A tribunal is precluded from hearing a claim that is not presented within the relevant time. Consequently, the jurisdictional provisions cannot be waived by the parties.

North Cumbria University Hospitals   [2010] IRLR 804 EAT
NHS Trust v
Fox

There was a stable employment relationship where, following implementation of Agenda for Change, the claimants continued to do the same work for the employer without any break in either the work itself or the succession of contracts. The only difference was that there were new terms and conditions, but there was no suggestion that the nature of their jobs changed materially.

National Power plc v   [2001] IRLR 32 CA
Young

The word "employment" in s.2(4) does not relate to the particular job on which the woman bases her claim to an equality clause. "Employed in the employment" means employed under a contract of service.

Slack v   [2009] IRLR 463 CA
Cumbria County Council

There was a new contract of employment where the claimant signed a document which included terms that differed from previous contracts and expressly stated that it superseded any previous contract of employment. However, the time limit is not triggered where the new contract was part of a succession of contracts in respect of the same employment within a stable employment relationship. A stable employment relationship is not confined to cases of a succession of contracts with breaks between the contracts. There can be a stable employment relationship where there is an unbroken succession of contracts.

Potter v   [2009] IRLR 900 EAT
North Cumbria Acute Hospitals NHS Trust (No.2)

Fundamental as well as minor contractual changes can be effected by consensual variation. Parties can agree both the content and the mechanism for effecting contractual change. Where parties do not expressly agree the mechanism for a change in terms and conditions of employment, their intention is to be objectively ascertained from all the relevant circumstances. In the present case, the changes in health service terms and condition brought about by Agenda for Change did not amount to a termination of the claimants' contracts of employment and replacement with new contracts, thereby triggering the time limit. The changes, which were restricted to pay, were not fundamental and were a variation to existing contracts of employment.

Powerhouse Retail Ltd v   **[2006] IRLR 381 HL**
Burroughs

Where there has been a relevant transfer under the Transfer of Undertakings Regulations, time begins to run under s.2(4) of the Equal Pay Act, for the purposes of an equal pay claim against a transferor, from the date of the relevant TUPE transfer rather than from the end of an employee's employment with the transferee.

Gutridge v   **[2009] IRLR 721 CA**
Sodexo Ltd

The *Powerhouse* judgment is not limited in its application to occupational pension schemes. Accordingly, where there is a transfer of an undertaking, a claim for breach of the equality clause by the transferor must be brought against the transferee within six months of the termination of her employment with the transferor. That time limit, however, does not apply to any discrimination by the transferee which occurs during the course of the transferred employment.

Kells v   **[2002] IRLR 693 EAT**
Pilkington plc

There is no rule of law restricting the period of events in respect of which an equal pay comparison can be made to six years before the date of the application.

Preston v   **[2000] IRLR 506 ECJ**
Wolverhampton Healthcare NHS Trust

Where there has been a stable employment relationship resulting from a succession of short-term contracts concluded at regular intervals in respect of the same employment to which the same pension scheme applies, Community law precludes a procedural rule, such as that contained in s.2(4) of the Equal Pay Act, which has the effect of requiring a claim for membership of an occupational pension scheme to be brought within six months of the end of each contract of employment to which the claim relates.

Preston v   **[2004] IRLR 96 EAT**
Wolverhampton Healthcare NHS Trust (No.3)

The features that characterise a "stable employment relationship" are that there is (1) a succession of short-term contracts, meaning three or more contacts for an academic year or shorter; (2) concluded at regular intervals, in that they are clearly predictable and can be calculated precisely, or where the employee is called upon frequently whenever a need arises; (3) relating to the same employment; and (4) to which the same pension scheme applies. A stable employment relationship ceases for this purpose when a succession of short-term contracts is superseded by a permanent contract.

Secretary of State for Health v   **[2007] IRLR 665 EAT**
Rance

In order for there to be a "stable employment relationship", the work done under the contract must be the same throughout. If there is a fundamental difference, time will begin to run.

Choice of comparator

Ainsworth v   **[1977] IRLR 74 EAT**
Glass Tubes & Components Ltd

An employment tribunal cannot substitute its own choice of comparator for the comparator selected by the claimant.

Thomas v   **[1978] IRLR 451 EAT**
National Coal Board

There is no requirement that the comparator selected by the claimant should be representative of a group.

Macarthys Ltd v   **[1980] IRLR 210 ECJ**
Smith

The principle of equal pay in Article 141 is not confined to situations in which men and women are contemporaneously doing equal work and therefore applies where it is established that, having regard to the nature of her services, a woman has received less pay than a man who was employed prior to her employment and who did equal work for the employer.

Walton Centre for Neurology and   **[2008] IRLR 588 EAT**
   Neurosurgery NHS Trust v
Bewley

A claimant cannot bring an equal pay claim using their successor as a comparator. The exercise of comparing with a successor is too hypothetical.

Pointon v   **[1979] IRLR 119 CA**
The University of Sussex

A complaint under the Equal Pay Act must relate to a term in the claimant's contract of employment that is less favourable than the equivalent term in the contract of the man with whom she is comparing herself. The Equal Pay Act cannot be used to establish a claim that a claimant should have been paid more than her comparator.

Macarthys Ltd v   **[1980] IRLR 210 ECJ**
Smith

Comparisons under Article 141 are confined to parallels which may be drawn on the basis of concrete appraisals of the work actually performed by employees of different sex within the same establishment or service.

Allonby v   **[2004] IRLR 224 ECJ**
Accrington & Rossendale College

Although Article 141 is not limited to situations in which men and women work for the same employer and may be invoked in cases of discrimination arising directly from legislative provisions or collective agreements, as well as in cases in which work is carried out in the same establishment or service, where the differences identified in the pay conditions of workers performing equal work or work of equal value cannot be attributed to a single source, there is no body which is responsible for the inequality and which could restore equal treatment. Such a situation does not come within the scope of Article 141. Therefore, a woman whose contract of employment was not renewed and who was immediately made available to her previous employer through another undertaking to provide the same services was not entitled to rely on Article 141 in a claim against the new employer, using as a basis for comparison the remuneration received for equal work or work of the same value by a man employed by the woman's previous employer.

Robertson v   **[2005] IRLR 363 CA**
Department for Environment, Food
   and Rural Affairs
Having a common employer is not necessarily the same as being "in the same employment" or having pay and conditions attributed to a "single source". The critical question is whether there is a single body responsible for the discriminatory pay differences of which complaint is made. This is not determined by only addressing the formal legal question of the identity of the employer.

Robertson v   **[2005] IRLR 363 CA**
Department for Environment, Food
   and Rural Affairs
The Crown is not the "single source" responsible for unequal pay as between employees who worked in different civil service departments, since pay and conditions of civil servants are no longer negotiated or agreed centrally on a civil service-wide basis but are the responsibility of each individual department.

Armstrong v   **[2006] IRLR 124 CA**
Newcastle Upon Tyne NHS Hospital Trust
Claimants employed by a hospital trust could not use employees at another hospital of the same trust as comparators notwithstanding that the hospital trust had taken some part in the negotiation of terms and conditions at departmental level and there was some evidence of the harmonisation of terms and conditions, in circumstances in which it was found that the trust had not assumed responsibility for the terms and conditions of all the employees for the purposes of the *Robertson* test.

Scullard v   **[1996] IRLR 344 EAT**
Knowles
The class of comparators under Article 141, as interpreted by the European Court of Justice, is broader than defined under s.1(6) of the Equal Pay Act. The crucial question for the purpose of Article 141, in accordance with the decision of the European Court in *Defrenne (No.2)*, is whether the claimant and her comparators are employed "in the same establishment or service". No distinction was drawn by the European Court between work carried out in the same establishment or service of limited companies and of other employers. To the extent that that is a wider class of comparators than is contained in s.1(6),

s.1(6) is displaced and must yield to the paramount force of Article 141, which has direct effect as between individuals.

North Cumbria Acute Hospitals   **[2009] IRLR 176 EAT**
  NHS Trust v
Potter
Section 1(6) does not require a single source for terms and conditions as between the claimant and her comparator.

South Ayrshire Council v   **[2002] IRLR 256 CS**
Morton
In determining whether men and women receive unequal pay for equal work, the scope of the inquiry is not always confined to the claimant's own workplace or to the claimant's own employer. If a case falls within para.21 of the decision in *Defrenne (No.2)*, as being direct discrimination having its origin in legislative provisions or in a collective agreement, a comparison is admissible and there is no need to apply the further test in para.22 of *Defrenne (No.2)* as to whether the work of the claimant and the work of the comparator is carried out in the same establishment or service.

South Ayrshire Council v   **[2002] IRLR 256 CS**
Morton
A claimant and her comparator who are in the same branch of public service and who are subject to a uniform system of national pay and conditions set by a statutory body whose decision is binding on their employers are engaged in the same "service" in the sense in which that expression is used in *Defrenne (No.2)*. Therefore, a female headteacher employed by a local education authority in Scotland was entitled to bring an equal pay claim relying on Article 141 to compare herself with a male headteacher employed by a different education authority in Scotland.

South Ayrshire Council v   **[2003] IRLR 153 CS**
Milligan
A comparator who is earning the same or less than the claimant is a valid comparator in a contingent equal pay claim, founded on the case of a comparator whose success in her own claim could result in discrimination against the claimant. Therefore, a male primary school headteacher was entitled to present his equal pay claim on a contingent basis, by naming as a comparator a female primary school headteacher whose pay currently was the same as his or less, and to have his case adjourned pending resolution of the comparator's equal pay claim comparing her work to that of male secondary school headteachers.

McLoughlin v   **[1978] IRLR 127 EAT**
Gordons (Stockport) Ltd
A comparison, once made and adjudicated upon under the Equal Pay Act, is *res judicata* and cannot be heard again unless there can be shown to be some appreciable difference in the facts.

Common terms and conditions

(6)(c) two employers are to be treated as associated if one is a company of which the other (directly or indirectly) has control or if both are companies of which a third person (directly or indirectly) has control,

[and men shall be treated as in the same employment with a woman if they are men employed by her employer or any associated employer at the same establishment or at establishments in Great Britain which include that one and at which common terms and conditions of employment are observed either generally or for employees of the relevant classes...]

EQUAL PAY ACT – s.1

➡ **EQUALITY ACT 2010 – s.83**

City of Edinburgh Council v **[2010] IRLR 756 EAT**
Wilkinson
Giving the word "establishment" a purposive construction so as to accord with the principles in Article 141, the question to ask is whether it is fair and reasonable to regard a particular group of employees as being a single establishment for comparison purposes in an equal pay claim.

City of Edinburgh Council v **[2010] IRLR 756 EAT**
Wilkinson
A local authority is prima facie a single establishment and that presumption will only be set aside if the facts demonstrate that there are subsets of its operation which ought properly to be regarded as separate establishments.

Lawson v **[1988] IRLR 53 EAT**
Britfish Ltd
The phrase "and at which common terms and conditions of employment are observed" in s.1(6) of the Equal Pay Act does not relate to employment at the same establishment. It relates to other establishments outside the establishment at which the claimant is employed. Once it is found that the claimants and the comparator are employed at the same establishment, whether there are common terms and conditions does not arise.

Leverton v **[1989] IRLR 28 HL**
Clwyd County Council
The comparison called for by s.1(6) is between the terms and conditions of employment observed at the establishment at which the woman is employed and the establishment at which the men are employed, and applicable either generally, ie to all the employees at the relevant establishments, or to a particular class or classes of employees to which both the woman and the men belong. The comparison is not between the terms and conditions of employment of the complainant on the one hand and of the comparators on the other. The concept of common terms and conditions of employment observed generally at different establishments necessarily contemplates terms and conditions applicable to a wide range of employees whose individual terms will vary greatly as between each other.

British Coal Corporation v **[1996] IRLR 404 HL**
Smith
"Common terms and conditions of employment" within the meaning of s.1(6) of the Equal Pay Act means terms and conditions which are substantially comparable on a broad basis, rather than the same terms and conditions subject only to de minimis differences. It is sufficient for the claimant to show that her comparator at another establishment and at her establishment were or would be employed on broadly similar terms.

South Tyneside Metropolitan **[2007] IRLR 715 CA**
Borough Council v
Anderson
"Common", as applied to terms and conditions, means sufficiently similar for a broad comparison to be made. Once it is found that the two employees' terms and conditions are "broadly similar", it is open to the employer to show a genuine material difference.

Leverton v **[1989] IRLR 28 HL**
Clwyd County Council
Terms and conditions of employment governed by the same collective agreement represent the paradigm, though not necessarily the only example, of the common terms and conditions of employment contemplated by s.1(6). Therefore, a nursery nurse was entitled to bring an equal value complaint comparing her work with that of male clerical workers employed by the respondents in different establishments where she and her comparators were employed on terms and conditions derived from the same collective agreement, notwithstanding that there were differences between her hours of work and holiday entitlement and those of her comparators.

City of Edinburgh Council v **[2010] IRLR 756 EAT**
Wilkinson
The intention of s.1(6) could be undermined if claimants were required to establish, as fact, that there was a real possibility of their comparators being employed at the same establishments as them. It is sufficient for claimants, in a case where employment of their comparators at the same establishment as them does not seem likely, to show that it is likely that those comparators would, wherever they worked, always be employed on the same terms and conditions because it is then legitimate to assume that they would be employed on those terms and conditions at the claimants' establishment. Circumstances where the comparators are always employed under the same collective agreement would be the paradigm.

Dumfries and Galloway Council v **[2009] IRLR 915 EAT**
North
The purpose of s.1(6) is to allow a woman to compare herself with a man in another of her employers' establishments, but only where there are factors that show that there is a commonality or uniformity of employment regime as between them. Where a woman seeks to use a male com-

parator that is not employed at her establishment, she must show a real possibility of him being employed there in the job he carries out at the other establishment or in a broadly similar job, and that the terms and conditions on which he would be employed at her establishment would be broadly similar to those under which the class of which he is a member are employed at his establishment.

Thomas v   **[1987] IRLR 451 EAT**
National Coal Board
There were "common terms and conditions of employment" between establishments for the relevant employees, notwithstanding that locally negotiated and varying bonus payments and concessionary entitlements formed a substantial part of remuneration, where the entitlement to bonuses and concessions was negotiated nationally, and it was only the amount which varied locally, so that the basic similarity of terms and conditions was not affected.

South Tyneside Metropolitan   **[2007] IRLR 715 CA**
  Borough Council v
Anderson
There were common terms and conditions as between local authority female school support staff and men employed by the local authority on the same grades, notwithstanding that none of the men worked in schools.

Associated employers

Hasley v   **[1989] IRLR 106 NICA**
Fair Employment Agency
The first limb of the statutory definition of associated employers, correctly interpreted, means that two employers are to be treated as associated if one employer is a company of which the other employer (not necessarily a company) has control. The second limb covers where both employers are companies of which a third person (not necessarily a company) has control.

Hasley v   **[1989] IRLR 106 NICA**
Fair Employment Agency
A statutory body corporate is not a "company" within the meaning of the statutory definition of associated employers.

LIKE WORK

(4) A woman is to be regarded as employed on like work with men if, but only if, her work and theirs is of the same or a broadly similar nature, and the differences (if any) between the things she does and the things they do are not of practical importance in relation to terms and conditions of employment; and accordingly in comparing her work with theirs regard shall be had to the frequency or otherwise with which any such differences occur in practice as well as to the nature and extent of the differences.

                 EQUAL PAY ACT – s.1
       ➡ **EQUALITY ACT 2010 – s.65**

General principles

Capper Pass Ltd v   **[1976] IRLR 366 EAT**
Lawton
Section 1(4) requires the determination of whether a man and a woman are employed on like work to be approached in two stages. First, is the work which she does and the work which he does of the same or of a broadly similar nature? This can be answered by a general consideration of the type of work involved and the skill and knowledge required to do it. Second, if it is work of a broadly similar nature, are the differences between the things she does and the things he does of practical importance in relation to terms and conditions of employment? Once it is determined that work is of a broadly similar nature, it should be regarded as being "like work" unless the differences are plainly of a kind which the employment tribunal in its experience would expect to find reflected in the terms and conditions of employment. Trivial differences, or differences not likely in the real world to be reflected in terms and conditions of employment, ought to be disregarded.

Capper Pass Ltd v   **[1976] IRLR 366 EAT**
Lawton
In deciding whether the work done by a woman and the work done by a man is "like work", the employment tribunal has to make a broad judgment. The intention is that the employment tribunal should not be required to undertake too minute an examination, nor be constrained to find that work is not like work, merely because of insubstantial differences.

Maidment and Hardacre v   **[1978] IRLR 462 EAT**
Cooper & Co (Birmingham) Ltd
The Equal Pay Act does not allow for a gap in remuneration to be narrowed so that it truly reflects the difference in the value of the work done by a claimant and her comparator. If the complainant and her comparator are not employed on like work, it is irrelevant that the gap in remuneration between them is in no way commensurate to the difference in the work which they do.

Differences of practical importance

E Coomes (Holdings) Ltd v   **[1978] IRLR 263 CA**
Shields

Section 1(4) requires a comparison to be made between the things that the woman and the man actually do and the frequency with which they are done, rather than between their respective contractual obligations.

Electrolux Ltd v   **[1976] IRLR 410 EAT**
Hutchinson

For differences in contractual obligations to amount to a difference of practical importance in relation to terms and conditions within the meaning of s.1(4), it must be shown that, as well as being contractually obliged to do additional different duties, the duties are performed to some significant extent.

British Leyland Ltd v   **[1978] IRLR 57 EAT**
Powell

In determining under s.1(4) whether differences in the things done by a man and those done by a woman are of "practical importance in relation to terms and conditions of employment", a practical guide is whether the differences (which ex hypothesi are not sufficient to make the work not of the same or a broadly similar nature) are such as to put the two employments into different categories or grades in an evaluation study.

Responsibility

Eaton Ltd v   **[1977] IRLR 71 EAT**
Nuttall

In considering whether there is like work, the circumstances in which the man and the woman do their work should not be disregarded. One of the circumstances properly to be taken into account is the degree of responsibility involved in carrying out the job. A factor such as responsibility may be decisive where it can be seen to put one employee into a different grade from another with whom comparisons are being made.

Waddington v   **[1977] IRLR 32 EAT**
Leicester Council for Voluntary
   Services

An obligation to supervise, to take responsibility or to control, if it is discharged, falls within the words "the things she does and the things they do".

Thomas v   **[1987] IRLR 451 EAT**
National Coal Board

The additional responsibility entailed in working permanently at night, alone and without supervision can amount to a "difference of practical importance in relation to terms and conditions of employment".

Time of work

Dugdale v   **[1976] IRLR 368 EAT**
Kraft Foods Ltd

In determining whether men and women are employed on like work, the mere time at which the work is performed should be disregarded when considering for the purposes of s.1(4), the differences between the things that the women do and the things which the men do.

Electrolux Ltd v   **[1976] IRLR 410 EAT**
Hutchinson

If the basic rate payable to the men, unlike that payable to the women, reflects some additional element of remuneration attributable to an obligation to work at nights or on Sundays (over and above any shift or Sunday shift premium payable), that fact can be reflected in the way in which the equality clause is applied – ie, it can be discounted so that the equality clause is applied not to produce equality, but so that the woman is not treated less favourably.

National Coal Board v   **[1978] IRLR 122 EAT**
Sherwin

If the man and the woman do the same work, the mere fact that they do it at different times is of no importance. The disadvantage of working at night, or at other inconvenient times, can be compensated by an additional night shift premium or other appropriate arrangement, but there is no reason why the man should receive by way of remuneration a sum which is greater than necessary to recognise the fact that he works at night, or at other inconvenient times, and if he does there is no reason why the woman should not be remunerated to the extent of the excess. An employment tribunal is entitled to adjust the woman's remuneration upon a claim by her so that it is at the same rate as the man's, discounting for the fact that he works at inconvenient hours, and she does not.

Maidment and Hardacre v   **[1978] IRLR 462 EAT**
Cooper & Co (Birmingham) Ltd

In applying the test of like work, it is not permissible to ignore some part of the work which the man actually does on the ground that his pay includes an additional element in respect of that work, which can be discounted. There is no warrant for the exclusion or hiving-off of some part of the activities of the comparator. There can be no question of discounting, or of applying the equality clause, until it has been established that the man and the woman are employed on like work, so that it cannot be right in order to determine that question to pray in aid a result which could only be arrived at after deciding that they were engaged on like work.

WORK RATED AS EQUIVALENT

(5) A woman is to be regarded as employed on work rated as equivalent with that of any men if, but only if, her job and their job have been given an equal value, in terms of the demand made on a worker under various headings (for instance effort, skill, decision), on a study undertaken with a view to evaluating in those terms the jobs to be done by all or any of the employees in an undertaking or group of undertakings, or would have been given an equal value but for the evaluation being made on a system setting different values for men and women on the same demand under any heading.

EQUAL PAY ACT – s.1
➡ **EQUALITY ACT 2010 – s.65**

Bromley v   **[1988] IRLR 249 CA**
H & J Quick Ltd

A job evaluation scheme must be "analytical" in order to comply with the provisions of s.1(5). The word "analytical" indicates conveniently the general nature of what is required by the section, viz that the jobs of each worker covered by the study must have been valued in terms of the demand made on the worker under various headings. It is not enough that benchmark jobs have been evaluated on a factor demand basis as required by s.1(5) if the jobs of the claimants and their comparators were not.

Bromley v   **[1988] IRLR 249 CA**
H & J Quick Ltd

Per Woolf LJ: In order to comply with s.1(5), employers can identify a group of jobs which when evaluated under the headings have no material difference. Then one of that group of jobs can be evaluated under headings and slotted into the rank in the appropriate position, having taken into account the factor value, and that job can then represent the other jobs within the group. If, however, a system of choosing a representative job for a group of jobs is adopted, then in relation to a job which has not been evaluated under headings it will be open to an employee to contend that his or her job is materially different from the alleged representative job and, if this is the case, the study will not comply with s.1(5).

Eaton Ltd v   **[1977] IRLR 71 EAT**
Nuttall

Section 1(5) can only apply to a valid evaluation study – that is, a study satisfying the test of being thorough in analysis and capable of impartial application. It should be possible by applying the study to arrive at the position of a particular employee at a particular point in a particular salary grade without taking other matters into account, except those unconnected with the nature of the work. An evaluation study which does not satisfy that test, and which requires the management to make a subjective judgment concerning the nature of the work before the employee can be fitted in at the appropriate place in the appropriate salary grade would not be a valid study for the purposes of s.1(5).

Arnold v   **[1982] IRLR 307 EAT**
Beecham Group Ltd

Before s.1(5) can be applied, there must be a completed job evaluation study, and there is no complete job evaluation study unless and until the parties who have agreed to carry out the study have accepted its validity. However, it is not the stage of implementing the study by using it as the basis of the payment of remuneration that makes it complete; it is the stage at which it is accepted as a study.

O'Brien v   **[1980] IRLR 373 HL**
Sim-Chem Ltd

Once a job evaluation study has been undertaken and has resulted in a conclusion that the job of a woman is of equal value with that of a man, then a comparison of their respective terms and conditions is made feasible and, subject to s.1(3), the equality clause can take effect. It is not necessary for the pay structure to have been adjusted as a result of the conclusions of the job evaluation study.

Springboard Sunderland Trust v   **[1992] IRLR 261 EAT**
Robson

In determining whether two jobs have been given an equal value within the meaning of s.1(5), so as to be work rated as equivalent, it is necessary to have regard to the full results of the job evaluation scheme, including the allocation to grade or scale at the end of the evaluation process.

Home Office v   **[2005] IRLR 757 EAT**
Bailey

Two jobs were not given an equal value under a job evaluation study within the meaning of s.1(5) in circumstances in which the claimants' work scored slightly lower than their comparators. The statutory formula, "if, but only if" her job and that of her comparator have been given equal value is precise.

Eaton Ltd v   **[1977] IRLR 71 EAT**
Nuttall

It is the duty of employers in Equal Pay Act cases to come to the employment tribunal hearing with the relevant information prepared in a comprehensive and readily assimilable form, including adequate details of any job evaluation system or other payment method in use.

EQUAL VALUE

(2) An equality clause is a provision which relates to terms (whether concerned with pay or not) of a contract under which a woman is employed (the "woman's contract"), and has the effect that –

> *[(c) where a woman is employed on work which, not being work in relation to which paragraph (a) or (b) above applies, is, in terms of the demands made on her (for instance under such headings as effort, skill and decision), of equal value to that of a man in the same employment –*
>> *(i) if (apart from the equality clause) any term of the woman's contract is or becomes less favourable to the woman than a term of a similar kind in the contract under which that man is employed, that term of the woman's contract shall be treated as so modified as not to be less favourable, and*
>> *(ii) if (apart from the equality clause) at any time the woman's contract does not include a term corresponding to a term benefiting that man included in the contract under which he is employed, the woman's contract shall be treated as including such a term.]*

EQUAL PAY ACT – s.1
➥ **EQUALITY ACT 2010 – s.65, s.66**

Commission of the European Communities v	**[1982] IRLR 333 ECJ**
United Kingdom of Great Britain and Northern Ireland	

Implementation of the EC principle of equal pay for work of equal value requires that where there is disagreement as to the application of that concept a worker must be entitled to claim before an appropriate authority that his work has the same value as other work and, if that is found to be the case, to have his rights under the EC Treaty and the Directive acknowledged by a binding decision. Any method which excludes that option prevents the aims of the Directive from being achieved.

Scope for comparison

Pickstone v	**[1988] IRLR 357 HL**
Freemans plc	

Section 1(2)(c) of the Equal Pay Act as amended does not preclude a woman employed on like work or work rated as equivalent with one man within the meaning of s.1(2)(a) or (b) of the Act from claiming that she is employed on work of equal value to that of another man. The words "not being work to which para. (a) or (b) above applies" in s.1(2)(c) have effect only where the particular man with whom the woman seeks to compare herself is employed on like work or work rated as equivalent.

Murphy v	**[1988] IRLR 267 ECJ**
Bord Telecom Eireann	

Article 141 of the EC Treaty must be interpreted as covering the case where a worker who relies on that provision to obtain equal pay within the meaning thereof is engaged in work of higher value than that of the person with whom a comparison is to be made.

Redcar & Cleveland Borough Council v	**[2007] IRLR 984 CA**
Bainbridge (No.1)	

Adopting a purposive construction, s.1(5) is to be read as if it said: "A woman is to be regarded as employed on work rated as equivalent with that of any men if, but only if, her job and their job have been given an equal value or her job has been given a higher value, in terms of the demand made on a worker under various headings (for instance effort, skill, decision), on a study undertaken with a view to evaluating in those terms the jobs to be done by all or any of the employees in an undertaking or group of undertakings, or would have been given an equal value, or her job would have been given a higher value, but for the evaluation being made on a system setting different values for men and women on the same demand under any heading."

Redcar & Cleveland Borough Council v	**[2008] IRLR 776 CA**
Bainbridge (No.2)	

Claimants are entitled to put forward all their equal pay claims cumulatively, although the amount of the arrears of pay recovered as a result of successfully putting the equal pay claim in one way will reduce the amount recoverable as a result of successfully putting the claim in a different way. There is nothing mutually inconsistent in the nature of the three different legal bases for an equal pay claim; nor is there anything in the Equal Pay Act explicitly or implicitly confining a claimant to only one way of putting her claim.

Redcar & Cleveland Borough Council v	**[2008] IRLR 776 CA**
Bainbridge (No.2)	

It is not permissible to allege a new cause of action in respect of a particular pay period in another action under the same head for the same pay period simply by selecting a different comparator. For a new cause of action for the same period it would be necessary to bring the equal pay claim under a different head, which would normally involve different comparators as well.

Job evaluation

(2) Subsection (2A) below applies in a case where –
> *(a) a tribunal is required to determine whether any work is of equal value as mentioned in s.1(2)(c) above, and*
> *(b) the work of the woman and that of the man in question have been given different values on a study such as is mentioned in s.1(5) above.*

(2A) The tribunal shall determine that the work of the woman and that of the man are not of equal value unless the tribunal has reasonable grounds for suspecting that the evaluation contained in the study –
> *(a) was (within the meaning of subsection (3) below) made on a system which discriminates on grounds of sex, or*
> *(b) is otherwise unsuitable to be relied upon.*

(3) An evaluation contained in a study such as is mentioned in s.1(5) above is made on a system which discriminates on grounds of sex where a difference, or coincidence, between values set by that system on different demands under the same or different headings is not justifiable irrespective of the sex of the person on whom those demands are made.

EQUAL PAY ACT (as amended) – s.2A
➡ EQUALITY ACT 2010 – s.131

The principle of equal pay for men and women outlined in Article 141 of the Treaty, hereinafter called "principle of equal pay", means, for the same work or for work to which equal value is attributed, the elimination of all discrimination on grounds of sex with regard to all aspects and conditions of remuneration.

In particular, where a job classification system is used for determining pay, it must be based on the same criteria for both men and women and so drawn up as to exclude any discrimination on grounds of sex.

EQUAL PAY DIRECTIVE – Article 1

Burden of proof

Dibro Ltd v   **[1990] IRLR 129 EAT**
Hore
Provided that a job evaluation scheme is analytical and a valid one within s.1(5) and relates to facts and circumstances existing at the time when the equal value proceedings were instituted, it does not matter that it came into existence after the initiation of proceedings. It is open to an employer to utilise such a scheme as evidence at any stage up to the final hearing, after the independent expert's report has been admitted, at which the tribunal gives its decision on the whole of the evidence.

Bainbridge v   **[2007] IRLR 494 EAT**
Redcar & Cleveland Borough Council (No.2)
An equal rating under a job evaluation scheme is not the same as establishing that the two jobs so rated are necessarily of equal value. There are two elements to a job evaluation study. There is the evaluation of the jobs; then there is the fixing of grade boundaries. It is not uncommon for jobs to be fitted into grades where there may be real distinctions in the value of the jobs.

Hovell v   **[2009] IRLR 734 CA**
Ashford and St Peter's Hospital NHS Trust
The fact that there is a small difference in the points given by a job evaluation study does not of itself establish that two jobs are of equal value. Equal value does not mean nearly equal value. However, jobs may be equal in value even though not precisely equal in points scored. It follows that a tribunal does not necessarily have to have the benefit of an independent expert before it can find equality where the claimant's job has been marked lower than the comparator's job in the job evaluation study.

Work rated unequal

Bromley v   **[1988] IRLR 249 CA**
H & J Quick Ltd
Section 1(5) requires a study undertaken with a view to evaluating jobs in terms of the demand made on a worker under various headings (for instance effort, skill, decision). It is necessary that both the work of the woman complainant and the work of her male comparator should have been valued in such terms of demand made on the worker under various headings.

Dibro Ltd v   **[1990] IRLR 129 EAT**
Hore
A job evaluation scheme advanced by the employer must compare the jobs as they were being carried out at the date the proceedings were issued and not compare a job or jobs which may have been changed since the initiation of proceedings.

McAuley v   **[1991] IRLR 467 NICA**
Eastern Health and Social
  Services Board
Per Sir Brian Hutton LCJ: A job evaluation study does not apply to employees unless they are employees in the undertaking or group of undertakings in respect of which the study was undertaken.

Bromley v   **[1988] IRLR 249 CA**
H & J Quick Ltd
There was not "a study such as is mentioned in s.1(5)" where the jobs of the women and their comparators were slotted into the structure on a "whole job" basis and no comparison was made by reference to the selected factors between the demands made on the individual workers under the selected headings. That at an appeal stage two of the women's jobs were evaluated in terms of their demands under the selected factors made no difference to the outcome in their cases, since there was never any appeal by their comparator. Nor was it sufficient that every worker covered by the study had a right of appeal which if exercised would have led to an analysis of their jobs.

Bromley v   **[1988] IRLR 249 CA**
H & J Quick Ltd
The good intentions of the parties to a job evaluation to avoid sex discrimination are of relatively minor importance when the question is whether the procedures followed in a job evaluation study matched up to the requirements of the Act as amended.

Avon County Council v   **[1989] IRLR 435 EAT**
Foxall
An employment tribunal has a discretion whether or not to grant a stay of proceedings pending implementation of a job evaluation scheme. However, a claimant has a prima facie right to prosecute her claim under the Act and there

was not much force in the argument that there was a risk of a job evaluation scheme being undermined if the results of the independent expert's report were more favourable to the claimant than the result of the job evaluation.

Discriminatory evaluation

Rummler v   **[1987] IRLR 32 ECJ**
Dato-Druck GmbH
[Article 4 of the Equal Treatment Directive], which provides that a job classification system "must be based on the same criteria for both men and women and so drawn up as to exclude any discrimination on grounds of sex", requires that the system must be based on criteria which do not differ according to whether the work is carried out by a man or by a woman and must not be organised, as a whole, in such a manner that it has the practical effect of discriminating generally against workers of one sex.

Rummler v   **[1987] IRLR 32 ECJ**
Dato-Druck GmbH
In determining rates of pay, it is consistent with the principle of non-discrimination to use a criterion based on the objectively measurable expenditure of effort necessary in carrying out the work or the degree to which, viewed objectively, the work is physically heavy, even where the criterion may in fact tend to favour male workers. A job classification system is not discriminatory within the meaning of [Article 4 of the Equal Treatment Directive] solely because one of its criteria is based on characteristics more commonly found among men than among women. However, if a job classification system is not to be discriminatory overall, it must be so designed, if the nature of the work so permits, as to take into account other criteria for which female employees may show particular aptitude.

Rummler v   **[1987] IRLR 32 ECJ**
Dato-Druck GmbH
The use of values reflecting the average performance of workers of one sex as a basis for determining the extent to which work makes demands or requires effort, or whether it is heavy, constitutes a form of discrimination on grounds of sex contrary to the [Equal Treatment Directive].

INDEPENDENT EXPERT'S REPORT

(1) Expert evidence shall be restricted to that which, in the opinion of the tribunal, is reasonably required to resolve the proceedings.
(3) No party may call an expert or put in evidence an expert's report without the permission of the tribunal. No expert report shall be put in evidence unless it has been disclosed to all other parties and any independent expert at least 28 days prior to the hearing.
(4) In proceedings in which an independent expert has been required to prepare a report on the question, the tribunal shall not admit evidence of another expert on the question unless such evidence is based on the facts relating to the question. Unless the tribunal considers it inappropriate to do so, any such expert report shall be disclosed to all parties and to the tribunal on the same date on which the independent expert is required to send his report to the parties and to the tribunal.

EMPLOYMENT TRIBUNALS (CONSTITUTION AND RULES OF PROCEDURE) REGULATIONS 2004: Schedule 6, rule 11

Leverton v   **[1989] IRLR 28 HL**
Clwyd County Council
An independent expert has to carry out what is, in effect, an ad hoc job evaluation study as between a complainant and her comparators and assess the demands of the job on a qualitative, rather than a quantitative, basis.

Leverton v   **[1989] IRLR 28 HL**
Clwyd County Council
Per Lord Bridge: Differences in hours of work and holidays between a complainant and her comparators are not a matter for assessment by the independent expert when considering the "demands" made upon them by their respective jobs.

Potter v   **[2009] IRLR 22 EAT**
North Cumbria Acute Hospitals NHS Trust
Whether a claimant's work and the work of comparator are of equal value must be considered in respect of every part of the claim period. Where there have, or may have, been material changes in a claimant's or comparator's job, or in its content, over the claim period, therefore, the facts will have to be found on a distinct basis in respect of the different parts of the period.

Tennants Textile Colours Ltd v   **[1989] IRLR 3 NICA**
Todd
The burden of proving a claim under the Equal Pay Act is on the claimant. The burden of proof is not transferred to the employer if the independent expert's report is in favour of the claimant.

Middlesbrough Borough Council v   **[2007] IRLR 981 EAT**
Surtees
Rule 11(4) does not deprive the tribunal of the power to hear an expert called by a party. What the party's expert can give

evidence about must exclude the facts that are not to be challenged and which represent a sacrosanct position following findings or agreement at an earlier stage in the proceedings. Given the restricted scope of challenge to facts, an expert is there to challenge methodology. The system of job evaluation is one which is susceptible to different methodologies.

DEFENCES

[(3) An equality clause shall not operate in relation to a variation between the woman's contract and the man's contract if the employer proves that the variation is genuinely due to a material factor which is not the difference of sex and that factor –

> *(a) in the case of an equality clause falling within subsection (2)(a) or (b) above, must be a material difference between the woman's case and the man's; and*
> *(b) in the case of an equality clause falling within subsection (2)(c) above, may be such a material difference.]*

EQUAL PAY ACT – s.1
➡ **EQUALITY ACT 2010 – s.69**

Burden of proof

Enderby v   [1993] IRLR 591 ECJ
Frenchay Health Authority and
  Secretary of State for Health
There is a prima facie case of sex discrimination where valid statistics disclose an appreciable difference in pay between two jobs of equal value, one of which is carried out almost exclusively by women and other predominantly by men. It is for the national court to assess whether the statistics appear to be significant in that they cover enough individuals and do not illustrate purely fortuitous or short-term phenomena.

Enderby v   [1993] IRLR 591 ECJ
Frenchay Health Authority and
  Secretary of State for Health
Where there is a prima facie case of discrimination, Article 141 of the EC Treaty requires the employer to show that the difference in pay is based on objectively justified factors unrelated to any discrimination on grounds of sex. Workers would be unable to enforce the principle of equal pay before national courts if evidence of a prima facie case did not shift to the employer the onus of showing that the pay differential is not in fact discriminatory.

Brunnhofer v   [2001] IRLR 571 ECJ
Bank der österreichischen Postsparkasse
If the employee adduces evidence to show that the criteria for establishing the existence of a difference in pay between a woman and a man and for identifying comparable work are satisfied, a prima facie case of discrimination would exist, and it is then for the employer to prove that there was no breach of the principle of equal pay. To do this, the employer could deny that the conditions for the application of the principle were met, by establishing that the activities actually performed by the two employees were not in fact comparable. The employer could also justify the difference in pay by objective factors, by proving that there was a difference unrelated to sex to explain the comparator's higher pay.

Glasgow City Council v   [2000] IRLR 272 HL
Marshall

An employer who proves the absence of sex discrimination, direct or indirect, is under no obligation to prove a "good" reason for the pay disparity.

Villalba v   [2006] IRLR 437 EAT
Merrill Lynch & Co Inc

There is no requirement of objective justification for differences in pay in circumstances where the employer has satisfactorily rebutted direct sex discrimination and there is no independent evidence of any kind to show that sex has had any influence on the difference in pay. The decision of the European Court of Justice in *Brunnhofer v Bank der Osterreichischen Postsparkasse* does not mean that once a woman is held to be working on work of equal value with a male comparator, the employer must show that there is an objective justification for the difference in pay, or else the claim must succeed. If it were enough to trigger the obligation objectively to justify the difference in pay that the claimant is a woman and the comparator a man employed on equal work, then the legislation would be concerned with fairness rather than with sex discrimination. The view of the EAT in *Sharp v Caledonia Group Services Ltd* that *Brunnhofer* altered the law and that House of Lords authorities ought not to be followed could not be agreed with.

Strathclyde Regional Council v   [1998] IRLR 146 HL
Wallace

Section 1(3) provides a defence if the employer shows that the variation between the woman's contract and the man's contract is "genuinely" due to a factor which is (a) material and (b) not the difference of sex. The requirement of genuineness is satisfied if the tribunal comes to the conclusion that the reason put forward was not a sham or pretence. For the matters relied upon to constitute "material factors", it has to be shown that they were in fact causally relevant to the difference in pay, ie that they were significant factors. This is a test which looks to the reason why there is a disparity in pay and not to whether there is an excuse for such disparity. Finally, the employer has to show that the disparity in pay is due to a factor "which is not the difference of sex", ie is not directly or indirectly sexually discriminatory.

Glasgow City Council v   [2000] IRLR 272 HL
Marshall

If there is any evidence of sex discrimination, such as evidence that the difference in pay has a disparately adverse impact on women, the employer will be called upon to satisfy the tribunal that the difference in pay is objectively justifiable.

Armstrong v   [2006] IRLR 124 CA
Newcastle Upon Tyne NHS Hospital Trust

Once disparate adverse impact has been established, the burden passes to the employer in respect of two issues. First, that the difference between the man's and the woman's con-tract is not discriminatory, in the sense of being attributable to a difference of gender. The burden of establishing an arguable case of discrimination is borne by the claimant, even though the employers bear the burden of persuasion. Second, if the employer cannot show that the difference in treatment was not attributable to a difference of gender, he must then demonstrate that there was nonetheless an objective justification for the difference between the woman's and the man's contract.

Gibson v   [2010] IRLR 311 CA
Sheffield City Council

A productivity bonus which applied only to men's work had a sexual taint and a disparately adverse effect on women's work as compared with men's work. Therefore, it had to be justified objectively by the employers.

Middlesbrough Borough Council v   [2007] IRLR 869 EAT
Surtees

Where the criterion which the employer chooses to differentiate pay scales impacts adversely on women because of the position of women in society, the pay arrangements are inevitably tainted by sex and the obligation to justify arises. Secondly, where the disadvantage to women as a group, typically gleaned from statistics, is sufficiently striking, it may be justified to draw the inference that the difference in pay reflects traditional attitudes about what is appropriate male and female work and pay, even though no obvious discriminatory factor is identified. A third situation is where the difference in pay is caused by a particular factor that is applied only to the predominantly male group. In those circumstances, it will be sex-tainted unless the employer can show that there are non-discriminatory reasons why the factor has been applied so as to only benefit the male group.

Coventry City Council v   [2009] IRLR 345 EAT
Nicholls

If it is possible to make a payment only to an almost exclusively male group, because of particular features of their job not shared by the female claimants, then it necessarily involves a form of prima facie indirect discrimination against those women in that the payment is being made by reference to characteristics of a job which in practice are held by job-holders who are predominantly of one sex only. Such payments will be unlawful unless they can be justified.

Cumbria County Council v   [2008] IRLR 91 EAT
Dow (No.1)

That there is job segregation along traditional sex lines does not inevitably mean that the particular differential must be sex tainted, but in such cases the difficulty of establishing otherwise will be a heavy one.

Barry v   [1999] IRLR 581 HL
Midland Bank plc

A claim of indirect discrimination contrary to Article 141 requires the claimant to show that she belongs to a group of employees which is differently and less well-treated than others, and that that difference affects considerably more women than men. If she can, the employer must show that the difference in treatment is objectively justified.

Grundy v [2008] IRLR 74 CA
British Airways plc

In determining whether a pay disparity has a disproportionate adverse impact on women, there is no principle of law which requires the tribunal always to base its test on the advantaged cohort. The pool must be one which suitably tests the particular discrimination complained of, but this does not mean that there is a single suitable pool for every case. Provided it tests the allegation in a suitable pool, the tribunal cannot be said to have erred in law even if a different pool, with a different outcome, could equally legitimately have been chosen.

Cheshire & Wirral Partnership [2006] IRLR 546 CA
NHS Trust v
Abbott

Although in a case of indirect sex discrimination in pay it is for the employee to identify a comparator group and to produce statistical evidence to show an appreciable difference in pay for jobs of equal value, the employee is not entitled to identify an artificial or arbitrary group. In principle, the comparison should be between the disadvantaged group and the advantaged group. As a matter of statistics, a more reliable result is likely to be forthcoming if one takes as large a group as possible, so long as that group shares the relevant characteristics and can be seen as doing work of equal value.

Bailey v [2005] IRLR 369 CA
Home Office

There is no clear difference between the approach in a condition or requirement case and cases where there is no condition or requirement but there is a pay disparity between two occupational groups. In each case, the employment tribunal is concerned to determine whether what on its face is a gender-neutral practice may be disguising the fact that female employees are being disadvantaged as compared with male employees to an extent that signifies that the disparity is prima facie attributable to a difference of sex.

Nelson v [2003] IRLR 428 CA
Carillion Services Ltd

In a case of alleged indirect discrimination under s.1(3), the complainant has the burden of proving on the balance of probabilities that the matter complained of has had a disproportionate adverse impact. It is for the claimant to provide the necessary statistics, seeking if necessary the relevant information from the employer.

Bailey v [2005] IRLR 369 CA
Home Office

Where there is one group of employees which contains a significant number, even though not a majority, of female workers whose work is evaluated as equal to that of another group of employees who are predominantly male and who receive greater pay, an employment tribunal is not precluded by the presence in the disadvantaged group of a significant number of men from holding that on the statistics of the proportions of women and men in the lower-paid group as a ratio of each other, there was a prima facie case of pay discrimination against women, so that the employers had to show that there was a genuine material factor which was not the difference of sex and which justified that disparity.

Schonheit v [2004] IRLR 983 ECJ
Stadt Frankfurt am Main

A difference in treatment between men and women may be justified, depending on the circumstances, by reasons other than those put forward when the measure introducing the differential treatment was adopted. It is for the Member State which has introduced such a measure, or the party who invokes it, to establish before the national court that there are objective reasons unrelated to any discrimination on grounds of sex such as to justify the measure concerned, and they are not bound in that respect by the intention expressed when the measure was adopted.

Cadman v [2004] IRLR 971 CA
Health and Safety Executive

There is no rule of law that the justification must have consciously and contemporaneously featured in the decision-making processes of the employer, and cannot be "after the event" arguments.

British Airways plc v [2008] IRLR 815 CA
Grundy (No.2)

There is a telling difference between cases in which the disparate impact of a new contractual provision has been recognised and its justifiability considered before adopting it, and cases in which the impact is initially not recognised, then denied, then found to exist and then sought to be justified. While justification in retrospect is perfectly admissible, it is probably going to start from a lower evidential base.

Tyldesley v [1996] IRLR 395 EAT
TML Plastics Ltd

A differential which is explained by careless mistake, which could not possibly be objectively justified, amounts to a defence, provided the tribunal is satisfied that the mistake was of sufficient influence to be significant or relevant. If a genuine mistake suffices, so must a genuine perception, whether reasonable or not, about the need to engage an individual with particular experience, commitment and skills.

Methven v [1980] IRLR 289 CA
Cow Industrial Polymers Ltd

The words "due to" in s.1(3) indicate that the question is one of causation, and like all questions of causation is a question of fact and degree.

Grounds for the pay difference

Bilka-Kaufhaus GmbH v   **[1986] IRLR 317 ECJ**
Weber von Hartz
A policy which applies independently of a worker's sex but in fact affects more women than men will not constitute an infringement of Article 141 if the employer shows that the policy is objectively justified on economic grounds. This requires a finding by the national court that the measures chosen by the employer correspond to a real need on the part of the undertaking, are appropriate with a view to achieving the objectives pursued and are necessary to that end.

Rainey v   **[1987] IRLR 26 HL**
Greater Glasgow Health Board
Although the European Court in the *Bilka-Kaufhaus* case referred to "economic" grounds objectively justified, read as a whole the ruling of the European Court would not exclude objectively justified grounds which are other than economic, such as administrative efficiency in a concern not engaged in commerce or business.

Cadman v   **[2004] IRLR 971 CA**
Health and Safety Executive
As reformulated by the Court of Appeal in *Barry v Midland Bank plc*, the test for objective justification set out in the *Bilka Kaufhaus* decision is whether the means used are "reasonably necessary". The difference between "necessary" and "reasonably necessary" is a significant one. The test does not require the employer to establish that the measure complained of was "necessary" in the sense of being the only course open to him.

Redcar & Cleveland Borough Council v   **[2007] IRLR 91 EAT**
   Bainbridge
It is inherent in the principle of proportionality that where different means of achieving a particular objective could be achieved, the one which has the least discriminatory impact should be chosen. A tribunal considering objective justification, therefore, is obliged to have regard to whether different and less discriminatory means could have been used to achieve the same objective.

Rainey v   **[1987] IRLR 26 HL**
Greater Glasgow Health Board
The true meaning and effect of Article 141 in the context of the employer's defence is the same as that correctly attributed to s.1(3) of the Equal Pay Act by the EAT in *Jenkins v Kingsgate (Clothing) Productions (No.2)*.

Specialarbejderforbundet   **[1995] IRLR 648 ECJ**
   i Danmark v
Dansk Industri,
   acting for Royal Copenhagen
It is for the national court to ascertain whether, in the light of the facts relating to the nature of the work carried out and the conditions in which it is carried out, equal value may be attributed to it, or whether those facts may be considered to be objective factors unrelated to discrimination on grounds of sex such as to justify any pay differentials.

Rainey v   **[1987] IRLR 26 HL**
Greater Glasgow Health Board
A difference between the woman's case and the man's must be "material", which means "significant and relevant".

Rainey v   **[1987] IRLR 26 HL**
Greater Glasgow Health Board
A relevant difference for the purposes of s.1(3) may relate to circumstances other than the personal qualifications or merits of the male and female workers who are the subject of comparison. Consideration of a difference between "her case and his" must necessarily involve consideration of all the circumstances of that case. These may go beyond the personal qualities by way of skill, experience or training which the individual brings to the job.

Waddington v   **[1977] IRLR 32 EAT**
Leicester Council for Voluntary
   Services
Usually the material difference within s.1(3) will be something other than the differences considered under s.1(4), and will not be differences between the things the woman does and the things the man does in the course of the work.

Davies v   **[1989] IRLR 439 EAT**
McCartneys
There is no limitation upon the factors relevant to a consideration of a defence under s.1(3). The factors which form the basis for a defence under s.1(3) can also be factors relevant in determining the demands of the jobs for the purpose of assessing equal value. However, an employer should not be allowed simply to say, "I value one demand factor so highly that I pay more," unless his true reason for so doing is one which is found by the tribunal to be genuine and not attributable to sex.

Christie v   **[2003] IRLR 670 EAT**
John E Haith
In accordance with the decision of the EAT in *Davies v McCartneys*, the mere fact that a particular factor may be relevant in the evaluation exercise to determine the question of equal value is no ground for excluding it as a defence which may be relied on by the employer under s.1(3), and may be taken into account by the tribunal in considering whether the employer's pay differential is justified or not on grounds other than sex. Therefore, an employment tribunal did not err in dismissing the appellants' equal value complaints on grounds that the physical effort and unpleasantness involved in the work of their male comparators was a genuine material difference accounting for the differential in pay within the meaning of s.1(3).

Benveniste v   **[1989] IRLR 123 CA**
University of Southampton

A material factor defence "evaporates" when the justification for it has disappeared.

Redcar & Cleveland Borough Council v   **[2008] IRLR 776 CA**
Bainbridge (No.2)

A tribunal has to find what the reason was for the pay differential and, if necessary, should look at the underlying reason and not merely the immediate reason or criterion for inclusion/exclusion. It is right to examine the underlying or historical position where that will throw light on the reason why one person is receiving an advantage and another is excluded from it.

Armstrong v   **[2006] IRLR 124 CA**
Newcastle Upon Tyne NHS Hospital Trust

It cannot be said that a failure to deprive male comparators of part of their income in the form of a bonus was discriminatory, if the assumption is that their original receipt of that part of their income was not discriminatory. Accordingly, an employment tribunal erred in finding that even if a disparity had been justified when it was introduced, the continuation over time of a system whereby more men than women received bonuses was indirectly discriminatory.

Sex discrimination

British Coal Corporation v   **[1994] IRLR 342 CA**
Smith
North Yorkshire County Council v
Ratcliffe

There cannot be a "material factor" defence under s.1(3) of the Equal Pay Act in any case where the facts establish direct discrimination within s.1(1)(a) of the Sex Discrimination Act, since an employer who treats a woman less favourably than a man "on the grounds of her sex" cannot assert that the difference between their terms of employment is due to a material factor which is not the difference of sex. Therefore, a "material factor" defence must fail if the employer cannot prove that the material factor relied upon was not tainted by sex.

Glasgow City Council v   **[2000] IRLR 272 HL**
Marshall

In order to discharge the burden of showing that the explanation for the variation is not tainted with sex the employer must satisfy the tribunal on several matters. First, that the proffered explanation, or reason, is genuine, and not a sham or pretence. Second, that the less favourable treatment is due to this reason. The factor relied upon must be the cause of the disparity. The factor must be "material" in a causative sense, rather than in a justificatory sense. Third, that the reason is not "the difference of sex", which is apt to embrace any form of sex discrimination, whether direct or indirect. Fourth, that the factor relied upon is a "material" difference, that is or, in

a case within s.1(2)(c), may be, a significant and relevant difference, between the woman's case and the man's case.

Redcar & Cleveland Borough Council v   **[2008] IRLR 776 CA**
Bainbridge (No.2)

In the context of an equal pay claim, the ways in which indirect discrimination can be proved are not limited to the method described in s.1(2)(b) of the Sex Discrimination Act. It is open to a court or tribunal to find indirect sex discrimination when the circumstances are such that they recognise it.

Ministry of Defence v   **[2004] IRLR 672 EAT**
Armstrong

The concept of indirect discrimination under the Equal Pay Act is broader than that which applies under the Sex Discrimination Act. In considering s.1(3), the fundamental question is whether there is a causative link between the claimant's sex and the fact that she is paid less than the true value of her job as reflected in the pay of her named comparator. If the material cause of the pay difference between the claimant and her comparator is tainted by sex-related factors, then the defence fails. This link may be established in a variety of different ways, depending on the facts of the case. There is no necessity for an employment tribunal, as a matter of law, always to adopt a formulaic approach, consistent with the provisions of s.1(1)(b) of the Sex Discrimination Act (and since 12 October 2001, s.1(2)), in considering whether there is sex-related pay discrimination and disparate impact for the purposes of s.1(3).

Snoxell v   **[1977] IRLR 123 EAT**
Vauxhall Motors Ltd

An employer can never establish that a variation between the woman's contract and the man's contract is genuinely due to a material difference (other than the difference of sex) between her case and his when it can be seen that past sex discrimination has contributed to the variation.

E Coomes (Holdings) Ltd v   **[1978] IRLR 263 CA**
Shields

The Equal Pay Act and the Sex Discrimination Act form two complementary parts of a single comprehensive code directed against sex discrimination. Both Acts should be construed and applied as a harmonious whole and in such a way that the broad principles which underlie the whole scheme of legislation are not frustrated by a narrow interpretation or restrictive application of particular provisions.

Coventry City Council v   **[2009] IRLR 345 EAT**
Nicholls

Union hostility to change is incapable of constituting a new explanation for a difference in pay such that it can be said that a pay differential the roots of which lay firmly in sex discrimination has at some indeterminate point ceased to have anything to do with sex. The union's stance may explain why the discrimination was not removed earlier, but it does not replace the original discriminatory explanation for the difference in pay.

Specific defences

Collective agreements

Enderby v [1993] IRLR 591 ECJ
Frenchay Health Authority and
** Secretary of State for Health**
The fact that the respective rates of pay of two jobs of equal value, one carried out almost exclusively by women and the other predominantly by men, were arrived at by collective bargaining processes which, although carried out by the same parties, were distinct, and conducted separately and without any discriminatory effect within each group, is not sufficient objective justification for the difference in pay between those two jobs.

British Road Services Ltd v [1997] IRLR 92 NICA
Loughran
Separate pay structures based on different collective agreements are not a sufficient defence under s.1(3) if the claimants are members of a class of which a "significant" number are female. The European Court's use of the term "almost exclusively" women in *Enderby* was merely a reference to the facts of that case and did not intend to propound a principle that unless the disadvantaged group could be described as being composed "almost exclusively" of females, a presumption of discrimination could not arise.

Specialarbejderforbundet [1995] IRLR 648 ECJ
** i Danmark v**
Dansk Industri, acting for Royal Copenhagen
The fact that rates of pay have been determined by collective bargaining or by negotiation at local level may be taken into account by the national court as a factor in its assessment of whether differences between the average pay of two groups of workers are due to objective factors unrelated to any discrimination on grounds of sex.

Redcar & Cleveland Borough Council v [2008] IRLR 776 CA
Bainbridge (No.2)
The fact that different jobs have been the subject of separate collective bargaining can be a defence to an equal pay claim in that the reason for the difference in pay for those jobs has been separate collective bargaining, not the difference of sex of the employees. Such a case could occur, for instance, where two different groups are of similar proportions by gender, but one of the groups earns less than the other. The position would be otherwise where there is a marked difference in the sex balance between the different groups, which would be evidence from which the tribunal could infer that the process was sex-tainted, unless the employer provided a different explanation.

Barber v [1993] IRLR 95 EAT
NCR (Manufacturing) Ltd
Evidence explaining the historical process by which a differ-ence in hourly rates had been arrived at did not show any objective factor which justified the result which had been produced.

Grading

National Vulcan Engineering [1978] IRLR 225 CA
** Insurance Group Ltd v**
Wade
A grading system according to skill, ability and experience is an integral part of good business management and as long as it is fairly and genuinely applied irrespective of sex, it cannot be held to infringe the Equal Pay Act.

Separate pay structures

British Coal Corporation v [1996] IRLR 404 HL
Smith
The simple existence of separate pay structures is not in itself a defence under s.1(3). What must be determined is whether the justification for the differences in benefits received by the claimants and their comparators satisfy objective criteria and was not one which occurred because of a difference of sex.

Administrative convenience

Barry v [1998] IRLR 138 CA
Midland Bank plc
Administrative convenience is an objective reason uncon-nected with the difference in sex.

Legal requirements

R v [1988] IRLR 22 HC
Secretary of State for Social Services
** ex parte Clarke**
That an employer is bound by statutory instrument to pay the salaries paid is not in itself a "material factor" defence to an equal pay claim.

Quality of work

Handels- og Kontorfunktionaerernes [1989] IRLR 532 ECJ
** Forbund i Danmark v**
Dansk Arbejdsgiverforening
** (acting for Danfoss)**
EC Equal Pay legislation must be interpreted as mean-ing that the quality of the work carried out by the worker

may not be used as a criterion for pay increments where its application shows itself to be systematically unfavourable to women. Where an assessment of the quality of work results in systematic unfairness to female workers, that could only be because the employer applied the criterion in an abusive manner. It is inconceivable that the work carried out by female workers would be generally of a lower quality.

Productivity

Hartlepool Borough Council v   **[2009] IRLR 168 EAT**
Dolphin
In order to be genuine, a productivity bonus scheme must be intended to, and in fact, achieve productivity improvements.

Cumbria County Council v   **[2008] IRLR 91 EAT**
Dow (No.1)
Improving productivity is a legitimate aim, but the means used must be proportionate to that aim. A tribunal is entitled to seek evidence that productivity had increased as a result of improvements in the performance of the workers themselves. Without a proper application of the scheme, the benefits were not being achieved. It cannot be proportionate to pay bonuses to achieve a legitimate objective if that objective is not in any meaningful way being realised. Where the payment cannot be justified, it is in essence part of the basic wage.

Additional obligations

Handels- og Kontorfunktionaerernes   **[1989] IRLR 532 ECJ**
    Forbund i Danmark v
Dansk Arbejdsgiverforening
    (acting for Danfoss)
EC Equal Pay legislation must be interpreted as meaning that where the adaptability of the employee to variable work schedules and places of work is used as a criterion for pay increments and this works systematically to the disadvantage of female workers who, as a result of household and family duties, may have greater difficulty than male workers in organising their working time in a flexible manner, the employer may justify the use of the criterion by demonstrating that such adaptability is important for the performance of the specific duties entrusted to the worker.

National Coal Board v   **[1978] IRLR 122 EAT**
Sherwin
While the mere fact that work is done at different times is irrelevant for the purposes of s.1(4), it does not follow that once like work has been established an employer, in seeking to set up an answer under s.1(3), cannot put forward as constituting a "material difference" circumstances which may include the fact that the man and the woman work at different times.

National Coal Board v   **[1978] IRLR 122 EAT**
Sherwin
An employment tribunal that found that a difference between the woman's pay and the pay of a man employed on like work was greater than could be justified by the fact that the man worked permanently on the night shift alone was entitled to conclude that the employers had failed to show that the difference to which the variation in pay was genuinely due was other than a difference of sex. The tribunal were therefore entitled to order that the women should be paid at the same rate as the man after making a proper, but not excessive, discount for the fact that he worked permanently at night alone.

Edmonds v   **[1977] IRLR 359 EAT**
Computer Services (South-West) Ltd
Higher pay because of the potential to exercise responsibility may be a "material difference" under s.1(3).

Training

Handels- og Kontorfunktionaerernes   **[1989] IRLR 532 ECJ**
    Forbund i Danmark v
Dansk Arbejdsgiverforening
    (acting for Danfoss)
EC Equal Pay legislation must be interpreted as meaning that where the worker's vocational training is used as a criterion for pay increments and this works systematically to the disadvantage of female workers, the employer may justify the use of the criterion of vocational training by demonstrating that such training is important for the performance of specific duties entrusted to the worker.

Service payments

Cadman v   **[2006] IRLR 969 ECJ**
Health & Safety Executive
An employer does not have to establish specifically that recourse to length of service as a determinant of pay is appropriate as regards a particular job to attain the legitimate objective of rewarding experience acquired which enables the worker to perform his duties better, unless the worker provides evidence capable of raising serious doubts in that regard.

Cadman v   **[2006] IRLR 969 ECJ**
Health & Safety Executive
Where the worker provides evidence capable of giving rise to serious doubts as to whether recourse to the criterion of length of service is, in the circumstances, appropriate to attain the objective of rewarding experience that enables the worker to perform his duties better, then it is for the employer to justify in detail recourse to the criterion of length of

service by proving, as regards the job in question, that length of service goes hand in hand with experience and that experience enables the worker to perform his duties better.

Cadman v   **[2006] IRLR 969 ECJ**
Health & Safety Executive
Where pay is based on a job evaluation system, if the objective pursued by using the criterion of length of service is to recognise experience, there is no need for the employer to show that an individual worker has acquired experience during the relevant period which has enabled him to perform his duties better.

Wilson v   **[2010] IRLR 59 CA**
Health & Safety Executive
An employer can be required to provide objective justification for use of a length of service criterion as well as its adoption in the first place. The employer must justify where the claimant has shown that there is evidence from which, if established at trial, it can properly be found that the general rule that a length of service criterion can be used should not apply because its adoption or use was disproportionate.

Hill v   **[1998] IRLR 466 ECJ**
Revenue Commissioners
Rules which treat full-time workers who previously job-shared at a disadvantage compared with other full-time workers by applying a criterion of service calculated by length of time actually worked in a post, and therefore placing them on the full-time pay scale at a level lower than that which they occupied on the pay scale applicable to job-sharing, must in principle be treated as contrary to Article 141, where 98% of those employed under jobsharing contracts are women.

Hill v   **[1998] IRLR 466 ECJ**
Revenue Commissioners
An employer cannot justify discrimination arising from a jobsharing scheme solely on the ground that avoidance of such discrimination would involve increased costs.

Protected pay

Snoxell v   **[1977] IRLR 123 EAT**
Vauxhall Motors Ltd
Where it can be shown that there is a group of employees who have had their wages protected for causes neither directly nor indirectly due to a difference of sex, and where male and female employees, doing the same work, who are not in this "red circle" are treated alike, an employer may succeed in establishing a defence under s.1(3).

Fearnon v   **[2009] IRLR 132 NICA**
Smurfit Corrugated Cases (Lurgan) Ltd
The judgment in *Snoxell* did not suggest that the length of

time that a discrepancy in salary has endured because of red-circling is irrelevant to the question of whether it can continue to be a genuine material factor. To qualify as a contemporaneous genuine material factor accounting for the discrepancy in salary, the reasons for red-circling at the time that the difference in earnings is challenged must be examined. Otherwise, it would be possible for an unscrupulous employer to allow a difference in earnings to persist while knowing that the initial reason for it no longer obtained. It is wrong to assume that because it was right to institute the system, it will remain right to maintain it indefinitely.

Redcar & Cleveland Borough Council v   **[2008] IRLR 776 CA**
Bainbridge (No.2)
Transitional arrangements that continue past indirect discrimination will not be unlawful if they can be justified. However, where the old indirect discrimination has been recognised, the employer will have great difficulty in justifying the continuation of any discriminatory element. That is because he must do his best to comply with the fundamental principle of equal pay. Nevertheless, it is still possible for an employer to justify where he is aware of the past discrimination by demonstrating that he had done all he could to minimise the effect of the continuing discrimination but was unable to eliminate it immediately. Where an employer is reorganising his pay structures and there is no reason to think that the old arrangements were directly or indirectly discriminatory, he will be entitled to bring in the new arrangements by transitional provisions. Thus, the employer's state of knowledge about the discriminatory effect of his provisions and the extent to which he tries to minimise that effect will be relevant considerations for whether the employer's discriminatory means are an appropriate and proportionate means of achieving his legitimate objective.

Redcar & Cleveland Borough Council v   **[2008] IRLR 776 CA**
Bainbridge (No.2)
Pay protection arrangements were rooted in past sex discrimination and had to be justified by the employer where the underlying reason the male comparators were receiving pay protection and the women claimants were not was because the women, unlike the men, did not suffer a drop in pay when a job evaluation scheme was implemented because they had previously been discriminated against in terms of pay. If they had been paid their wage entitlement, they too would have suffered a drop in pay and would have been entitled to pay protection.

Redcar & Cleveland Borough Council v   **[2008] IRLR 776 CA**
Bainbridge (No.2)
A large public employer might be able to demonstrate that the constraints on its finances were so pressing that it could not do other than it did and that it was justified in putting the need to cushion the men's pay reduction ahead of the need to bring the women up to parity with the men. However, that result is not a foregone conclusion and the employer must prove that what was done was objectively justified in the individual case.

United Biscuits Ltd v   **[1978] IRLR 15 EAT**
Young

Where an employer seeks to discharge the onus of proof under s.1(3) by a "red circle" defence, he must do so with respect to each employee who, it is claimed, is within the circle. The employer must prove that at the time when the employee was admitted to the circle his higher pay was related to a consideration other than sex.

Outlook Supplies Ltd v   **[1978] IRLR 12 EAT**
Parry

It is relevant for an employment tribunal to take into account the length of time which has elapsed since a "red circle" was introduced, and whether the employer has acted in accordance with good industrial practice in the continuation of the practice, for the purpose of determining whether the employer has discharged the onus under s.1(3).

Home Office v   **[2005] IRLR 757 EAT**
Bailey

Although red-circling of the practice of doubling pensionable years of service of prison officers for every year of service after 20 years was objectively justified when it was introduced in 1987, an employment tribunal was entitled to find that the Prison Service had not established a genuine material factor defence as regards retaining its practice when it relied upon the original 1987 justification in 1999.

Financial constraints

Benveniste v   **[1989] IRLR 123 CA**
University of Southampton

That a woman was appointed at a lower point on a salary scale than men doing like work due to financial constraints did not constitute a material difference to justify her lower salary once the reason for the lower payment disappeared. The material difference between her case and the case of her comparators evaporated when the financial constraints were removed.

Redcar & Cleveland Borough   **[2007] IRLR 91 EAT**
   Council v
Bainbridge

Although budgetary considerations cannot be the sole justification for failing to give effect to the principle of equal pay, they can be a factor to be weighed with other considerations when determining whether the difference in pay could be objectively justified, provided that if there are cost constraints, they are allocated in a way that limits any discriminatory impact as much as possible. For example, transitional arrangements to cushion the pay of those moving to lower pay will sometimes be appropriate. It would be theoretically possible to confer the benefit of the higher pay on everyone, but the cost may reinforce the justification limiting the benefit.

Location

Navy, Army & Air Force   **[1976] IRLR 408 EAT**
   Institutes v
Varley

A difference in weekly hours of work between employees on like work in London and in Nottingham was based on a long-standing geographical distinction and was a genuine material difference within s.1(3).

Other contractual terms

Hayward v   **[1988] IRLR 257 HL**
Cammell Laird Shipbuilders Ltd

Per the Lord Chancellor [Lord Mackay]: Section 1(3) would not provide a defence to an employer against whom it was shown that a term in the woman's contract was less favourable to her than a corresponding term in the man's contract, on the basis that there was another term in the woman's contract which was more favourable to her than the corresponding term in the man's contract. At the very least, for s.1(3) to operate, it would have to be shown that the unfavourable character of the term in the woman's contract was in fact due to the difference in the opposite sense in the other term and that the difference was not due to the reason of sex.

Hours of work

Leverton v   **[1989] IRLR 28 HL**
Clwyd County Council

Where a woman's and a man's regular annual working hours, unaffected by any significant additional hours of work, can be translated into a notional hourly rate which yields no significant difference, it is a legitimate, if not a necessary, inference that the difference in their annual salaries is both due to and justified by the difference in the hours they work in the course of a year and has nothing to do with the difference in sex.

Bilka-Kaufhaus GmbH v   **[1986] IRLR 317 ECJ**
Weber von Hartz

An employer who excludes part-time workers from an occupational pension scheme is in breach of Article 141 if this exclusion affects significantly more women than men, unless the employer can show that the exclusion is based on objectively justified factors unrelated to any discrimination on grounds of sex.

Bilka-Kaufhaus GmbH v   **[1986] IRLR 317 ECJ**
Weber von Hartz

An employer may justify the exclusion of part-time workers, irrespective of their sex, from an occupational pension scheme on the ground that it seeks to employ as few part-time workers as possible, where it is found that the means chosen for achieving that objective correspond to a real need on the part of the undertaking, are appropriate with a view to achieving the objective in question and are necessary to that end.

Kowalska v   **[1990] IRLR 447 ECJ**
Freie und Hansestadt Hamburg
Article 141 precludes the application of a provision of a collective agreement under which part-time workers are excluded from the benefit of a severance payment in the case of termination of the employment relationship, when it is clear that in fact a considerably smaller percentage of men than of women work part time, unless the employer shows that the provision is justified by objective factors unrelated to any discrimination on grounds of sex.

Market forces

Enderby v   **[1993] IRLR 591 ECJ**
Frenchay Health Authority and
   Secretary of State for Health
The state of the employment market, which may lead an employer to increase the pay of a particular job in order to attract candidates, may constitute an objectively justified economic ground for a difference in pay. If the national court is able to determine precisely what proportion of the increase in pay is attributable to market forces, it must necessarily accept that the pay differential is objectively justified to the extent of that proportion. If that is not the case, it is for the national court to assess whether the role of market forces in determining the rate of pay was sufficiently significant to provide objective justification for part or all of the difference. Therefore, it must determine, if necessary by applying the principle of proportionality, whether and to what extent the shortage of candidates for a job and the need to attract them by higher pay constitutes an objectively justi-fied economic ground for the difference in pay between the jobs in question.

Rainey v   **[1987] IRLR 26 HL**
Greater Glasgow Health Board
A difference in pay between a female prosthetist and her male comparator, employed on like work but recruited from the private sector on his existing terms and conditions when the prosthetic service was established prior to her employ-ment, was "genuinely due to a material difference (other than the difference of sex) between her case and his", where the fact that the new service could never have been estab-lished within a reasonable time if the employees of private contractors had not been offered a scale of remuneration no less favourable than that which they were then enjoying was a good and objectively justified ground for offering that scale of remuneration. There was no suggestion that it was unreasonable to place the prosthetists on the particular point

on the salary scale which was in fact selected, and it was not a question of the women being paid less than the norm but of the comparator being paid more because of the necessity to attract him.

Ratcliffe v   **[1995] IRLR 439 HL**
North Yorkshire County Council
A difference in pay, between the female school catering assistants and their male comparators employed in local government on work rated as equivalent, which resulted from a reduction in the women's wages from the local gov-ernment rate because of the employer's need to tender for work at a commercially competitive rate, was not genuinely due to a material factor which was not the difference of sex. To reduce the women's wages below that of their male com-parators was the very kind of discrimination in relation to pay which the Act sought to remove.

Cumbria County Council v   **[2008] IRLR 91 EAT**
Dow (No.1)
It is not enough for an employer to establish that some dif-ferential is justified by market forces without giving the tri-bunal a proper evidential basis for determining whether it is the whole amount or something short of that.

Cumbria County Council v   **[2008] IRLR 91 EAT**
Dow (No.1)
Lack of recruitment problems does not establish that the market rate was being paid. That is equally consistent with the employer paying over the odds. It is for the employer to show that the market dictated higher pay. It is not for the claimants to show that the pay is too high.

Albion Shipping Agency v   **[1981] IRLR 525 EAT**
Arnold
A change in an employer's trading position leading to reduced profitability was capable of constituting a defence to a woman's claim for equal pay with her male predecessor, provided the employers could show that they were not tak-ing advantage of the complainant's sex to get the work done at a rate less than that for which a man would have worked.

EFFECT OF THE EQUALITY CLAUSE

[(1) If the terms of a contract under which a woman is employed at an establishment in Great Britain do not include (directly or by reference to a collective agreement or otherwise) an equality clause they shall be deemed to include one.

(2) An equality clause is a provision which relates to terms (whether concerned with pay or not) of a contract under which a woman is employed (the "woman's contract"), and has the effect that –

(a) where the woman is employed on like work with a man in the same employment –

(i) if (apart from the equality clause) any term of the woman's contract is or becomes less favourable to the woman than a term of a similar kind in the contract under which that man is employed, that term of the woman's contract shall be treated as so modified as not to be less favourable, and

(ii) if (apart from the equality clause) at any time the woman's contract does not include a term corresponding to a term benefiting that man included in the contract under which he is employed, the woman's contract shall be treated as including such a term;

(b) where the woman is employed on work rated as equivalent with that of a man in the same employment –

(i) if (apart from the equality clause) any term of the woman's contract determined by the rating of the work is or becomes less favourable to the woman than a term of a similar kind in the contract under which that man is employed, that term of the woman's contract shall be treated as so modified as not to be less favourable, and

(ii) if (apart from the equality clause) at any time the woman's contract does not include a term corresponding to a term benefiting that man included in the contract under which he is employed and determined by the rating of the work, the woman's contract shall be treated as including such a term;

(c) where a woman is employed on work which, not being work in relation to which paragraph (a) or (b) above applies, is, in terms of the demands made on her (for instance under such headings as effort, skill and decision), of equal value to that of a man in the same employment –

(i) if (apart from the equality clause) any term of the woman's contract is or becomes less favourable to the woman than a term of a similar kind in the contract under which that man is employed, that term of the woman's contract shall be treated as so modified as not to be less favourable, and

(ii) if (apart from the equality clause) at any time the woman's contract does not include a term corresponding to a term benefiting that man included in the contract under which he is employed, the woman's contract shall be treated as including such a term.]

EQUAL PAY ACT – s.1
➡ **EQUALITY ACT 2010 – s.66**

(1) [Any claim in respect of the contravention of a term modified or included by virtue of an equality clause, including a claim for arrears of remuneration or damages in respect of the contravention, may be presented by way of a complaint to an employment tribunal.]

EQUAL PAY ACT – s.2
➡ **EQUALITY ACT 2010 – s.127**

Barber v   **[1990] IRLR 240 ECJ**
Guardian Royal Exchange Assurance Group
The application of the principle of equal pay must be ensured in respect of each element of remuneration and not only on the basis of a comprehensive assessment of the consideration paid to workers.

Jämställdhetsombudsmannen v   **[2000] IRLR 421 ECJ**
Örebro Läns Landsting
In comparing the pay of midwives and a clinical technician for the purpose of Article 141, the appropriate comparison was between the monthly basic salary of the two groups. No account was to be taken of a supplement paid to the midwives for working inconvenient hours. Genuine transparency, permitting effective judicial review, is assured only if the principle of equal pay applies to each of the elements of remuneration.

Hayward v   **[1988] IRLR 257 HL**
Cammell Laird Shipbuilders Ltd
The natural meaning of the word "term" in the context of s.1(2)(c) is a distinct provision or part of the contract which has sufficient content to make it possible to compare it, from the point of view of the benefits it confers, with a similar provision or part in another contract. Therefore, on the correct construction of s.1(2)(c)(i), if in the contract of a woman and the contract of a man employed on work of equal value there is "a term of a similar kind" – ie a term making a comparable provision for the same subject-matter – the two must be compared and if, on that comparison, the term of the woman's contract proves to be less favourable than the term of the man's contract, then the term in the woman's contract is to be treated as modified so as to make it not less favourable.

Hayward v   **[1988] IRLR 257 HL**
Cammell Laird Shipbuilders Ltd
If a contract contains provisions relating to basic pay, benefits in kind such as the use of a car, cash bonuses and sickness benefits, on the natural and ordinary meaning of the word "term", all these different terms cannot be lumped together as one "term" of the contract, simply because they can all together be considered as providing for the total "remuneration" for the services to be performed under the contract.

Degnan v   **[2005] IRLR 615 CA**
Redcar and Cleveland Borough Council
Attendance allowances paid to men employed on work rated as equivalent to that of the claimant women were a single term together with the hourly rate and fixed bonuses, rather than

being a separate term of the men's contract for the purpose of the comparison with the terms of the women's contracts. The EAT correctly held that all monetary payments received by male comparators for normal working hours should be aggregated and divided by the number of hours in the working week, to give an hourly rate; if it is greater, the woman's hourly rate should be increased to eliminate the difference.

Brownbill v   **[2010] EqLR 4 EAT**
St Helens & Knowsley Hospital NHS Trust
Since the Equal Pay Act is not a fair wages statute, it is impermissible for the tribunal to select the terms as to pay to be compared, for the purposes of achieving a broadly equitable outcome. What is important is to ensure transparency and the provision of non-discriminatory pay structures, not to seek to amalgamate distinct components of remuneration in order to see whether, viewed in this way, any particular claimant is as well paid or better paid than her chosen comparator. Accordingly, in this case, the fact that both elements in issue concerned "pay", namely basic rates of pay and enhanced rates of pay contingent on unsociable hours being worked, did not prevent them from being considered and compared separately as distinct terms.

Brownbill v   **[2010] EqLR 4 EAT**
St Helens & Knowsley Hospital NHS Trust
The key to the Court of Appeal's decision in *Degnan* is that it turned on its own particular facts.

Hayward v   **[1988] IRLR 257 HL**
Cammell Laird Shipbuilders Ltd
On the correct construction of s.1(2)(c) of the Equal Pay Act as amended, a woman who can point to a term of her contract which is less favourable than a term of a similar kind in the man's contract is entitled to have that term made not less favourable irrespective of whether she is as favourably treated as the man when the whole of her contract and the whole of his contract are considered. Therefore, a woman employee on work of equal value was entitled to the same basic hourly wage and overtime rates as her comparator, notwithstanding that she received additional holidays and better sickness benefits.

Dugdale v   **[1976] IRLR 368 EAT**
Kraft Foods Ltd
An equality clause has effect so as to modify any less favourable term of the women's contract so as to make it not less favourable. It need not produce equality if, though they are engaged on like work, the payment to the men includes something affecting them and not the woman, such as working at night.

Evesham v   **[2000] IRLR 257 CA**
North Hertfordshire Health Authority
A claimant's entitlement under s.1(2)(c) to have the relevant term of her contract of employment modified so as to be not less favourable than that of her male comparator means that she should mirror her comparator on the incremental pay scale, and therefore enter the scale at the lowest level,

rather than that she should be placed on the pay scale for his post at a level appropriate to her actual years of service.

Sorbie v   **[1976] IRLR 371 EAT**
Trust House Forte Hotels Ltd
The effect of an equality clause is to strike out the less favourable rate and substitute the higher rate. Once a contract of employment has been modified in accordance with an equality clause, it is a contract providing remuneration at the higher rate. That contract remains so modified until something else happens, such as a further agreement between the parties, a further collective agreement, or a further statutory modification by reason of a further operation of the equality clause. Therefore, a modification to a woman's contract providing equal pay with a male comparator did not cease to operate when the man was no longer employed on like work.

Hartlepool Borough Council v   **[2009] IRLR 796 EAT**
Llewellyn
A male claimant is entitled under the Equal Pay Act to the benefit of a contractual term enjoyed by a female comparator even though the comparator herself has only acquired the benefit of that term as a result of the operation of the Act. The reference in s.1(2) to a "term" in the man's (ie the comparator's) contract should be construed as a reference to either a term in the contract as actually agreed between the parties or a term acknowledged by the employer or declared by a tribunal to have been inserted or modified following a claim under the Act.

REMEDIES

(5) A woman shall not be entitled, in proceedings brought in respect of a contravention of a term modified or included by virtue of an equality clause (including proceedings before an employment tribunal), to be awarded any payment by way of arrears of remuneration or damages –

(a) in proceedings in England and Wales, in respect of a time earlier than the arrears date (determined in accordance with section 2ZB below), and

(b) in proceedings in Scotland, in respect of a time before the period determined in accordance with section 2ZC below."

EQUAL PAY ACT (as amended) – s.2(5)
➡ **EQUALITY ACT 2010 – s.132**

(1) This section applies for the purpose of determining the arrears date, in relation to an award of any payment by way of arrears of remuneration or damages in proceedings in England and Wales in respect of a woman's employment, for the purposes of section 2(5)(a) above.

(2) In this section –

"concealment case" means a case where –

(a) the employer deliberately concealed from the woman any fact –

(i) which is relevant to the contravention to which the proceedings relate, and

(ii) without knowledge of which the woman could not reasonably have been expected to institute the proceedings, and

(b) the woman instituted the proceedings within six years of the day on which she discovered the fact (or could with reasonable diligence have discovered it);

"disability case" means a case where –

(a) the woman was under a disability at the time of the contravention to which the proceedings relate, and

(b) the woman instituted the proceedings within six years of the day on which she ceased to be under a disability;

"standard case" means a case which is not –

(a) a concealment case,

(b) a disability case, or

(c) both.

(3) In a standard case, the arrears date is the date falling six years before the day on which the proceedings were instituted.

(4) In a case which is a concealment or a disability case or both, the arrears date is the date of the contravention.

EQUAL PAY ACT (as amended) – s.2ZB
➡ **EQUALITY ACT 2010 – s.132, s.135**

(1) This section applies, in relation to an award of any payment by way of arrears of remuneration or damages in proceedings in Scotland in respect of a woman's employment, for the purpose of determining the period mentioned in s.2(5)(b) above.

(2) Subject to subsection (3) below, that period is the period of five years which ends on the day on which the proceedings were

instituted, except that the five years shall not be regarded as running during –

(a) any time when the woman was induced, by reason of fraud on the part of, or error induced by the words or conduct of, the employer or any person acting on his behalf, to refrain from commencing proceedings (not being a time after she could with reasonable diligence have discovered the fraud or error), or

(b) any time when she was under a disability.

(3) If, after regard is had to the exceptions in subsection (2) above, that period would include any time more than twenty years before the day mentioned in that subsection, that period is instead the period of twenty years which ends on that day."

EQUAL PAY ACT (as amended) – s.2ZC
➡ **EQUALITY ACT 2010 – s.132, s.135**

Preston v   **[2000] IRLR 506 ECJ**
Wolverhampton Healthcare NHS Trust

The fact that a worker can claim retroactively to join an occupational pension scheme does not allow him to avoid paying the contributions relating to the period of membership concerned.

Council of the City of   **[2005] IRLR 504 EAT**
   Newcastle upon Tyne v
Allan

Compensation for non-economic loss, such as for injury to feelings, aggravated or exemplary damages, is not recoverable in a claim brought under the Equal Pay Act.

Redcar & Cleveland Borough Council v **[2008] IRLR 776 CA**
Bainbridge (No.2)

That work has been rated as equivalent for the purposes of s.1(5) does not conclusively determine that they must be taken to be of equal value for the purposes of s.1(2)(c).

Redcar & Cleveland Borough Council v **[2008] IRLR 776 CA**
Bainbridge (No.2)

A job evaluation scheme does not have retroactive effect so as to entitle the claimant to rely on a person of the opposite sex, who is rated as equivalent under the job evaluation scheme, as a comparator for the purposes of a rated as equivalent claim for a period prior to the implementation of the job evaluation scheme.

3. DISABILITY DISCRIMINATION

EC DISABILITY DISCRIMINATION LAW

Chacon Navas v   [2006] IRLR 706 ECJ
Eurest Colectividades SA
The concept of "disability" for the purpose of Directive 2000/78 must be understood as referring to a limitation which results in particular from physical, mental or psychological impairments and which hinders the participation of the person concerned in professional life.

Chacon Navas v   [2006] IRLR 706 ECJ
Eurest Colectividades SA
A person who has been dismissed by his employer solely on account of sickness is not protected by the prohibition against discrimination on grounds of disability in Framework Employment Equality Directive 2000/78.

Coleman v   [2008] IRLR 722 ECJ
Attridge Law
The prohibition of direct discrimination laid down by Framework Employment Equality Directive 2000/78 is not limited only to people who are themselves disabled. Where an employer treats an employee who is not himself disabled less favourably than another employee is, has been or would be treated in a comparable situation, and it is established that the less favourable treatment of that employee is based on the disability of his child, whose care is provided primarily by that employee, such treatment is contrary to the prohibition of direct discrimination laid down by Article 2(2)(a).

STATUTORY EXCLUSIONS AND EXCEPTIONS

Meaning of "employment"

"Employment" means, subject to any prescribed provision, employment under a contract of service or of apprenticeship or a contract personally to do any work, and related expressions are to be construed accordingly.

           DISABILITY DISCRIMINATION ACT – s.68(1)
           ➡ EQUALITY ACT 2010 – s.83

Burton v   [2003] IRLR 257 EAT
Higham t/a Ace Appointments
All that s.68 requires is for there to be an obligation to do work. In this case, those engaged by an employment agency under a temporary worker's contract fell within the wider definition of "employment", notwithstanding that they provided their services to the client. The obligations set out in their contract corresponded to those envisaged in s.68. The temporary worker's contract required them, when accepting an assignment, to do work. They could not substitute another person to take their place. That the work was performed for the client did not take it outside the scope of s.68.

X v   [2010] IRLR 101 EAT
Mid Sussex Citizens Advice Bureau
There is no requirement under the Framework Employment Equality Directive for a national government to make provisions for those voluntary workers who are not protected by a contract within the meaning of the statutory definition of "employment". There is no authority that suggests that "occupation", as used in the Directive, means "unpaid employment" as opposed to a profession or qualification or area of work.

Claim in time

(1) An employment tribunal shall not consider a complaint under s.8 unless it is presented before the end of the period of three months beginning when the act complained of was done.

(2) A tribunal may consider any such complaint which is out of time if, in all the circumstances of the case, it considers that it is just and equitable to do so.

           DISABILITY DISCRIMINATION ACT – Sch. 3, para. 3
           ➡ EQUALITY ACT 2010 – s.123

Department for Constitutional Affairs v   [2008] IRLR 128 CA
Jones
Although there is no general principle that a person with mental health problems is entitled to delay as a matter of course in bringing a claim, there is an additional factor in

disability discrimination not present when some of the other discretions come to be exercised, which is that the disability, to come within s.1, must be a 12-month disability as defined in the Act. Any person with a mental condition has therefore to predict whether he is likely to come within the definition. In this case, an employment judge was entitled to exercise his discretion to extend time where the true reason for the delay which occurred in presenting the claim was that the claimant did not want to admit to himself or to others that he was disabled within the meaning of the Act.

Robinson v   **[2000] IRLR 904 EAT**
Post Office

An employment tribunal was entitled to find that it was not just and equitable to extend the time limit for presenting the claimant's disability discrimination complaint in respect of his dismissal, notwithstanding that his complaint was out of time because he was pursuing an internal appeal against dismissal. Parliament deliberately has not provided that the running of time should be delayed until the end of the domestic processes. When delay on account of an incomplete internal appeal is relied upon as a reason for failing to lodge a tribunal application in time, it will ordinarily suffice for the employment tribunal to put this into the balance when the justice and equity of the matter is being considered.

British Gas Services Ltd v   **[2001] IRLR 60 EAT**
McCaull

Time does not run in respect of a discriminatory dismissal until the notice of dismissal expires and the employment ceases. In dismissal cases, it is when the individual finds himself out of a job that he suffers detriment as a result of the discrimination.

Matuszowicz v   **[2009] IRLR 288 CA**
Kingston upon Hull City Council

A failure to make reasonable adjustments is an omission, not an act. The time-limit provisions relating to "deliberate omissions" apply even where the failure to make a reasonable adjustment is inadvertent. In such a case, where a person has not done an act inconsistent with making a reasonable adjustment, the tribunal must determine when, if the employer had been acting reasonably, it would have made the reasonable adjustment.

Work ordinarily done outside Great Britain

(6) This section applies only in relation to employment at an establishment in Great Britain.
DISABILITY DISCRIMINATION ACT 1995 (as amended) – s.4
[Note: these provisions are no longer in force]

(2A) This subsection applies if –
    (a) the employer has a place of business at an establishment in Great Britain,

(b) the work is for the purposes of the business carried on at that establishment, and
(c) the employee is ordinarily resident in Great Britain –
    (i) at the time when he applies for or is offered the employment, or
    (ii) at any time during the course of the employment.
DISABILITY DISCRIMINATION ACT 1995 (as amended) – s.68
[Note: these provisions are no longer in force]

Williams v   **[2007] IRLR 660 EAT**
University of Nottingham

In determining whether "the work is for the purposes of the business carried on at the establishment" within the meaning of s.68(2A)(b), the words should be regarded as meaning the same as the phrase used by Lord Hoffmann in *Lawson v Serco* in the context of unfair dismissal, "for the purposes of a business carried on in Great Britain". It would be extraordinary if Lord Hoffmann had intended that the self-same words should be given different interpretations depending on the particular context in which those words were being used.

MEANING OF DISABILITY

(1) Subject to the provisions of Schedule 1, a person has a disability for the purposes of this Act if he has a physical or mental impairment which has a substantial and long-term adverse effect on his ability to carry out normal day-to-day activities.

(2) In this Act "disabled person" means a person who has a disability.

DISABILITY DISCRIMINATION ACT – s.1
➡ EQUALITY ACT 2010 – s.6

General approach

Goodwin v   **[1999] IRLR 4 EAT**
The Patent Office
When faced with an issue as to whether a person has a disability within the meaning of the Act, the tribunal should adopt an inquisitorial or interventionist role. There is a risk of a "Catch 22" situation, in that some disabled persons may be unable or unwilling to accept that they have a disability. Without the direct assistance of the tribunal at the hearing, there may be cases where the claimant, for a reason related to his disability, is unwilling to support the claim.

Rugamer v   **[2001] IRLR 644 EAT**
Sony Music Entertainment UK Ltd
McNicol v
Balfour Beatty Rail Maintenance
An employment tribunal is not an inquisitorial body in the same sense as a medical or other tribunal dealing with a disablement issue as part of the statutory machinery for determining benefit claims. The observations of Morison J in *Goodwin v Patent Office* that the role of tribunals in a disability discrimination case contains "an inquisitorial element" mean no more than that the tribunal is obliged to conduct the hearing in a fair and balanced manner, intervening and making its own inquiries in the course of the hearing of such persons appearing before it and such witnesses as are called before it as it considers appropriate, so as to ensure due consideration of the issues raised by, or necessarily implicit in, the complaint being made. The role of the tribunal is not thereby extended so as to place on it the duty to conduct a freestanding inquiry of its own, or to require it to attempt to obtain further evidence beyond that placed in front of it on the issues raised by the parties, or to cause the parties to raise additional issues they have not sought to rely on at all.

Goodwin v   **[1999] IRLR 4 EAT**
The Patent Office
The tribunal should adopt a purposive approach to construction, construing the statutory language in a way which gives effect to the stated or presumed intention of Parliament, but with due regard to the ordinary and natural meaning of the words in question. Explicit reference should always be made to any relevant provision of the Guidance issued by the Secretary of State or of the Code of Practice, which the tribunal has taken into account. However, the Guidance should not be used as an extra hurdle over which the claimant must jump.

Ministry of Defence v   **[2008] IRLR 928 EAT**
Hay
The statutory approach is self-evidently a functional one directed towards what a claimant cannot, or can no longer, do at a practical level.

Meaning of impairment

McNicol v   **[2002] IRLR 711 CA**
Balfour Beatty Rail Maintenance Ltd
The term "impairment" in s.1 of the Act bears its ordinary and natural meaning. It is clear from Schedule 1 that impairment may result from an illness or it may consist of an illness. The essential question in each case is whether, on a sensible interpretation of the relevant evidence, including the expert medical evidence and reasonable inferences which can be made from all the evidence, the claimant can fairly be described as having a physical or mental impairment. Such a decision can and should be made without substituting for the statutory language a different word or form of words in an attempt to describe or define the concept of "impairment".

Ministry of Defence v   **[2008] IRLR 928 EAT**
Hay
A "disability" is not the same as an "impairment".

McNicol v   **[2002] IRLR 711 CA**
Balfour Beatty Rail Maintenance Ltd
The onus is on the claimant to prove the impairment on the conventional balance of probabilities.

Millar v   **[2006] IRLR 112 CS**
Inland Revenue Commissioners
Physical impairment can be established without reference to causation, and, in particular, without reference to any form of "illness". Many forms of physical impairment result from conditions that cannot be described as "illness".

Hospice of St Mary of Furness v   **[2007] IRLR 944 EAT**
Howard
It is not necessary for a claimant to establish the cause of an alleged physical impairment, but where there is an issue as to the existence of a physical impairment, it is open to a respondent to seek to disprove the existence of such impairment, including by seeking to prove that the

impairment is not genuine or is a mental and not a physical impairment.

J v   **[2010] IRLR 936 EAT**
DLA Piper UK LLP   **[2010] EqLR 164 EAT**

It is good practice in every case for a tribunal to state conclusions separately on the questions of impairment and of adverse effect, and in the case of adverse effect, the questions of substantiality and long-term effect arising under it.

J v   **[2010] IRLR 936 EAT**
DLA Piper UK LLP   **[2010] EqLR 164 EAT**

There are sometimes cases where identifying the nature of the impairment from which a claimant may be suffering involves difficult medical questions. In cases where there may be a dispute about the existence of an impairment, it will make sense to start by making findings about whether the claimant's ability to carry out normal day-to-day activities is adversely affected (on a long-term basis), and to consider the question of impairment in the light of those findings. If the tribunal finds that the claimant's ability to carry out normal day-to-day activities has been adversely affected on a long-term basis, it will in many or most cases follow as a matter of common-sense inference that the claimant is suffering from a condition which has produced that adverse effect – ie, an "impairment". If that inference can be drawn, it will be unnecessary for the tribunal to try to resolve difficult medical issues.

J v   **[2010] IRLR 936 EAT**
DLA Piper UK LLP   **[2010] EqLR 164 EAT**

If a tribunal finds that the claimant's ability to carry out normal day-to-day activities has been substantially impaired by symptoms characteristic of depression for 12 months or more, it would in most cases be likely to conclude that he or she was suffering "clinical depression" rather than simply a reaction to adverse circumstances.

Morgan v   **[2002] IRLR 190 EAT**
Staffordshire University

Medical notes which refer to "anxiety", "stress" and "depression" do not amount to proof of a mental impairment within the meaning of the DDA.

Dunham v   **[2005] IRLR 608 EAT**
Ashford Windows

A tribunal hearing a mental impairment case based on learning difficulties should look for expert evidence as to the nature and degree of the impairment claimed and for evidence of a particular identified condition (which may have a specific or a generalised effect on function). It is unlikely to be sufficient for a claimant to put his case only on the basis that he had difficulties at school or is "not very bright".

Dunham v   **[2005] IRLR 608 EAT**
Ashford Windows

In a case of learning difficulties, there is no reason why the essential evidence which establishes the nature of the

claimant's condition should not be provided by a suitably qualified psychologist. What is important is that there should be evidence from a suitably qualified expert who can speak, on the basis of their experience and expertise, as to the relevant condition.

J v   **[2010] IRLR 936 EAT**
DLA Piper UK LLP   **[2010] EqLR 164 EAT**

A GP is fully qualified to express an opinion on whether a patient is suffering from depression, and on any associated questions arising under the disability discrimination legislation. Depression is a condition very often encountered in general practice.

Leonard v   **[2001] IRLR 19 EAT**
Southern Derbyshire
   Chamber of Commerce

An employment tribunal misdirected themselves as to the manner in which the Guidance on the definition of disability should be applied by taking examples from the Guidance of what the claimant could do, such as being able to eat and drink, and catch a ball and then weighing that against what she could not do, such as negotiate pavement edges safely. This was inappropriate, since her ability to catch a ball did not diminish her inability to negotiate pavement edges safely.

Excluded conditions

(1) Subject to para. (2) below, addiction to alcohol, nicotine or any other substance is to be treated as not amounting to an impairment for the purposes of the Act.

(2) Para. (1) above does not apply to addiction which was originally the result of administration of medically prescribed drugs or other medical treatment.

DISABILITY DISCRIMINATION (MEANING OF DISABILITY)
REGULATIONS 1996 – reg. 3
➡ EQUALITY ACT 2010 (DISABILITY) REGULATIONS 2010
– reg. 3

Power v   **[2003] IRLR 151 EAT**
Panasonic UK Ltd

It is not material to a decision as to whether a person has a disability within the meaning of the Act to consider how the impairment which they have was caused. What is material is to ascertain whether the disability which they have at the material time is a disability within the meaning of the Act or whether, where it is relevant, it is an impairment which is excluded by reason of the Regulations from being treated as such a disability. In this case, the tribunal erred in not considering whether the claimant's depression had a substantial and long-term adverse effect on her ability to carry out normal day-to-day activities, but by considering instead whether alcoholism caused her depression, and concluding that her case fell within reg.3(1), which provides that "addiction to alcohol ... is to be treated as not amounting to an impairment for the purposes of the Act."

(1) For the purposes of the Act the following conditions are to be treated as not amounting to impairments –
  (a) a tendency to set fires,
  (b) a tendency to steal,
  (c) a tendency to physical or sexual abuse of other persons,
  (d) exhibitionism, and
  (e) voyeurism.

DISABILITY DISCRIMINATION (MEANING OF DISABILITY) REGULATIONS 1996 – reg. 4
➡ **EQUALITY ACT 2010 (DISABILITY) REGULATIONS 2010 – reg. 4**

Governing Body of X Endowed   **[2009] IRLR 1007 HC**
  Primary School v
Special Educational Needs and Disability Tribunal
The exclusion in respect of a "condition" within the meaning of para. 4(1) includes both an independent, free-standing condition and symptoms or manifestations of an underlying impairment.

Long-term effects

2. (1) The effect of an impairment is a long-term effect if –
  (a) it has lasted at least 12 months;
  (b) the period for which it lasts is likely to be at least 12 months; or
  (c) it is likely to last for the rest of the life of the person affected.

(2) Where an impairment ceases to have a substantial adverse effect on a person's ability to carry out normal day-to-day activities, it is to be treated as continuing to have that effect if that effect is likely to recur.

DISABILITY DISCRIMINATION ACT – Sch. 1
➡ **EQUALITY ACT 2010 – Sch. 1**

Richmond Adult Community College v   **[2008] IRLR 227 CA**
McDougall
The point in time for determining whether the effect of an impairment is likely to last for at least 12 months is the time of the decision complained of. The tribunal should make its judgment on the basis of evidence as to the circumstances prevailing at the time of that decision.

Patel v   **[2010] IRLR 280 EAT**
Oldham Metropolitan Borough Council
The effect of an illness or condition likely to develop or which has developed from another illness or condition forms part of the assessment of whether the effect of the original impairment is likely to last or has lasted at least 12 months.

Normal day-to-day activities

4. – (1) An impairment is to be taken to affect the ability of the person concerned to carry out normal day-to-day activities only if it affects one of the following –
  (a) mobility;
  (b) manual dexterity;
  (c) physical co-ordination;
  (d) continence;
  (e) ability to lift, carry or otherwise move everyday objects
  (f) speech, hearing or eyesight;
  (g) memory or ability to concentrate, learn or understand; or
  (h) perception of the risk of physical danger.

DISABILITY DISCRIMINATION ACT – Sch. 1
[Note: this provision was not included in the Equality Act 2010]

Goodwin v   **[1999] IRLR 4 EAT**
The Patent Office
The Act is concerned with a person's ability to carry out activities. The fact that a person can carry out such activities does not mean that his ability to carry them out has not been impaired. The focus of the Act is on the things that the claimant either cannot do or can only do with difficulty, rather than on the things that the person can do.

Ekpe v   **[2001] IRLR 605 EAT**
Commissioner of Police
  of the Metropolis
What is "normal" for the purposes of the Act may be best understood by defining it as anything which is not abnormal or unusual (or, in the words of the Guidance issued by the Secretary of State, "particular" to the individual claimant). What is normal cannot sensibly depend on whether the majority of people do it. The antithesis for the purposes of the Act is between that which is "normal" and that which is "abnormal" or "unusual" as a regular activity, judged by an objective population standard.

Ekpe v   **[2001] IRLR 605 EAT**
Commissioner of Police of the Metropolis
Anything done by most women, or most men, is a normal day-to-day activity. Therefore, an employment tribunal erred in discounting the fact that the claimant could not put rollers in her hair and that she could not always use her right hand to apply make-up on grounds that neither was a "normal day-to-day activity" because they are activities carried out almost exclusively by women.

Law Hospital NHS Trust v   **[2001] IRLR 611 CS**
Rush
Evidence of the nature of a claimant's duties at work, and the way in which they are performed, particularly if they include "normal day-to-day activities, can be relevant to the assessment which the tribunal has to make of the claimant's case.

Chief Constable of Dumfries &   **[2009] IRLR 612 EAT**
  Galloway Constabulary v
Adams
The European Court of Justice's use of the term "participation in professional life" in *Chacon Navas* means that when assessing whether a person is limited in their normal day-to-day activities, it is relevant to consider whether they are limited in an activity which is to be found across a range of employment situations. Although work of a particular form is not a "normal day-to-day activity", something that a per-

son does only at work may be classed as normal if it is common to different types of employment.

Paterson v   [2007] IRLR 763 EAT
Commissioner of Police of the Metropolis

Section 1 can be read in a way which gives effect to EU law by giving a meaning to day-to-day activities that encompasses the activities that are relevant to participation in professional life. Where it is not disputed that the employee is suffering a substantial disadvantage because of the effects of his or her disability in the procedures adopted for deciding between candidates for promotion, the only proper inference is that those effects must involve more than a trivial effect on his ability to undertake normal day-to-day activities.

Paterson v   [2007] IRLR 763 EAT
Commissioner of Police of the Metropolis

Carrying out an assessment or examination is properly to be described as a normal day-to-day activity.

Chief Constable of Lothian and   [2010] IRLR 109 EAT
Borders Police v
Cumming

Paterson and *Chacon* are not authority for the broad proposition that being afforded general participation in or access to professional life is a day-to-day activity. The status of disability for the purposes of the statute cannot be dependent on the decision of the employer as to how to react to the employee's impairment.

Chief Constable of Dumfries &   [2009] IRLR 612 EAT
Galloway Constabulary v
Adams

There are enough people working on night shifts for it to be a normal day-to-day activity.

Cruickshank v   [2002] IRLR 24 EAT
VAW Motorcast Ltd

In a case where, as a result of a medical condition, the effects of an impairment on ability to carry out normal day-to-day activities fluctuate and may be exacerbated by conditions at work, the tribunal should consider whether the impairment has a substantial and long-term adverse effect on the employee's ability to perform normal day-to-day activities both while actually at work and while not at work. If, while at work, a claimant's symptoms are such as to have a significant and long-term effect on his ability to perform day-to-day tasks, such symptoms are not to be ignored simply because the work itself may be specialised and unusual, so long as the disability and its consequences can be measured in terms of the ability of a claimant to undertake day-to-day tasks.

Vicary v   [1999] IRLR 680 EAT
British Telecommunications plc

It is not for a doctor to express an opinion as to what is a normal day-to-day activity. Nor is it for the medical expert to tell the tribunal whether the impairments which had been found proved were or were not substantial. Those are matters for the employment tribunal to arrive at its own assessment.

Ekpe v   [2001] IRLR 605 EAT
Commissioner of Police
of the Metropolis

An employment tribunal is entitled to have regard to its own observation of the claimant in determining the extent of a claimant's disability. A decision as to whether a disability has an adverse impact on normal day-to-day activities and whether that impact is substantial may properly be influenced by the behaviour of a claimant as demonstrated before the tribunal, although any tribunal considering whether to draw any conclusion from such behaviour would be expected to raise that possibility at the hearing.

Kapadia v   [2000] IRLR 699 CA
London Borough of Lambeth

An employment tribunal was obliged to conclude that a claimant's mental impairment had a substantial adverse effect on his normal day-to-day activities, in circumstances in which there was direct medical evidence that his anxiety, neuroses and depression would have had such an effect but for the fact that he had received medical treatment, and there was no contrary expert medical evidence or challenge to the factual bases of those opinions.

Recurring conditions

2(2) Where an impairment ceases to have a substantial adverse effect on a person's ability to carry out normal day-to-day activities, it is to be treated as continuing to have that effect if that effect is likely to recur.

DISABILITY DISCRIMINATION ACT 1995 – Sch.1
➡ EQUALITY ACT 2010 – Sch. 1

Swift v   [2004] IRLR 540 EAT
Chief Constable of Wiltshire Constabulary

In considering the application of para.2(2), a tribunal should ask itself the following questions: first, was there at some stage an impairment which had a substantial adverse effect on the claimant's ability to carry out normal day-to-day activities? Secondly, did the impairment cease to have a substantial adverse effect on the claimant's ability to carry out normal day-to-day activities, and if so when? Thirdly, what was the substantial adverse effect? Fourthly, is that substantial adverse effect likely to recur. The tribunal must be satisfied that the same effect is likely to recur and will again amount to a substantial adverse effect on the claimant's ability to carry out normal day-to-day activities.

Swift v   [2004] IRLR 540 EAT
Chief Constable of Wiltshire Constabulary

Although the tribunal must be satisfied that the substantial adverse effect is likely to recur, it need not be satisfied that the recurrence is likely to last for at least 12 months. The effect of para.2(2) is that the impairment is treated as continuing for as long as its substantial adverse effect is likely to recur. Even if the impairment has ceased to have a substantial adverse effect, it "lasts" for as long as its substantial adverse effect is likely to recur.

Swift v   **[2004] IRLR 540 EAT**
Chief Constable of Wiltshire Constabulary
The question for the tribunal is whether the substantial adverse effect is likely to recur, not whether the illness is likely to recur. The Act contemplates that an illness may run its course to a conclusion but leave behind an impairment.

J v   **[2010] IRLR 936 EAT**
DLA Piper UK LLP   **[2010] EqLR 164 EAT**
If a woman over a five-year period suffers several short episodes of depression which have a substantial adverse impact on her ability to carry out normal day-to-day activities but who between those episodes is symptom-free and does not require treatment, it may be appropriate to regard her as suffering from a mental impairment throughout the period in question, ie even between episodes. The model would be of a single condition producing recurrent symptomatic episodes.

Substantial adverse effects

Goodwin v   **[1999] IRLR 4 EAT**
The Patent Office
"Substantial" means "more than minor or trivial" rather than "very large". The tribunal may take into account how the claimant appears to the tribunal to "manage", although it should be slow to regard a person's capabilities in the relatively strange adversarial environment as an entirely reliable guide to the level of ability to perform normal day-to-day activities.

Paterson v   **[2007] IRLR 763 EAT**
Commissioner of Police of the Metropolis
In the population at large there will be differences in such things as manual dexterity, ability to lift objects or to concentrate. In order to be substantial, the effect must fall outwith the normal range of effects that one might expect from a cross-section of the population. However, when assessing the effect, the comparison is not with the population at large. What is required is to compare the difference between the way in which the individual in fact carries out the activity in question and how he would carry it out if not impaired.

Abadeh v   **[2001] IRLR 23 EAT**
British Telecommunications plc
It is not the task of the medical expert to tell the tribunal whether an impairment was or was not substantial. That is a question which the tribunal itself has to answer. The medical report should deal with the doctor's diagnosis of the

impairment, the doctor's observation of the claimant carrying out day-to-day activities and the ease with which he was able to perform those functions, together with any relevant opinion as to prognosis and the effect of medication.

Vicary v   **[1999] IRLR 680 EAT**
British Telecommunications plc
Having concluded that the ability of the claimant to do a number of activities was impaired, the tribunal should have concluded that she had a disability within the meaning of the Act.

Paterson v   **[2007] IRLR 763 EAT**
Commissioner of Police of the Metropolis
In some cases, coping strategies will prevent the impairment having adverse effects, but only where they can be relied on in all circumstances.

Abadeh v   **[2001] IRLR 23 EAT**
British Telecommunications plc
An assessment of disability by a Medical Appeal Tribunal is clearly relevant evidence for an employment tribunal to take into account as part of the evidence before them on the issue of disability.

Goodwin v   **[1999] IRLR 4 EAT**
The Patent Office
An employment tribunal erred in finding that a paranoid schizophrenic who was dismissed after complaints relating to his behaviour, was not a "disabled person" because the adverse effect of the impairment on his ability to carry out normal day-to-day activities was not "substantial". The claimant was unable to carry on a normal day-to-day conversation with work colleagues, which was good evidence that his capacity to concentrate and communicate had been adversely affected in a significant manner.

Severe disfigurement

3(1) An impairment which consists of a severe disfigurement is to be treated as having a substantial adverse effect on the ability of the person concerned to carry out normal day-to-day activities.
             DISABILITY DISCRIMINATION ACT – Sch.1
             ➡ EQUALITY ACT 2010 – Sch. 1

Cosgrove v   **[2007] IRLR 397 NICA**
Northern Ireland Ambulance Service
An impairment "consisting of" disfigurement means that the impairment relates solely to the cosmetic aspect of the condition, and not to a condition, one aspect of which is disfigurement. Therefore, the severe disfigurement provisions did not protect a claimant with psoriasis, where the reason he was not employed as an ambulance worker was not as a result of his disfigurement but because it was judged that he was at risk of infection and that his condition carried the danger that he would infect others.

Effect of medical treatment

6(1) An impairment which would be likely to have a substantial adverse effect on the ability of the person concerned to carry out normal day-to-day activities, but for the fact that measures are being taken to treat or correct it, is to be treated as having that effect.

(2) In sub-paragraph (1) "measures" includes, in particular, medical treatment and the use of a prosthesis or other aid.

(3) Sub-paragraph (1) does not apply –
(a) in relation to the impairment of a person's sight, to the extent that the impairment is, in his case, correctable by spectacles or contact lenses or in such other ways as may be prescribed; or
(b) in relation to such other impairments as may be prescribed, in such circumstances as may be prescribed.

DISABILITY DISCRIMINATION ACT – Sch. 1
➡ **EQUALITY ACT 2010 – Sch. 1**

SCA Packaging Ltd v   **[2009] IRLR 746 HL**
Boyle
The word "likely" in para. 6(1) is used in the sense of "could well happen" rather than whether it is more probable than not.

SCA Packaging Ltd v   **[2009] IRLR 746 HL**
Boyle
Paragraph 6(1) is a far-reaching provision. Where it applies, the individual's actual situation with the benefit of the course of treatment must be ignored, and she must be considered as if she was not having the treatment and the impairment was completely unchecked.

Woodrup v   **[2003] IRLR 111 CA**
London Borough of Southwark
The question to be asked is whether, if treatment were stopped at the relevant date, would the person then, notwithstanding such benefit as had been obtained from prior treatment, have an impairment which would have the relevant adverse effect?

Abadeh v   **[2001] IRLR 23 EAT**
British Telecommunications plc
Para. 6 of Schedule 1 applies only to continuing medical treatment, ie to measures that "are being taken" and not to concluded treatment where the effects of such treatment may be more readily ascertained. Where treatment has ceased, the effects of that treatment should be taken into account in order to assess the disability.

Abadeh v   **[2001] IRLR 23 EAT**
British Telecommunications plc
Where the medical evidence satisfies the tribunal that the effect of continuing medical treatment is to create a permanent improvement, the effects of that treatment should be taken into account in order to assess the disability as measures are no longer needed to treat or correct it once the permanent improvement has been established.

Woodrup v   **[2003] IRLR 111 CA**
London Borough of Southwark
In a deduced effects case similar to the present one, in which the claimant was claiming that if her psychotherapy treatment for anxiety neurosis had been discontinued, her impairment would have had a substantial adverse effect on her ability to carry out normal day-to-day activities, the claimant should be required to prove his or her alleged disability with some particularity. Ordinarily, one would expect clear medical evidence to be necessary.

Kapadia v   **[2000] IRLR 14 EAT**
London Borough of Lambeth
Counselling sessions with a consultant clinical psychologist constitute "medical treatment" within the meaning of para. 6 of Schedule 1.

Carden v   **[2005] IRLR 720 EAT**
Pickerings Europe Ltd
A plate and pins surgically inserted in the claimant's ankle and requiring no further treatment could be regarded as an "other aid" within the definition of "measures" in para. 6(2), which includes "in particular, medical treatment and the use of a prosthesis or other aid" so as to fall within the deduced effects provisions, so long as there was continuing support or assistance being given by the pins and plate to the functioning of the claimant's ankle.

Progressive conditions

6A(1) Subject to sub-paragraph (2), a person who has cancer, HIV infection or multiple sclerosis is to be deemed to have a disability, and hence to be a disabled person.
(2) Regulations may provide for sub-paragraph (1) not to apply in the case of a person who has cancer if he has cancer of a prescribed description.
(3) A description of cancer prescribed under sub-paragraph (2) may (in particular) be framed by reference to consequences for a person of his having it.

8(1) Where –
(a) a person has a progressive condition (such as cancer, multiple sclerosis or muscular dystrophy or HIV infection),
(b) as a result of that condition, he has an impairment which has (or had) an effect on his ability to carry out normal day-to-day activities, but
(c) that effect is not (or was not) a substantial adverse effect,
he shall be taken to have an impairment which has such a substantial adverse effect if the condition is likely to result in his having such an impairment."

9. In this Schedule "HIV infection" means infection by a virus capable of causing the Acquired Immune Deficiency Syndrome.

DISABILITY DISCRIMINATION ACT (as amended) – Sch. 1
➡ **EQUALITY ACT 2010 – Sch. 1**

Mowat-Brown v   [2002] IRLR 235 EAT
University of Surrey

It is not enough simply for a claimant to establish that he has a progressive condition and that it has or has had an effect on his ability to carry out normal day-to-day activities. He must go on and show that it is more likely than not that at some stage in the future he will have an impairment which will have a substantial adverse effect on his ability to carry out normal day-to-day activities. In some cases it may be possible to produce medical evidence of his likely prognosis. In other cases it may be possible to discharge the onus of proof by statistical evidence.

Kirton v   [2003] IRLR 353 CA
Tetrosyl Ltd

The words "as a result of that condition" should not be so narrowly construed as to exclude an impairment which results from a standard and common form of operative procedure for cancer. Impairment in this context also includes the ordinary consequences of an operation to relieve the disease. Therefore, a claimant who had an operation for prostate cancer which led to urinary incontinence fell within the definition of disability relating to a "progressive condition", notwithstanding that his incontinence was not a direct result of the progressive condition, but was a result of the surgery by which the progressive condition was treated.

EMPLOYMENT DISCRIMINATION

Direct discrimination

(5) A person directly discriminates against a disabled person if, on the ground of the disabled person's disability, he treats the disabled person less favourably than he treats or would treat a person not having that particular disability whose relevant circumstances, including his abilities, are the same as, or not materially different from, those of the disabled person.
DISABILITY DISCRIMINATION ACT 1995 (as amended) – s.3A
➡ **EQUALITY ACT 2010 – s.13**

Aylott v   [2010] IRLR 994 CA
Stockton on Tees Borough Council   [2010] EqLR 69 CA

Direct discrimination can occur when assumptions are made that a claimant, as an individual, has characteristics associated with a group to which the claimant belongs, irrespective of whether the claimant or most members of the group have those characteristics.

High Quality Lifestyles Ltd v   [2006] IRLR 850 EAT
Watts

In order to establish direct discrimination, it is not sufficient for the claimant to show that his treatment was on the grounds of his disability. It also has to be established that the treatment was less favourable than the treatment which would be afforded to a hypothetical comparator in circumstances that are "not materially different".

Aylott v   [2010] IRLR 994 CA
Stockton on Tees Borough Council   [2010] EqLR 69 CA

There are dangers in attaching too much importance to constructing a hypothetical comparator and to less favourable treatment as a separate issue. If a claimant was dismissed on the ground of disability, then it is likely that he was treated less favourably than a hypothetical comparator not having the particular disability would have been treated in the same relevant circumstances. The finding of the reason for the dismissal supplies the answer to the question whether he received less favourable treatment.

Eagle Place Services Ltd v   [2010] IRLR 486 EAT
Rudd

It is not open to an employer to say that it has not discriminated against a claimant because it would have behaved unreasonably in dismissing a comparator. It is unreasonable to suppose that it in fact would have dismissed the comparator for what amounts to an irrational reason. It is one thing to find, as in *Bahl v Law Society*, that a named individual has behaved unreasonably to both the claimant and named comparators; it is quite another to find that a corporate entity would behave unreasonably to a hypothetical comparator when it had no good reason to do so.

EBR Attridge Law LLP v Coleman (No.2)

[2010] IRLR 10 EAT

There was nothing "impossible" about adding words to the provisions of the Disability Discrimination Act so as to cover associative discrimination. The proscription of associative discrimination is an extension of the scope of the legislation as enacted, but it is in no sense repugnant to it. On the contrary, it is an extension fully in conformity with the aims of the legislation as drafted. The Act would be interpolated so as to give effect to the reasoning of the European Court of Justice by adding a new subsection in the following terms: "A person also directly discriminates against a person if he treats him less favourably than he treats or would treat another person by reason of the disability of another person."

EBR Attridge Law LLP v Coleman (No.2)

[2010] IRLR 10 EAT

Although the phrase "associative discrimination" is a convenient shorthand, the concept of association is not central to the reasoning of the European Court of Justice. What matters is that the putative victim has suffered adverse treatment on a proscribed ground, namely disability, and the fact that the disability is not his own is not of the essence.

Duty to make reasonable adjustment

(1) Where –
  (a) a provision, criterion or practice applied by or on behalf of an employer, or
  (b) any physical feature of premises occupied by the employer,
places the disabled person concerned at a substantial disadvantage in comparison with persons who are not disabled, it is the duty of the employer to take such steps as it is reasonable, in all the circumstances of the case, for him to have to take in order to prevent the provision, criterion or practice, or feature, having that effect.

(2) In subsection (1), "the disabled person concerned" means –
  (a) in the case of a provision, criterion or practice for determining to whom employment should be offered, any disabled person who is, or has notified the employer that he may be, a claimant for that employment;
  (b) in any other case, a disabled person who is –
    (i) a claimant for the employment concerned, or
    (ii) an employee of the employer concerned.

(3) Nothing in this section imposes any duty on an employer in relation to a disabled person if the employer does not know, and could not reasonably be expected to know –
  (a) in the case of a claimant or potential claimant, that the disabled person concerned is, or may be, a claimant for the employment; or

  (b) in any case, that that person has a disability and is likely to be affected in the way mentioned in subsection (1).

DISABILITY DISCRIMINATION ACT 1995 (as amended) – s.4A
➡ **EQUALITY ACT 2010 – s.20, Sch. 8**

(1) In determining whether it is reasonable for a person to have to take a particular step in order to comply with a duty to make reasonable adjustments, regard shall be had, in particular, to –
  (a) the extent to which taking the step would prevent the effect in relation to which the duty is imposed;
  (b) the extent to which it is practicable for him to take the step;
  (c) the financial and other costs which would be incurred by him in taking the step and the extent to which taking it would disrupt any of his activities;
  (d) the extent of his financial and other resources;
  (e) the availability to him of financial or other assistance with respect to taking the step;
  (f) the nature of his activities and the size of his undertaking;
  (g) where the step would be taken in relation to a private household, the extent to which taking it would –
    (i) disrupt that household, or
    (ii) disturb any person residing there.

(2) The following are examples of steps which a person may need to take in relation to a disabled person in order to comply with a duty to make reasonable adjustments –
  (a) making adjustments to premises;
  (b) allocating some of the disabled person's duties to another person;
  (c) transferring him to fill an existing vacancy;
  (d) altering his hours of working or training;
  (e) assigning him to a different place of work or training;
  (f) allowing him to be absent during working or training hours for rehabilitation, assessment or treatment;
  (g) giving, or arranging for, training or mentoring (whether for the disabled person or any other person);
  (h) acquiring or modifying equipment;
  (i) modifying instructions or reference manuals;
  (j) modifying procedures for testing or assessment;
  (k) providing a reader or interpreter;
  (l) providing supervision or other support.

DISABILITY DISCRIMINATION ACT 1995 (as amended) – s.18B
➡ **EQUALITY ACT 2010 – s.22**

Provision, criterion or practice

Archibald v Fife Council

[2004] IRLR 651 HL

The duty to make an adjustment is triggered where an employee becomes so disabled that she can no longer meet the requirements of her job description. The duty applies to the job description for a post and the liability of anyone who becomes incapable of fulfilling the job description to be dismissed, as much as it applies to an employer's arrangements for deciding who gets what job or how much each is paid.

O'Hanlon v   **[2006] IRLR 840 EAT**
Commissioners for HM Revenue and Customs
The whole premise of the reasonable adjustment provisions is that the disabled employee may be disadvantaged by the application of common rules.

Smith v   **[2006] IRLR 41 CS**
Churchills Stairlifts plc
The proper comparator is readily identified by reference to the disadvantage caused by the relevant arrangements. It is not with the population generally who do not have a disability.

Kenny v   **[1999] IRLR 76 EAT**
Hampshire Constabulary
An employer's duty to make a reasonable adjustment to arrangements on which employment is offered or afforded is restricted to "job related" matters. Not every failure to make an arrangement which deprives an employee of a chance to be employed is unlawful.

When duty applies

Archibald v   **[2004] IRLR 651 HL**
Fife Council
A claimant was placed "at a substantial disadvantage in comparison with persons who are not disabled" where her job description required her to be physically fit, which she was no longer able to meet, and that exposed her to a condition that if she was physically unable to do the job she was employed to do, she was liable to be dismissed.

Paul v   **[2004] IRLR 190 EAT**
National Probation Service
The existence of a disability does not of itself substantially disadvantage a disabled person who is subject to a general requirement of clearance from an occupational health adviser. In many cases, having a disability does not adversely affect an individual's general health and an occupational health assessment will not lead to a refusal of employment unless the disability affects the claimant's ability to do the work and no reasonable adjustments can be made.

Archibald v   **[2004] IRLR 651 HL**
Fife Council
The duty to make adjustments is not linked to the employee's particular employment and can arise even if there is nothing that the employer can do to prevent the disabled person from being placed at a disadvantage in their particular employment.

Archibald v   **[2004] IRLR 651 HL**
Fife Council
The duty to make adjustments may require the employer to treat a disabled person more favourably to remove the disad-

vantage which is attributable to the disability. This necessarily entails a measure of positive discrimination.

Chief Constable of South   **[2010] IRLR 744 EAT**
   Yorkshire Police v
Jelic
Employers are required to take reasonable steps to help disabled people, which they are not required to take for others, in order to achieve for them substantive equality and to assist their integration in the working environment.

Archibald v   **[2004] IRLR 651 HL**
Fife Council
The comparison under [s.4A(1)] with persons who are not disabled is not confined to non-disabled people doing the same job. Therefore, the steps which the employer might have to take in order to prevent the arrangements placing a disabled employee at a substantial disadvantage in comparison with non-disabled persons include transferring her to another job, a possibility expressly contemplated by [s.18B(2)(c)].

Fareham College Corporation v   **[2009] IRLR 991 EAT**
Walters
It is not necessary for a claimant in a reasonable adjustment case to satisfy the tribunal that someone who did not have a disability but whose circumstances were otherwise the same as hers would have been treated differently. The more general comparative exercise required in a reasonable adjustment claim, involving a class or group of non-disabled comparators, differs from the individual, like-for-like comparison required in cases of direct discrimination. In many cases the facts will speak for themselves and the identity of the non-disabled comparators will be clearly discernible from the provision, criterion or practice found to be in play.

Archibald v   **[2004] IRLR 651 HL**
Fife Council
The duty to take such steps as it is reasonable in all the circumstances for the employer to have to take could include transferring without competitive interview a disabled employee from a post she can no longer do to a post which she can do. The employer's duty may require moving the disabled person to a post at a slightly higher grade. A transfer can be upwards as well as sideways or downwards.

Chief Constable of South   **[2010] IRLR 744 EAT**
   Yorkshire Police v
Jelic
A tribunal is not precluded as a matter of law from holding that it would be a reasonable adjustment to create a new job for a disabled employee, if the particular facts of the case support such a finding.

Tarbuck v   **[2006] IRLR 664 EAT**
Sainsbury's Supermarkets Ltd
There is no obligation on an employer to create a post spe-

cifically, which is not otherwise necessary, merely to create a job for a disabled person.

Beart v   [2003] IRLR 238 CA
HM Prison Service

The test of reasonableness under [s.4A] is directed to the steps to be taken to prevent the employment from having a detrimental effect on the disabled employee.

British Gas Services Ltd v   [2001] IRLR 60 EAT
McCaull

The test under [s.4A] is an objective one: did the employer take such steps as it is reasonable in all the circumstances of the case for him to have to take in order to prevent the arrangements made by the employer from placing the disabled person at a substantial disadvantage in comparison with those who are not disabled? The test of whether it was reasonable for an employer to have to take a particular step does not relate to what the employer considered but to what he did and did not do. That is for the tribunal to consider. If Parliament had intended an employer to be in breach of statutory duty because he failed to consider what steps he might reasonably take, it would have so provided in the Act.

Secretary of State for Work and   [2010] IRLR 283 EAT
Pensions v
Alam

To ascertain whether the statutory exemption from the obligation to make reasonable adjustments applies, two questions arise: Did the employer know both that the employee was disabled and that his disability was liable to affect him in the manner set out in the legislation? If "no", ought the employer to have known both that the employee was disabled and that his disability was liable to place him at a substantial disadvantage as compared with a non-disabled person in the manner set out in the legislation? If the employer could not reasonably have been expected to be aware of the relevant effect, no duty to make reasonable adjustments arises because the reasonableness of his ignorance would make it unreasonable to impose on him the duty to adjust.

Morse v   [1999] IRLR 352 EAT
Wiltshire County Council

The purpose of [s.18B(2)] is to focus the mind of the employer on possible steps which it might take in compliance with its duty under [s.4A(1)], and to focus the mind of the tribunal when considering whether an employer has failed to comply with a [s.4A] duty.

Ridout v   [1999] IRLR 628 EAT
T C Group

The duty to make a reasonable adjustment is to be construed in the light of [s.4A(3)]. This requires a tribunal to measure the extent of the duty, if any, against the actual or assumed knowledge of the employer both as to the disability and its

likelihood of causing the individual a substantial disadvantage in comparison with persons who are not disabled.

Matuszowicz v   [2009] IRLR 288 CA
Kingston upon Hull City Council

There may be inadvertent and non-deliberate omissions on the part of the employer which are breaches of the duty to make reasonable adjustments.

Nottinghamshire County Council v   [2004] IRLR 703 CA
Meikle

Payment of full sick pay by an employer can be an adjustment falling within the scope of [s.4A].

O'Hanlon v   [2006] IRLR 840 EAT
Commissioners for HM Revenue
and Customs

It will be a very rare case where giving higher sick pay than would be payable to a non-disabled person who in general does not suffer the same disability-related absence would be considered necessary as a reasonable adjustment.

O'Hanlon v   [2007] IRLR 404 CA
Commissioners for HM Revenue and Customs

The employers did not have a duty as a reasonable adjustment to disaggregate entitlement for disability-related absence and absence for a non-disability-related reason, and not count disability-related absence against entitlement to full pay under the employers' sick pay rules.

Kenny v   [1999] IRLR 76 EAT
Hampshire Constabulary

Employers are not under a statutory duty to provide carers to attend to their employees' personal needs, such as assistance in going to the toilet. A line has to be drawn on the extent of the employer's responsibilities in providing adjustments to accommodate a disabled employee.

British Gas Services Ltd v   [2001] IRLR 60 EAT
McCaull

There is no automatic breach of the duty of reasonable adjustment because an employer is unaware of that duty. The question is what steps the employer took and did not take. An employer might take all reasonable steps as contemplated by the statute while remaining ignorant of the statutory provision itself.

Ridout v   [1999] IRLR 628 EAT
T C Group

Tribunals should be careful not to impose upon disabled people a duty to give a long detailed explanation as to the effects of their disability merely to cause the employer to make adjustments which it probably should have made in the first place. On the other hand, it is equally undesirable that an employer should be required to ask a number of questions as to whether a person with a disability feels disadvantaged merely to protect themselves from liability.

Failure to make reasonable adjustment

(2) For the purposes of this Part, a person also discriminates against a disabled person if he fails to comply with a duty to make reasonable adjustments imposed on him in relation to the disabled person.

(6) If, in a case falling within subsection (1), a person is under a duty to make reasonable adjustments in relation to a disabled person but fails to comply with that duty, his treatment of that person cannot be justified under subsection (3) unless it would have been justified even if he had complied with that duty.

DISABILITY DISCRIMINATION ACT 1995 (as amended) – s.3A

➡ EQUALITY ACT 2010 – s.21

| Clark v | [1999] IRLR 318 CA |
| TDG Ltd t/a Novacold | |

A claim for a breach of a duty of reasonable adjustment is not dependent on successfully establishing a claim for less favourable treatment for a reason related to disability.

| Smith v | [2006] IRLR 41 CA |
| Churchills Stairlifts plc | |

Sections [3A(3)] and [4A(1)] of the DDA call for different tests and the difference is such that something that might otherwise have been justifiable in the context of [s.3A(3)] nevertheless results in a duty to make an adjustment pursuant to [s.4A(1)].

| Smith v | [2006] IRLR 41 CA |
| Churchills Stairlifts plc | |

The test under [s.4A(1)] is an objective test. The employer must take "such steps as ... is reasonable, in all the circumstances of the case". The objective nature of the test is further illustrated by [s.18B(1)], which provides that in determining whether it is reasonable for an employer to have to take a particular step, regard is to be had, amongst other things, to "the financial and other costs which could be incurred by the employer in taking the step and the extent to which taking it would disrupt any of his activities." It is significant that the concern is with the extent to which the step would disrupt any of the employer's activities, not the extent to which the employer reasonably believes that such disruption would occur. The position is noticeably different as regards the question of justification. Whereas, in relation to the duty of adjustment, it is ultimately the employment tribunal's view of what is reasonable that matters, in relation to justification, the task of the employment tribunal is to consider the materiality and substantiality of the employer's reason.

| Environment Agency v | [2008] IRLR 20 EAT |
| Rowan | |

An employment tribunal considering a claim that an employer has discriminated against an employee by failing to comply with the duty of reasonable adjustment must identify: (a) the provision, criterion or practice applied by or on behalf of an employer, or (b) the physical feature of premises occupied by the employer, (c) the identity of non-disabled comparators (where appropriate) and (d) the nature and extent of the substantial disadvantage suffered by the claimant. Identification of the substantial disadvantage suffered by the claimant may involve a consideration of the cumulative effect of both the "provision, criterion or practice applied by or on behalf of an employer" and the "physical feature of premises". Unless the tribunal has gone through that process, it cannot go on to judge if any proposed adjustment is reasonable because it will be unable to say what adjustments were reasonable to prevent the provision, criterion or practice, or feature, placing the disabled person concerned at a substantial disadvantage.

| HM Prison Service v | [2007] IRLR 951 EAT |
| Johnson | |

A tribunal deciding whether an employer is in breach of its duty under s.4A must identify with some particularity what "step" it is that the employers are said to have failed to take.

| Morse v | [1999] IRLR 352 EAT |
| Wiltshire County Council | |

A tribunal hearing an allegation of failure to make a reasonable adjustment must go through a number of sequential steps:

– It must decide whether the provisions of [s.4A] impose a duty on the employer in the circumstances of the particular case.

– If such a duty is imposed, it must next decide whether the employer has taken such steps as it is reasonable, in all the circumstances of the case, for him to have to take in order to prevent the arrangements or feature having the effect of placing the disabled person concerned at a substantial disadvantage in comparison with persons who are not disabled.

– This, in turn, involves the tribunal inquiring whether the employer could reasonably have taken any of the steps set out in [s.18B(1)].

– At the same time the tribunal must have regard to the factors set out in [s.18B(2)].

| Beart v | [2003] IRLR 238 CA |
| HM Prison Service | |

It is not an error of law for a tribunal to have failed to follow sequentially the series of steps indicated in *Morse*, provided that it is apparent from the tribunal's decision that they properly applied themselves to considering whether the requirements of the statute were satisfied.

| Project Management Institute v | [2007] IRLR 579 EAT |
| Latif | |

The claimant must not only establish that the duty of reasonable adjustment has arisen, but that there are facts from which it could reasonably be inferred, absent an explanation, that it has been breached. By the time the case is heard by the tribunal, there must be evidence of some apparently reasonable adjustment that could be made, even though the claimant does not have to identify the proposed adjustment until after the alleged failure to implement it. Although the claimant does not have to provide the detailed adjustment that would need to be made, it is necessary for the respondent to understand the broad nature of the adjustment proposed and to be given sufficient detail to enable him to engage with the question of whether or not it could reasonably be achieved. It would be an impossible burden to place on a respondent to prove a negative, that there is no adjustment that could reasonably be made.

Tarbuck v   **[2006] IRLR 664 EAT**
Sainsbury's Supermarkets Ltd
There is no separate and distinct duty of reasonable adjustment on an employer to consult the disabled employee about what adjustment might be made. The reasoning to this effect in *Mid Staffordshire General Hospitals NHS Trust v Cambridge* was incorrect. The only question is, objectively, whether the employer has complied with his obligations or not (even though it will always be good practice for the employer to consult and it will potentially jeopardise the employer's legal position if he does not do so, because the employer cannot use the lack of knowledge that would have resulted from consultation as a shield to defend a complaint that he has not made reasonable adjustments). If the employer does what is required of him, then the fact that he failed to consult about it or did not know that the obligation existed is irrelevant. It may be an entirely fortuitous and unconsidered compliance, but that is enough. Conversely, if he fails to do what is reasonably required, it avails him nothing that he has consulted the employee.

HM Prison Service v   **[2007] IRLR 951 EAT**
Johnson
That the disability from which the claimant was suffering was caused, at least in substantial part, by the employer's failings is potentially relevant to the assessment of reasonableness under s.4A. It may require an employer to do more by way of reasonable adjustment than would be necessary in other circumstances, but it cannot give rise to an unlimited obligation to accommodate the employee's needs.

Fareham College Corporation v   **[2009] IRLR 991 EAT**
Walters
Dismissing the claimant was itself an unlawful act of disability discrimination by reason of a failure to make reasonable adjustments allowing her to return to work

Eagle Place Services Ltd v   **[2010] IRLR 486 EAT**
Rudd
Once adjustments have been considered to be reasonable, an employer cannot then assert that because of their perceived financial implications he is entitled to dismiss the employee because he would dismiss any employee who was not disabled whose adjustments gave rise to the same financial implications. Such an argument would give the employer a "second bite of the cherry" and drive a coach

and horses through the statutory protection given to disabled employees. An employer could always disregard the need to make reasonable adjustments with impunity by dismissing the employee and asserting that he would have dismissed a non-disabled employee requiring the same adjustments, on financial grounds, notwithstanding that the adjustments had been adjudged to be "reasonable".

DISABILITY DISCRIMINATION BY EMPLOYERS

(1) It is unlawful for an employer to discriminate against a disabled person –

    (a) in the arrangements which he makes for the purpose of determining to whom he should offer employment;

    (b) in the terms on which he offers that person employment; or

    (c) by refusing to offer, or deliberately not offering, him employment.

(2) It is unlawful for an employer to discriminate against a disabled person whom he employs –

    (a) in the terms of employment which he affords him;

    (b) in the opportunities which he affords him for promotion, a transfer, training or receiving any other benefit;

    (c) by refusing to afford him, or deliberately not affording him, any such opportunity; or

    (d) by dismissing him, or subjecting him to any other detriment.

(3) It is also unlawful for an employer, in relation to employment by him, to subject to harassment –

    (a) a disabled person whom he employs; or

    (b) a disabled person who has applied to him for employment.

(4) Subsection (2) does not apply to benefits of any description if the employer is concerned with the provision (whether or not for payment) of benefits of that description to the public, or to a section of the public which includes the employee in question, unless –

    (a) that provision differs in a material respect from the provision of the benefits by the employer to his employees;

    (b) the provision of the benefits to the employee in question is regulated by his contract of employment; or

    (c) the benefits relate to training.

(5) The reference in subsection (2)(d) to the dismissal of a person includes a reference –

    (a) to the termination of that person's employment by the expiration of any period (including a period expiring by reference to an event or circumstance), not being a termination immediately after which the employment is renewed on the same terms; and

    (b) to the termination of that person's employment by any act of his (including the giving of notice) in circumstances such that he is entitled to terminate it without notice by reason of the conduct of the employer.

(6) This section applies only in relation to employment at an establishment in Great Britain.

DISABILITY DISCRIMINATION ACT 1995 (as amended) – s.4

➡ EQUALITY ACT 2010 – s.39, s.40

Dismissal

British Sugar plc v Kirker   **[1998] IRLR 624 EAT**

An employment tribunal was entitled to take into account the history of the claimant's treatment prior to the Disability Discrimination Act coming into force by way of background in order to determine whether or not old perceptions of the claimant's value as an employee, based on his disability, were carried through to when he was assessed for redundancy selection purposes.

H J Heinz Co Ltd v Kenrick   **[2000] IRLR 144 EAT**

An employer who does not adequately consider alternative employment or shorter hours may find that the dismissal is held not to be justified, on the basis that a reason for the dismissal such as continuing incapability would not be material to the circumstances so long as part-time or lighter duties might have fitted the bill.

Fu v London Borough of Camden   **[2001] IRLR 186 EAT**

In deciding whether an employer was justified in dismissing rather than making reasonable adjustments on the basis that they would not enable the employee off work ill to return to work, an employment tribunal should arrive at its conclusion by examining the adjustments proposed and the extent to which they could have overcome the medical symptoms which otherwise prevented the employee's return to work.

Kent County Council v Mingo   **[2000] IRLR 90 EAT**

The employers unlawfully discriminated against the claimant when, notwithstanding his disability, they treated him less favourably for the purposes of redeployment than employees at risk of redundancy. A redeployment policy of giving preferential treatment to redundant or potentially redundant employees does not adequately reflect the statutory duty on employers under the Disability Discrimination Act, since it means that those with disabilities are relatively handicapped in the redeployment system.

Nottinghamshire County Council v Meikle   **[2004] IRLR 703 CA**

A persistent failure by a local authority to carry out reasonable adjustments amounted to a fundamental breach of the obligation of trust and confidence entitling the employee to claim that she was constructively dismissed.

Discrimination against contract workers

(1) It is unlawful for a principal, in relation to contract work, to discriminate against a disabled person who is a contract worker (a "disabled contract worker") –

(a) in the terms on which he allows him to do that work;

(b) by not allowing him to do it or continue to do it;

(c) in the way he affords him access to any benefits or by refusing or deliberately omitting to afford him access to them; or

(d) by subjecting him to any other detriment.

(6) Section 4A applies to any principal, in relation to contract work, as if he were, or would be, the employer of the disabled contract worker and as if any contract worker supplied to do work for him were an employee of his.

(7) However, for the purposes of s.4A as applied by subsection (6), a principal is not required to take a step in relation to a disabled contract worker if under that section the disabled contract worker's employer is required to take the step in relation to him.

(9) In this section –

"principal" means a person ("A") who makes work available for doing by individuals who are employed by another person who supplies them under a contract made with A;

"contract work" means work so made available; and

"contract worker" means any individual who is supplied to the principal under such a contract.

DISABILITY DISCRIMINATION ACT 1995 (as amended) – s.4B

➡ **EQUALITY ACT 2010 – s.41, Sch. 8**

Abbey Life Assurance Co Ltd v Tansell   **[2000] IRLR 387 CA**

[Section 4B] does not require a direct contractual relationship between the employer and the principal. It applies to a case where there is no direct contract between the person making the work available and the employer of the individual who is supplied to do that work. The statutory definition only requires the supply of the individual to be "under a contract made with 'A'." It does not expressly stipulate who is to be the party who contracts with 'A'. Although in many cases the contract with the end-user will be made by the employer who supplies the individual, the definition in s.4B does not require that to be the case.

Abbey Life Assurance Co Ltd v Tansell   **[2000] IRLR 387 CA**

A claimant, who was employed by a company which supplied him to an agency, which in turn supplied him to an end-user, was a "contract worker" within the meaning of s.4B who could present a claim against the end-user as being a "principal".

REMEDIES

(1) A complaint by any person that another person –

(a) has discriminated against him in a way which is unlawful under this Part, or

(b) is, by virtue of section 57 or 58, to be treated as having discriminated against him in such a way,

may be presented to an employment tribunal.

(2) Where an employment tribunal finds that a complaint presented to it under this section is well-founded, it shall take such of the following steps as it considers just and equitable –

(a) making a declaration as to the rights of the complainant and the respondent in relation to the matters to which the complaint relates;

(b) ordering the respondent to pay compensation to the complainant;

(c) recommending that the respondent take, within a specified period, action appearing to the tribunal to be reasonable, in all the circumstances of the case, for the purpose of obviating or reducing the adverse effect on the complainant of any matter to which the complaint relates.

(3) Where a tribunal orders compensation under subsection (2)(b), the amount of the compensation shall be calculated by applying the principles applicable to the calculation of damages in claims in tort or (in Scotland) in reparation for breach of statutory duty.

(4) For the avoidance of doubt it is hereby declared that compensation in respect of discrimination in a way which is unlawful under this Part may include compensation for injury to feelings whether or not it includes compensation under any other head.

(5) If the respondent to a complaint fails, without reasonable justification, to comply with a recommendation made by an employment tribunal under subsection (2)(c) the tribunal may, if it thinks it just and equitable to do so –

(a) increase the amount of compensation required to be paid to the complainant in respect of the complaint, where an order was made under subsection (2)(b); or

(b) make an order under subsection (2)(b).

DISABILITY DISCRIMINATION ACT 1995 (as amended) – s.17A

➡ **EQUALITY ACT 2010 – s.119, s.124**

Compensation

Buxton v Equinox Design Ltd   **[1999] IRLR 158 EAT**

An employment tribunal's finding that the period of loss should be one year for an employee with multiple sclerosis who was dismissed lacked a sufficient evidential basis, since it involved making a finding as to the outcome of a risk assessment in the context of a disease which has variable effects. Without medical evidence, the tribunal was not in a position to say what the outcome would be.

HM Prison Service v   [2005] IRLR 568 CA
Beart (No.2)

An unfair dismissal does not break the chain of causation, thereby terminating the liability for the earlier wrong of disability discrimination so that all further losses have to be assessed under the unfair dismissal regime with its statutory cap on compensation. That would be contrary to the principle that a defendant cannot rely on its own further wrong to break the chain of causation.

Sheffield Forgemasters v   [2009] IRLR 192 EAT
  International Ltd
Fox

Receipt of incapacity benefit does not preclude a claimant from obtaining compensation for loss of earnings in respect of the same period, since the fact that they have obtained incapacity benefit does not in itself show that they were not able to work and earn money during that period.

Da'bell v   [2010] IRLR 19 EAT
NSPCC

The guidelines for awarding compensation for injury to feelings set out by the Court of Appeal in *Chief Constable of West Yorkshire Police v Vento (No.2)* would be updated in line with inflation so that the bottom band would be increased from £5,000 to £6,000; the top of the middle band would be increased from £15,000 to £18,000; and the top of the higher band would be increased from £25,000 to £30,000.

Da'bell v   [2010] IRLR 19 EAT
NSPCC

Disputes about the placement within a band of an award are likely to be about fact and impression. They are more likely to raise questions of law if they are about placement in the wrong band or at the extremes.

Al Jumard v   [2008] IRLR 345 EAT
Clywd Leisure Ltd

It would not necessarily be wrong in an appropriate case for a tribunal to fix a separate sum for the injury to feelings flowing from acts of direct disability discrimination and the failure to make reasonable adjustments respectively.

Purves v   [2003] IRLR 420 Sheriff Principal
Joydisc Ltd

Damages for injury to feelings should be awarded in a case of discrimination in relation to goods, facilities and services on the same basis as in employment tribunal cases. Whether the ground of discrimination is race or sex or disability, and whether the context is the field of employment or some other field, a person may suffer injury to his or her feelings as a result. It would be erroneous to assume that the measure of damages in an action based on one ground or in one context must necessarily always be greater or smaller than in an action based on some other ground or in another context. The precise ground and context of the act of discrimination in respect of which damages are claimed are not of primary importance.

4. RELIGION OR BELIEF DISCRIMINATION

MEANING OF RELIGION OR BELIEF

(1) In these Regulations –
(a) "religion" means any religion,
(b) "belief" means any religious or philosophical belief,
(c) a reference to religion includes a reference to lack of religion, and
(d) a reference to belief includes a reference to lack of belief.

EMPLOYMENT EQUALITY (RELIGION OR BELIEF)
REGULATIONS 2003 – reg. 2
➡ **EQUALITY ACT 2010 – s.10**

Eweida v   **[2009] IRLR 78 EAT**
British Airways plc
The protection afforded to those holding a religious or philosophical belief is a broad one. The belief can be intensely personal and subjective. Accordingly, it is not necessary for a belief to be shared by others in order for it to be a religious belief, nor need a specific belief be a mandatory requirement of an established religion for it to qualify as a religious belief.

Grainger plc v   **[2010] IRLR 4 EAT**
Nicholson
There must be some limits placed upon the definition of "philosophical belief" for the purposes of the Religion or Belief Regulations. These are that the belief must be genuinely held; it must be a belief and not an opinion or viewpoint based on the present state of information available; it must be a belief as to a weighty and substantial aspect of human life and behaviour; it must attain a certain level of cogency, seriousness, cohesion and importance; and it must be worthy of respect in a democratic society, be not incompatible with human dignity and not conflict with the fundamental rights of others. Moreover, in order for a belief to be protected, it is necessary for it to have a similar status or cogency to a religious belief. It is not a bar, however, to a philosophical belief being protected that it is a one-off belief, not shared by others.

McClintock v   **[2008] IRLR 29 EAT**
Department for Constitutional Affairs
To constitute a belief there must be a religious or philosophical viewpoint in which one actually believes. It is not enough to have an opinion based on some real or perceived logic or based on information or lack of information available.

Grainger plc v   **[2010] IRLR 4 EAT**
Nicholson
There is nothing in the make-up of a philosophical belief which would disqualify a belief based on a political philosophy. Therefore, belief in the political philosophies of socialism, Marxism, communism or free-market capitalism might qualify.

Grainger plc v   **[2010] IRLR 4 EAT**
Nicholson
A belief in man-made climate change and the environment is capable, if genuinely held, of being a "philosophical belief" for the purposes of the Regulations.

EXCLUSIONS OR EXCEPTIONS

Meaning of "employment"

(3)..."employment" *means employment under a contract of service or apprenticeship or a contract personally to do any work, and related expressions shall be construed accordingly.*

EMPLOYMENT EQUALITY (RELIGION OR BELIEF) REGULATIONS 2003 – reg.2
➡ **EQUALITY ACT 2010 – s.83**

Jivraj v   **[2010] IRLR 797 CA**
Hashwani

The Religion or Belief Regulations apply to the appointment of an arbitrator, because the relationship is normally supported by a contract of some kind. Since an arbitrator (or any professional person) contracts to do work personally, the provision of his services falls within the definition of "employment", and it follows that the person making the appointment must be an employer within the meaning of reg. 6(1).

DIRECT DISCRIMINATION

(1) For the purposes of these Regulations, a person ("A") discriminates against another person ("B") if – (a) on grounds of religion or belief, A treats B less favourably than he treats or would treat other persons;

(3) A comparison of B's case with that of another person under para. (1) must be such that the relevant circumstances in the one case are the same, or not materially different, in the other.

EMPLOYMENT EQUALITY (RELIGION OR BELIEF) REGULATIONS 2003 – reg. 3
➡ **EQUALITY ACT 2010 – s.13, s.23**

London Borough of Islington v   **[2009] IRLR 154 EAT**
Ladele

There will be unlawful discrimination where the prohibited ground contributes to an act or decision even though it is not the sole or principal reason for the act or decision. It follows that there will inevitably be circumstances where an employee has a claim for unlawful discrimination even though he would have been subject to precisely the same treatment even if there had been no discrimination, because the prohibited ground merely reinforces a decision that would have been taken for lawful reasons.

London Borough of Islington v   **[2009] IRLR 154 EAT**
Ladele

It cannot constitute direct discrimination to treat all employees in precisely the same way.

McFarlane v   **[2010] IRLR 872 CA**
Relate Avon Ltd

There is an important distinction between the law's protection of the right to hold and express a belief and the law's protection of that belief's substance or content. The common law and Article 9 of the European Convention on Human Rights offer vigorous protection of every person's right to hold and express his or her beliefs. They do not offer any protection whatever of the substance or content of those beliefs on the ground only that they are based on religious precepts.

McFarlane v   **[2010] IRLR 196 EAT**
Relate Avon Ltd

The right to hold religious beliefs and the right to manifest them in conduct are not inseparable. There will be cases in which the fact that the employee's motivation for the conduct in question may be found in his wish to manifest his religious belief does not mean that that belief is the ground of the employer's action.

Statutory comparison

London Borough of Islington v Ladele
[2009] IRLR 154 EAT

The proper hypothetical or statutory comparator for a registrar claiming that she was discriminated against on grounds of religion or belief by being disciplined for refusing to conduct civil partnerships was another registrar who refused to conduct civil partnership work because of antipathy to the concept of same-sex relationships but which antipathy was not based upon religious belief. If such a person would equally have been required to carry out civil partnership duties and would have been subject to the similar disciplinary process if they had refused, there would be no direct discrimination on grounds of religion or belief.

INDIRECT DISCRIMINATION

(1) For the purposes of these Regulations, a person ('A') discriminates against another person ('B') if –

(b) A applies to B a provision, criterion or practice which he applies or would apply equally to persons not of the same religion or belief as B, but –

(i) which puts or would put persons of the same religion or belief as B at a particular disadvantage when compared with other persons,

(ii) which puts B at that disadvantage, and

(iii) which A cannot show to be a proportionate means of achieving a legitimate aim.

EMPLOYMENT EQUALITY (RELIGION OR BELIEF) REGULATIONS 2003 – reg. 3
➡ **EQUALITY ACT 2010 – s.19**

Disproportionate impact

Eweida v British Airways plc
[2010] IRLR 322 CA

The test of indirect discrimination requires that some identifiable section of a workforce, quite possibly a small one, must be shown to suffer a particular disadvantage which the claimant shares. Solitary disadvantage is not sufficient.

Eweida v British Airways plc
[2009] IRLR 78 EAT

In order for indirect discrimination to be established, it must be possible to make some general statements which would be true about a religious group such that an employer ought reasonably to be able to appreciate that any particular provision may have a disparate adverse impact on the group.

Eweida v British Airways plc
[2010] IRLR 322 CA

The purpose of the phrase "would put persons ... at a particular disadvantage" is to include in the disadvantaged group not only employees to whom the condition has actually been applied but those to whom it potentially applies.

Justifiable

London Borough of Islington v Ladele
[2009] IRLR 154 EAT

The proportionality test is not to be determined by a vague attempt to balance irreconcilable positions. The focus should be on whether the means adopted are a proportionate way of achieving a legitimate aim.

Eweida v   [2010] IRLR 322 CA
British Airways plc
BA's staff dress code, which forbade the wearing of visible neck adornment and so prevented a Christian from wearing with her uniform a small, visible cross, was not disproportionate in circumstances in which the employee's objection to the dress code was entirely personal, neither arising from any doctrine of her faith nor interfering with her observance of it, and never raised by any other employee.

Ladele v   [2010] IRLR 211 CA
London Borough of Islington
The fact that a Christian registrar's refusal to perform civil partnerships was based on her religious views of marriage could not justify the conclusion that the local authority should not be allowed to implement its aim to the full, namely that all registrars should perform civil partnerships as part of its Dignity for All policy. The claimant was employed in a public job and was working for a public authority; she was being required to perform a purely secular task, which was being treated as part of her job; her refusal to perform that task involved discriminating against gay people in the course of that job; she was being asked to perform the task because of the council's Dignity for All policy, whose laudable aim was to avoid, or at least minimise, discrimination both among the council's employees and as between it (and its employees) and those in the community they served. The claimant's refusal was causing offence to at least two of her gay colleagues; her objection was based on her view of marriage, which was not a core part of her religion; and the council's requirement in no way prevented her from worshipping as she wished.

McFarlane v   [2010] IRLR 872 CA
Relate Avon Ltd
A requirement that counsellors should be prepared to make their services available without differentiation to same-sex and heterosexual couples was justified, notwithstanding that it put those holding traditional Christian views at a disadvantage. There was no real difference between the position of a body such as Relate and the situation considered in *Ladele*, in which the EAT held that an employer may properly insist on all employees participating in the services in question, even if to do so is in conflict with their religious beliefs, because to do otherwise would be inconsistent with the principle which it regards as fundamental to its own ethos.

HARASSMENT

(1) For the purposes of these Regulations, a person ("A") subjects another person ("B") to harassment where, on grounds of religion or belief, A engages in unwanted conduct which has the purpose or effect of –
> *(a) violating B's dignity; or*
> *(b) creating an intimidating, hostile, degrading, humiliating or offensive environment for B.*

(2) Conduct shall be regarded as having the effect specified in para. (1)(a) or (b) only if, having regard to all the circumstances, including in particular the perception of B, it should reasonably be considered as having that effect.
EMPLOYMENT EQUALITY (RELIGION OR BELIEF) REGULATIONS 2003 – reg. 5
➡ **EQUALITY ACT 2010 – s.26**

Saini v   [2009] IRLR 74 EAT
All Saints Haque Centre
The prohibition on harassment on grounds of religion or belief in reg. 5(1)(b) will be breached not only where an employee is harassed on the grounds that he holds certain religious or other relevant beliefs but also where he is harassed because someone else holds certain religious or other beliefs. To use an employee in any manner in the implementation of a discriminatory policy is caught if the effect on the employee falls within any of the descriptions set out in reg. 5(1)(b).

EXCLUSIONS AND EXCEPTIONS

Genuine occupational requirements

(1) In relation to discrimination falling within reg. 3 (discrimination on grounds of religion or belief) –

(a) reg. 6(1)(a) or (c) does not apply to any employment;

(b) reg. 6(2)(b) or (c) does not apply to promotion or transfer to, or training for, any employment; and

(c) reg. 6(2)(d) does not apply to dismissal from any employment,

where para. (2) or (3) applies.

(2) This paragraph applies where, having regard to the nature of the employment or the context in which it is carried out –

(a) being of a particular religion or belief is a genuine and determining occupational requirement;

(b) it is proportionate to apply that requirement in the particular case; and

(c) either –

(i) the person to whom that requirement is applied does not meet it, or

(ii) the employer is not satisfied, and in all the circumstances it is reasonable for him not to be satisfied, that that person meets it,

and this paragraph applies whether or not the employer has an ethos based on religion or belief.

(3) This paragraph applies where an employer has an ethos based on religion or belief and, having regard to that ethos and to the nature of the employment or the context in which it is carried out –

(a) being of a particular religion or belief is a genuine occupational requirement for the job;

(b) it is proportionate to apply that requirement in the particular case; and

(c) either –

(i) the person to whom that requirement is applied does not meet it, or

(ii) the employer is not satisfied, and in all the circumstances it is reasonable for him not to be satisfied, that that person meets it.

EMPLOYMENT EQUALITY (RELIGION OR BELIEF) REGULATIONS 2003 – reg. 7
➡ **EQUALITY ACT 2010 – Sch. 9**

Glasgow City Council v McNab   [2007] IRLR 476 EAT

The local education authority was not entitled to have recourse to the genuine occupational requirement exception in reg. 7(3) in respect of a teaching post in a maintained Roman Catholic school because they could not show that they were an employer who had "an ethos based on religion or belief". An education authority does not have a religious ethos. The fact that it operates a statutory system under which it enables denominations to advance their ethos through schools maintained by it, does not mean that they espouse the same ethos at all.

Glasgow City Council v McNab   [2007] IRLR 476 EAT

Had it been intended that an employer could qualify for the protection afforded by reg. 7(3) if only part of their organisation had a religious ethos, it would have been expected that such a right would have been expressly stated by the legislature.

5. SEXUAL ORIENTATION DISCRIMINATION

EC SEXUAL ORIENTATION DISCRIMINATION LAW

Maruko v   **[2008] IRLR 450 ECJ**
Versorgungsanstalt der Deutschen Bühnen
Recital 22 of the preamble to the Framework Employment Equality Directive, which provides that the Directive is "without prejudice to national laws on marital status and the benefits dependent thereon", cannot affect application of the Directive.

Maruko v   **[2008] IRLR 450 ECJ**
Versorgungsanstalt der Deutschen Bühnen
The Framework Employment Equality Directive precludes legislation under which, after the death of his life partner, the surviving partner does not receive a survivor's benefit equivalent to that granted to a surviving spouse.

EXCLUSIONS AND EXCEPTIONS

Genuine occupational requirements

(1) In relation to discrimination falling within reg.3 (discrimination on grounds of sexual orientation) –

(a) reg. 6(1)(a) or (c) does not apply to any employment;

(b) reg. 6(2)(b) or (c) does not apply to promotion or transfer to, or training for, any employment; and

(c) reg. 6(2)(d) does not apply to dismissal from any employment,

where para. (2) or (3) applies.

(2) This paragraph applies where, having regard to the nature of the employment or the context in which it is carried out –

(a) being of a particular sexual orientation is a genuine and determining occupational requirement;

(b) it is proportionate to apply that requirement in the particular case; and

(c) either –

(i) the person to whom that requirement is applied does not meet it, or

(ii) the employer is not satisfied, and in all the circumstances it is reasonable for him not to be satisfied, that that person meets it,

and this paragraph applies whether or not the employment is for purposes of an organised religion.

EMPLOYMENT EQUALITY (SEXUAL ORIENTATION)
REGULATIONS 2003 – reg. 7
➡ EQUALITY ACT 2010 – Sch. 9

R (on the application of Amicus –   **[2004] IRLR 430 HC**
MSF section) v
Secretary of State for Trade and Industry
Regulation 7(2) is compatible with the Framework Employment Directive, even though the exception applies not only where a person does not in fact meet the requirement as to sexual orientation but also, by virtue of reg. 7(2)(c)(ii), where it is "reasonable" for the employer "not to be satisfied" that the person meets it. The derogation in Article 4(1) of the Directive, which refers to a difference of treatment "based on a characteristic related to" sexual orientation, is wide enough to cover reg. 7(2), even allowing for the need to construe derogations strictly. Regulation 7(2)(c)(ii) has a sensible rationale. In those cases where being of a particular sexual orientation is a genuine and determining occupational requirement, it cannot be right that an employer, having asked the plainly permissible initial question whether a person meets that requirement, is bound in all circumstances to accept at face value the answer given or is precluded from forming his own assessment if no answer is given. The requirement of reasonableness ensures that decisions cannot lawfully be based on mere assumptions or social stereotyping.

Organised religion

(3) This paragraph applies where –

(a) the employment is for purposes of an organised religion;

(b) the employer applies a requirement related to sexual orientation –

(i) so as to comply with the doctrines of the religion, or

(ii) because of the nature of the employment and the context in which it is carried out, so as to avoid conflicting with the strongly held religious convictions of a significant number of the religion's followers; and

(c) either –

(i) the person to whom that requirement is applied does not meet it, or

(ii) the employer is not satisfied, and in all the circumstances it is reasonable for him not to be satisfied, that that person meets it.

EMPLOYMENT EQUALITY (SEXUAL ORIENTATION) REGULATIONS 2003 – reg. 7

➡ **EQUALITY ACT 2010 – Sch. 9**

R (on the application of Amicus –   [2004] IRLR 430 HC
    MSF section) v
Secretary of State for Trade and Industry
Regulation 7(3) is compatible with the Framework Employment Directive. The exception in reg. 7(3) is very narrow. It has to be construed strictly since it is a derogation from the principle of equal treatment; and it has to be construed purposively so as to ensure, so far as possible, compatibility with the Directive. When its terms are considered in light of those interpretative principles, they can be seen to afford an exception only in very limited circumstances. The fact that the exception applies "for the purposes of an organised religion" is an important initial limitation since that is a narrower expression than "for the purposes of a religious organisation" or "an ethos based on religion or belief" as used in the Regulations relating to discrimination on grounds of religion or belief. Thus, employment as a teacher in a faith school is likely to be for the "purposes of a religious organisation" but not for the "purposes of an organised religion".

R (on the application of Amicus –   [2004] IRLR 430 HC
    MSF section) v
Secretary of State for Trade and Industry
The condition in reg. 7(3)(b)(i) that the employer must apply the requirement "so as to comply with the doctrines of the religion" is an objective test whereby it must be shown that employment of a person not meeting the requirement would be incompatible with the doctrines of the religion. That is very narrow in scope.

R (on the application of Amicus –   [2004] IRLR 430 HC
    MSF section) v
Secretary of State for Trade and Industry
The condition in reg. 7(3)(b)(ii), which refers to an employer applying a requirement related to sexual orientation "because of the nature of the employment and the context in which it is carried out, so as to avoid conflicting with the strongly held religious convictions of a significant number of the religion's followers", requires careful examination of the precise nature of the employment and is to be read as an objective, not subjective, test. It will be a very far from easy test to satisfy in practice

R (on the application of Amicus –   [2004] IRLR 430 HC
    MSF section) v
Secretary of State for Trade and Industry
The protection against discrimination on grounds of sexual orientation relates as much to the manifestation of that orientation in the form of sexual behaviour as it does to sexuality as such.

HARASSMENT

(1) For the purposes of these Regulations, a person ("A") subjects another person ("B") to harassment where, on grounds of religion or belief, A engages in unwanted conduct which has the purpose or effect of –

(a) violating B's dignity; or

(b) creating an intimidating, hostile, degrading, humiliating or offensive environment for B.

(2) Conduct shall be regarded as having the effect specified in para. (1)(a) or (b) only if, having regard to all the circumstances, including in particular the perception of B, it should reasonably be considered as having that effect.

EMPLOYMENT EQUALITY (SEXUAL ORIENTATION)
REGULATIONS 2003 – reg. 5
➡ **EQUALITY ACT 2010 – s.26**

English v   **[2009] IRLR 206 CA**
Thomas Sanderson Blinds Ltd

A person who is taunted by "homophobic banter" is subject to harassment on the ground of sexual orientation within the meaning of reg. 5, even though he is not gay; he is not perceived or assumed to be gay by his colleagues; and he accepts they do not believe him to be gay. Harassment is on grounds of sexual orientation where the claimant's sexual orientation, whether real or supposed, is the basis of the harassment directed at him or her.

HM Land Registry v   **[2010] IRLR 583 EAT**
Grant

If an employment tribunal comes to the conclusion that a gay employee has been "outed" against his wishes to those whom he would rather not know of his orientation, that fact alone may well constitute an act of sexual orientation discrimination or harassment. However, an employment tribunal which found that making a gay employee's sexual orientation known to other employees was unlawful harassment which had the effect of creating a humiliating working environment for him erred by failing to recognise the implications of the fact that the employee had "come out" in his last posting at another office and that the manager knew this.

DISCRIMINATION BY EMPLOYERS

(1) It is unlawful for an employer, in relation to employment by him at an establishment in Great Britain, to discriminate against a person –

(a) in the arrangements he makes for the purpose of determining to whom he should offer employment;

(b) in the terms on which he offers that person employment; or

(c) by refusing to offer, or deliberately not offering, him employment.

(2) It is unlawful for an employer, in relation to a person whom he employs at an establishment in Great Britain, to discriminate against that person –

(a) in the terms of employment which he affords him;

(b) in the opportunities which he affords him for promotion, a transfer, training, or receiving any other benefit;

(c) by refusing to afford him, or deliberately not affording him, any such opportunity; or

(d) by dismissing him, or subjecting him to any other detriment.

EMPLOYMENT EQUALITY (SEXUAL ORIENTATION)
REGULATIONS 2003 – reg. 6
➡ **EQUALITY ACT 2010 – s.39**

Access to benefits

Benefits defined by reference to marital status

Nothing in Part II or III shall render unlawful anything which prevents or restricts access to a benefit by reference to marital status.

EMPLOYMENT EQUALITY (SEXUAL ORIENTATION)
REGULATIONS 2003 – reg. 25

R (on the application of Amicus –   **[2004] IRLR 430 HC**
MSF section) v
Secretary of State for Trade and Industry

Regulation 25, which has the effect that employment benefits defined by reference to marital status, such as a surviving spouse's pension, are not prohibited by the Regulations, reflects a limitation in the scope of the Directive itself. Recital 22 to the Directive, which says that "this Directive is without prejudice to national laws on marital status and the benefits dependent thereon", is of general application, covering all benefits that are dependent on marital status. It is not limited to State benefits.

Institutions of further and higher education

(1) It is unlawful, in relation to an educational establishment to which this regulation applies, for the governing body of that establishment to discriminate against a person –

    (a) in the terms on which it offers to admit him to the establishment as a student;

    (b) by refusing or deliberately not accepting an application for his admission to the establishment as a student; or

    (c) where he is a student of the establishment –

        (i) in the way it affords him access to any benefits,

        (ii) by refusing or deliberately not affording him access to them, or

        (iii) by excluding him from the establishment or subjecting him to any other detriment.

(3) Paragraph (1) does not apply if the discrimination only concerns training which would help fit a person for employment which, by virtue of reg. 7 (exception for genuine occupational requirement etc), the employer could lawfully refuse to offer the person in question.

**EMPLOYMENT EQUALITY (SEXUAL ORIENTATION)
REGULATIONS 2003 – reg. 20
➥ EQUALITY ACT 2010 – Sch. 12**

R (on the application of Amicus –   **[2004] IRLR 430 HC**
  MSF section) v
Secretary of State for Trade and Industry
For training to come within the exception in reg. 20(3), it must be training that would only help fit a person for a relevant employment. If training has a broader purpose, as in the case of a degree course in theology, it cannot come within the exception. The expression "would help fit ... for employment" is likewise to be strictly construed, as referring to vocational training rather than to training of a more general nature. Construed in that way, the exception has a narrow scope, being tied closely to training directed specifically and solely towards an employment to which an occupational requirement can lawfully be applied.

6. AGE DISCRIMINATION

EC AGE DISCRIMINATION LAW

(1) For the purposes of this Directive, the "principle of equal treatment" shall mean that there shall be no direct or indirect discrimination whatsoever on any of the grounds referred to in Article 1.

FRAMEWORK EMPLOYMENT EQUALITY
DIRECTIVE 2000/78 – Article 2

Within the limits of the areas of competence conferred on the Community, this Directive shall apply to all persons, as regards both the public and private sectors, including public bodies, in relation to:

(a) conditions for access to employment, to self-employment or to occupation, including selection criteria and recruitment conditions, whatever the branch of activity and at all levels of the professional hierarchy, including promotion;

(b) access to all types and to all levels of vocational guidance, vocational training, advanced vocational training and retraining, including practical work experience;

(c) employment and working conditions, including dismissals and pay;

(d) membership of, and involvement in, an organisation of workers or employers, or any organisation whose members carry on a particular profession, including the benefits provided for by such organisations.

FRAMEWORK EMPLOYMENT EQUALITY
DIRECTIVE 2000/78 – Article 3

(1) Notwithstanding Article 2(2), Member States may provide that differences of treatment on grounds of age shall not constitute discrimination, if, within the context of national law, they are objectively and reasonably justified by a legitimate aim, including legitimate employment policy, labour market and vocational training objectives, and if the means of achieving that aim are appropriate and necessary.

Such differences of treatment may include, among others:

(a) the setting of special conditions on access to employment and vocational training, employment and occupation, including dismissal and remuneration conditions, for young people, older workers and persons with caring responsibilities in order to promote their vocational integration or ensure their protection;

(b) the fixing of minimum conditions of age, professional experience or seniority in service for access to employment or to certain advantages linked to employment;

(c) the fixing of a maximum age for recruitment which is based on the training requirements of the post in question or the need for a reasonable period of employment before retirement.

FRAMEWORK EMPLOYMENT EQUALITY
DIRECTIVE 2000/78 – Article 6

Kücüdeveci v   **[2010] IRLR 346 ECJ**
Swedex GmbH & Co LG
The principle of non-discrimination on grounds of age is a general principle of EU law. The Framework Employment Equality Directive 2000/78 merely gives expression to, but does not lay down, the principle of equal treatment in employment and occupation. Accordingly, it is for the national court, faced with a national provision falling within the scope of EU law which it considers to be incompatible with that principle, and which cannot be interpreted in conformity with that principle, to disapply that provision.

Occupational requirements

(1) Notwithstanding Article 2(1) and (2), member states may provide that a difference of treatment which is based on a characteristic related to any of the grounds referred to in Article 1 shall not constitute discrimination where, by reason of the nature of the particular occupational activities concerned or of the context in which they are carried out, such a characteristic constitutes a genuine and determining occupational requirement, provided that the objective is legitimate and the requirement is proportionate.

Wolf v   **[2010] IRLR 244 ECJ**
Stadt Frankfurt am Main
German national legislation which sets a maximum age of 30 for recruitment to intermediate career posts in the fire service was justifiable as a genuine and determining occupational requirement under Article 4(1) of the Framework Employment Equality Directive 2000/78. The maximum age was appropriate to the objective of ensuring the operational capacity and proper functioning of the fire service and did not go beyond what was necessary to achieve that objective. Possession of especially high physical capacities is a genuine and determining occupational requirement for such a post in the fire service. This need is related to age in that some of the tasks, such as fighting fires or rescuing persons, can be performed only by young employees. Scientific data shows that respiratory capacity, musculature and endurance diminish with age. Very few employees over age 45 have sufficient physical capacity to perform fire-fighting duties. Accordingly, recruitment at an older age than 30 would have the consequence that too large a number of employees could not be assigned to the most physically demanding duties. Similarly, such recruitment would not allow the employees thus recruited to be assigned to those duties for a sufficiently long period.

R (on the application of the   **[2009] IRLR 373 ECJ**
National Council on Ageing) v
Secretary of State for Business, Enterprise
and Regulatory Reform
The scope of the Framework Employment Equality Directive 2000/78 extends to national rules, such as those in the Age Discrimination Regulations, which permit employers to dismiss employees aged 65 or over by reason of retirement.

Direct discrimination

Palacios de la Villa v   [2007] IRLR 989 ECJ
Cortefiel Servicios SA

National legislation under which the fact that a worker has reached the retirement age laid down by the legislation leads to automatic termination of his employment contract must be regarded as directly imposing less favourable treatment for all workers who have reached that age as compared with all other persons in the labour force. Such legislation therefore establishes a difference in treatment directly based on age within the meaning of Article 2 of Directive 2000/78.

Justification

R (on the application of the   [2009] IRLR 373 ECJ
   National Council on Ageing) v
Secretary of State for Business, Enterprise
   and Regulatory Reform

Article 6(1) of Directive 2000/78 does not require a member state to draw up, in their measures of transposition, a specific list of the differences in treatment which may be justified by a legitimate aim. However, Article 6(1) offers the option to derogate from the principle of prohibiting discrimination on grounds of age only in respect of measures justified by legitimate social policy objectives, such as those related to employment policy, the labour market or vocational training. By their public interest nature, those legitimate aims are distinguishable from purely individual reasons particular to the employer's situation, such as cost reduction or improving competitiveness, although it cannot be ruled out that a national rule may recognise, in the pursuit of those legitimate aims, a certain degree of flexibility for employers.

R (on the application of the   [2009] IRLR 373 ECJ
   National Council on Ageing) v
Secretary of State for Business, Enterprise
   and Regulatory Reform

In choosing the means capable of achieving their social policy objectives, member states enjoy broad discretion. However, that discretion cannot have the effect of frustrating the implementation of the principle of non-discrimination on grounds of age. Mere generalisations concerning the capacity of a specific measure to contribute to employment policy, labour market or vocational training objectives are not enough to show that the aim of that measure is capable of justifying derogation from that principle and do not constitute evidence on the basis of which it could reasonably be considered that the means chosen are suitable for achieving that aim. Article 6(1) imposes on member states, notwithstanding their broad discretion in matters of social policy, the burden of establishing to a high standard of proof the legitimacy of the aim pursued.

R (on the application of Age UK) v   [2009] IRLR 1017 HC
Secretary of State for Business,
   Innovation & Skills

In a challenge to the legality and sufficiency of a transposition of EU legislation, the question is principally determined by reference to the social policy aims identified by the Government at the time of transposition. Subsequent developments may show that the Government is required to review those aims and their impact upon the class who suffer equal treatment, but just as there is a broad measure of discretion as to the adoption of social policy aims, and the best means of giving effect to them, so there is a broad measure of discretion afforded to governments as to when those aims and the methods of giving effect to them need to be reviewed.

Kücüdeveci v   [2010] IRLR 346 ECJ
Swedex GmbH & Co LG

EU law precludes national legislation which provides that periods of employment completed by an employee before reaching the age of 25 are not taken into account in calculating the notice period for dismissal. Although the aim of the legislation is to afford employers greater flexibility in dismissing young workers, the legislation is not appropriate for achieving that aim since it applies to all employees who joined the undertaking before the age of 24, whatever their age at the time of dismissal.

Ingeniørforeningen i Danmark   [2010] EqLR 345 ECJ
   (acting for Andersen) v
Region Syddanmark

A national law which excluded workers from receipt of a severance allowance on dismissal in circumstances where they were entitled to claim a pension was incompatible with the Framework Employment Equality Directive 2000/78 because it entailed an unjustifiable difference of treatment directly on grounds of age. Although the aim pursued by the severance allowance of protecting workers with many years of service and helping them to find new employment fell within the category of legitimate labour market objectives, the measure went beyond what is necessary to attain the objective pursued in that it treated those who will actually receive an old-age pension from their employer in the same way as those who are eligible for such a pension. The measure actually made it more difficult for workers who are eligible for an old-age pension to exercise their right to work because they are not entitled to the severance allowance when seeking new employment.

Rosenbladt v   [2010] EqLR 365 ECJ
Gebäudereinigungsges mbH

Article 6(1) of the Framework Employment Equality Directive 2000/78 does not preclude legislation covering the cleaning industry in Germany which provides for automatic termination of employment contracts at age 65, the age at which an employee is eligible to retire and claim a retirement pension. The aims described by the German Government, based on the notion of sharing employment between generations, must, in principle, be regarded as "objectively and reasonably justifying" a difference in treatment on grounds of age such as that in this case. Those aims included the fact that the automatic termination of the employment contracts on reaching retirement age directly benefits young workers by making it easier for them to find work. The rights of older workers are adequately protected as most of them wish to stop working as soon as they are able to retire and the pension they receive serves as a replacement income once they lose their salary. The automatic termination of employment contracts also has the advantage of not requiring employers to dismiss employees on the ground that they are no longer capable of working, which may be humiliating for those who have reached an advanced age. It was not unreasonable for the German Government to take the view that the measure was appropriate and necessary to achieve these legitimate aims.

Palacios de la Villa v   [2007] IRLR 989 ECJ
Cortefiel Servicios SA

The aim of Spanish legislation providing for compulsory retirement at age 65 – to create opportunities for persons seeking employment – was a legitimate aim of social policy which, in principle, must be regarded as objectively and reasonably justifying a difference in treatment on grounds of age.

Palacios de la Villa v   [2007] IRLR 989 ECJ
Cortefiel Servicios SA

It could not reasonably be maintained that national legislation providing for compulsory retirement at age 65 was incompatible with the requirements of Directive 2000/78, where the member state reasonably took the view that the measure was appropriate and necessary in order to achieve a legitimate aim in the context of national employment policy, consisting of the promotion of full employment by facilitating access to the labour market, the legislation took account of the fact that the persons concerned were entitled to a retirement pension, and the legislation had the flexibility of allowing the social partners to opt by way of collective agreement to apply the compulsory retirement mechanism to take account of the specific features of the jobs in question.

Petersen v   [2010] IRLR 254 ECJ
Berufungsausschuss für Zahnärzte für
den Bezirk Westfalen-Lippe

A national measure setting a maximum age of 68 for practising as a panel dentist does not fall within the scope of Article 2(5) of the Framework Employment Equality Directive 2000/78, which provides that the Directive is without prejudice to measures which are "necessary ... for the protection of health", notwithstanding that the aim of the measure was to protect the health of patients against the decline in performance of those dentists after that age, in circumstances in which the age limit did not apply to dentists practising outside the panel system.

Petersen v   [2010] IRLR 254 ECJ
Berufungsausschuss für Zahnärzte für
den Bezirk Westfalen-Lippe

Article 6(1) of the Framework Employment Equality Directive 2000/78 does not preclude a national measure in Germany setting a maximum age of 68 for practising as a panel dentist where its aim was to share out employment opportunities among the generations, if, taking into account the situation in the labour market concerned, the measure was appropriate and necessary for achieving that aim. The difference in treatment on grounds of age resulting from such an aim may be regarded as objectively and reasonably justified by that aim, and the means of achieving that aim as appropriate and necessary, provided that there was a situation in which there was an excessive number of panel dentists or a latent risk that such a situation would occur.

EXCLUSIONS AND EXCEPTIONS

Pensions

(2) Member States may provide that the fixing for occupational social security schemes of ages for admission or entitlement to retirement or invalidity benefits, including the fixing under those schemes of different ages for employees or groups or categories of employees, and the use, in the context of such schemes, of age criteria in actuarial calculations, does not constitute discrimination on the grounds of age.

FRAMEWORK EMPLOYMENT DIRECTIVE 2000/78 – Article 6

R (on the application of Unison) v   **[2006] IRLR 926 HC**
First Secretary of State

The Government was entitled to conclude that the "rule of 85" in the Local Government Pension Scheme, which allowed scheme members to take early retirement and receive full benefits if the sum of their age and length of service was 85 years or more, was age discriminatory because it produced different outcomes where the distinguishing characteristic is age, and that it did not come within the derogation in Article 6(2) of the Framework Employment Directive. This stipulates that: "Member States may provide that the fixing for occupational social security schemes of ages for … entitlement to retirement … does not constitute discrimination on the grounds of age …" The rule of 85 adopted a formula which was based on two elements: age at retirement and the age at which the member joined the scheme. To fall within the derogation, the other criteria used to define the categories of employees cannot be ones that are themselves age-related, such as, in the present case, age at the date of joining the scheme. Accordingly, the Government was entitled to take the view that the rule of 85 had to be abolished in order to implement the Directive's prohibition on age discrimination.

Default retirement age

(1) This regulation applies in relation to an employee within the meaning of s.230(1) of the 1996 Act, a person in Crown employment, a relevant member of the House of Commons staff, and a relevant member of the House of Lords staff.

(2) Nothing in Part 2 or 3 shall render unlawful the dismissal of a person to whom this regulation applies at or over the age of 65 where the reason for the dismissal is retirement.

**EMPLOYMENT EQUALITY (AGE DISCRIMINATION)
REGULATIONS 2006, reg. 30
➡ EQUALITY ACT 2010 – Sch. 9**

R (on the application of Age UK) v   **[2009] IRLR 1017 HC**
Secretary of State for Business,
   Innovation & Skills

The decision to adopt a default retirement age was not a dis-proportionate way of giving effect to the social aim of labour market confidence. The idea of a default retirement age is not inherently arbitrary and illegitimately discriminatory but is the making of a social choice in the light of a number of social and economic factors which point either way as to the desirability of such a measure or its actual effect upon future employment practices.

R (on the application of Age UK) v   **[2009] IRLR 1017 HC**
Secretary of State for Business,
   Innovation & Skills

The selection of age 65 as the default retirement age in 2006 was not beyond the competence of the Government in applying the Directive, although if it had been adopted for the first time in 2009, or there had been no indication of an imminent review, the selection of age 65 would not have been proportionate in that it creates greater discriminatory effect than is necessary on a class of people who both are able to and want to continue in their employment.

DIRECT DISCRIMINATION

(1) For the purposes of these Regulations, a person ("A") discriminates against another person ("B") if – (a) on grounds of B's age, A treats B less favourably than he treats or would treat other persons ... and A cannot show the treatment ... to be a proportionate means of achieving a legitimate aim.

EMPLOYMENT EQUALITY (AGE DISCRIMINATION)
REGULATIONS 2006 – reg. 3
➡ EQUALITY ACT 2010 – s.13

R (on the application of Age UK) v   **[2009] IRLR 1017 HC**
Secretary of State for Business,
   Innovation & Skills
Regulation 3(1), which applies the test for justification of indirect discrimination to direct discrimination, is compatible with the Directive in that the Government had legitimate social policy concerns in protecting the integrity of the labour market by allowing employers flexibility in endeavouring to justify discriminatory treatment. Whereas the social aims that the Government relied on were ones in which the states enjoy a wide margin of appreciation, the individual employer justifying particular practices or treatment in reliance upon that social aim has a much more rigorous task.

MacCulloch v   **[2008] IRLR 846 EAT**
Imperial Chemical Industries plc
Where direct age discrimination is reflected in general rules or policies, the discriminatory effect of the measure will necessarily be greater than where a rule is cast in apparently neutral terms but has indirect discriminatory adverse effects. To that extent, direct discrimination may be harder to justify.

Seldon v   **[2009] IRLR 267 EAT**
Clarkson Wright & Jakes
In determining whether direct age discrimination is justified, tribunals should apply the normal principles of legitimate aim and proportionality. However, the overall discriminatory effect of a measure will necessarily be greater when there is direct as opposed to indirect discrimination and this will be a material factor to bear in mind when applying the test of proportionality.

Seldon v   **[2010] IRLR 865 CA**
Clarkson Wright & Jakes   **[2010] EqLR 89 CA**
In order to justify a mandatory retirement age provision, an employer does not need to have a "social policy objective". It would be inconsistent with upholding the justification for the derogation allowed by regs.3 and 30, that it is in the interests of young would-be employees and/or actual employees that employers should have a retirement age providing a greater likelihood of employment for young persons and reasonable prospects of promotion, to hold that a compulsory retirement age whose aim was consistent with

that social policy was not legitimate. If an employer's aim is to provide employment prospects for young people and encourage young people to seek employment by holding out good promotion prospects, that is consistent with the Government's social policy.

London Borough of Tower Hamlets v **[2009] IRLR 980 EAT**
Wooster
In a case of alleged direct discrimination (where the act complained of is not inherently discriminatory), the tribunal is required in principle to consider the "mental processes" of the relevant decision-maker(s). It is accordingly necessary to identify who the decision-maker(s) was or were.

Seldon v   **[2010] IRLR 865 CA**
Clarkson Wright & Jakes   **[2010] EqLR 89 CA**
A discriminatory measure may be justified by a legitimate aim other than that which was specified at the time when the measure was introduced. There is no difference in principle in this respect between indirect discrimination which can be justified and direct discrimination which in the context of age can also be justified.

Pulham v   **[2010] IRLR 184 EAT**
London Borough of Barking & Dagenham
It would be wrong in principle to exclude a defence of justification on the basis that the employer had not himself articulated or recognised the matters relied on at the time that he did the act complained of. The fact that a justification is produced long after the event may entitle a tribunal to treat it with some scepticism, but that depends on the circumstances of the particular case.

Seldon v   **[2010] IRLR 865 CA**
Clarkson Wright & Jakes   **[2010] EqLR 89 CA**
Once a clause or rule is justified, its application will need little justification.

Pulham v   **[2010] IRLR 184 EAT**
London Borough of Barking & Dagenham
The task of any tribunal in attempting to weigh the discriminatory impact of a particular measure against the cost of eliminating that impact is not an easy one, particularly since there is no objective measure common to both elements in the equation. The employer's budget is a relevant factor, but employers cannot automatically justify a failure to eliminate discrimination by allocating the costs of doing so to a particular budget and then declaring that budget to be exhausted.

Seldon v   **[2010] IRLR 865 CA**
Clarkson Wright & Jakes   **[2010] EqLR 89 CA**
An aim intended to produce a happy workplace is consistent with the Government's social policy objective for the Regulations. It may be thought better to have a cut-off age rather than force an assessment of a person's falling off in performance as they get older. It is a justification for having a cut-off age that people will be allowed to retire with dignity.

Seldon v   [2010] IRLR 865 CA
Clarkson Wright & Jakes   [2010] EqLR 89 CA

Recital 14 of the Directive contemplates the legitimacy of a retirement age and thus it cannot have envisaged that it would be impossible to justify one age because a different age would be less discriminatory to persons of the age chosen. If it is proportionate to choose age 65, the fact that it would be less discriminatory to some to have chosen 66 cannot render the clause unlawful.

Loxley v   [2008] IRLR 853 EAT
BAE Systems (Munitions & Ordnance) Ltd

The fact that an agreement is made with a trade union does not render an otherwise unlawful scheme lawful, but in determining whether treatment is proportionate, it is right to attach some significance to the fact that the collective parties have agreed a scheme which they consider to be fair.

Pulham v   [2010] IRLR 184 EAT
London Borough of Barking & Dagenham

While a tribunal is entitled to have regard, in assessing the justifiability of a discriminatory measure, to the fact that it has been negotiated with the representatives of the workforce, it cannot abdicate the responsibility of itself carrying out the necessary proportionality exercise.

Canadian Imperial Bank   [2010] EqLR 120 EAT
   of Commerce v
Beck

The deliberate adoption by the employers in a briefing document to a recruitment consultant of the description of the person being sought for a new role replacing the claimant as "younger" was a flagrant instance of potential age discrimination that shifted the burden of proof to the respondent bank, and the respondents had not discharged the burden of showing that a decision to dismiss was not significantly influenced by the claimant's age.

Pulham v   [2010] IRLR 184 EAT
London Borough of Barking & Dagenham

Pay protection arrangements following withdrawal of an incremental pay scheme based on age and length of service are capable in principle of being justified notwithstanding that they perpetuate age discrimination.

INDIRECT DISCRIMINATION

(1) For the purposes of these Regulations, a person ("A") discriminates against another person ("B") if – …

(b) A applies to B a provision, criterion or practice which he applies or would apply equally to persons not of the same age group as B, but –

(i) which puts or would put persons of the same age group as B at a particular disadvantage when compared with other persons, and

(ii) which puts B at that disadvantage,

and A cannot show the treatment or, as the case may be, provision, criterion or practice to be a proportionate means of achieving a legitimate aim.

(2) A comparison of B's case with that of another person under para. (1) must be such that the relevant circumstances in the one case are the same, or not materially different, in the other.

**EMPLOYMENT EQUALITY (AGE DISCRIMINATION)
REGULATIONS 2006 – reg. 3
➡ EQUALITY ACT 2010 – s.19**

Homer v   [2010] IRLR 619 CA
Chief Constable of West Yorkshire Police

The introduction of a requirement that to be in the top grade for legal adviser an employee had to obtain a law degree did not cause any particular disadvantage for employees between age 60 and 65 without law degrees even though they were close to retirement. Whatever the employee's age was when the provision, criterion or practice was introduced, he would have failed to achieve the top grade until he obtained the degree.

---

(1) It is unlawful for an employer, in relation to employment by him at an establishment in Great Britain, to discriminate against a person –
    (a) in the arrangements he makes for the purpose of determining to whom he should offer employment;
    (b) in the terms on which he offers that person employment; or
    (c) by refusing to offer, or deliberately not offering, him employment.

(2) It is unlawful for an employer, in relation to a person whom he employs at an establishment in Great Britain, to discriminate against that person –
    (a) in the terms of employment which he affords him;
    (b) in the opportunities which he affords him for promotion, a transfer, training, or receiving any other benefit;
    (c) by refusing to afford him, or deliberately not affording him, any such opportunity; or
    (d) by dismissing him, or subjecting him to any other detriment.

(3) It is unlawful for an employer, in relation to employment by him at an establishment in Great Britain, to subject to harassment a person whom he employs or who has applied to him for employment.

          EMPLOYMENT EQUALITY (AGE DISCRIMINATION)
                         REGULATIONS 2006 – reg. 7
           ➥ **EQUALITY ACT 2010 – s.39, s.40**

Dismissal

London Borough of Tower Hamlets v   **[2009] IRLR 980 EAT**
Wooster

It is plainly a legitimate aim for an employer to dismiss employees who are genuinely redundant. Where an employer no longer has work for an employee, he is not obliged to postpone the dismissal for however long is necessary in order to entitle the employee to qualify for an age-related benefit which has not yet accrued.

London Borough of Tower Hamlets v   **[2009] IRLR 980 EAT**
Wooster

A local authority unlawfully discriminated on grounds of age when it dismissed an employee instead of redeploying him or extending his employment because it was motivated by a desire to terminate his employment before he reached age 50 and became eligible for an early retirement pension, which the authority would have had to fund.

Rolls-Royce plc v   **[2009] IRLR 576 EAT**
Unite the Union

Length of service as one of the criteria for redundancy selection is a proportionate means of achieving a legitimate aim. The legitimate aim is the reward of loyalty, and the overall desirability of achieving a stable workforce in the context of a fair process of redundancy selection. Proportionate means was amply demonstrated where length of service was only one of a substantial number of criteria for measuring employee suitability for redundancy and was by no means determinative.

Seldon v   **[2009] IRLR 267 EAT**
Clarkson Wright & Jakes

It is a legitimate consideration that a rule requiring an equity partner in a law firm to retire after reaching age 65 was agreed by parties with equal bargaining power. Furthermore, to the extent that the rule benefits the partnership as a whole, the retired partner may have derived advantage from the provision when he was an equity partner.

Seldon v   **[2009] IRLR 267 EAT**
Clarkson Wright & Jakes

A partnership is in principle entitled to take the view that it does not want to have a performance regime leading to expulsion, and that factor could in principle justify a compulsory retirement age, but in such a case the partnership needs to analyse very carefully the age at which performance falls off. It requires evidence of a considered and reasoned explanation as to why the particular age had been chosen. Mere assertion would not be enough. In this case, there was a stereotyped assumption that partners will by age 65 be more likely to be underperforming than partners of a younger age. It is not self-evident that performance will dip in that way at that age, and there was no evidence to support that proposition before the tribunal.

Benefits based on length of service

(1) Subject to para. (2), nothing in Part 2 or 3 shall render it unlawful for a person ("A"), in relation to the award of any benefit by him, to put a worker ("B") at a disadvantage when compared with another worker ("C"), if and to the extent that the disadvantage suffered by B is because B's length of service is less than that of C.

(2) Where B's length of service exceeds five years, it must reasonably appear to A that the way in which he uses the criterion of length of service, in relation to the award in respect of which B is put at a disadvantage, fulfils a business need of his undertaking (for example, by encouraging the loyalty or motivation, or rewarding the experience, of some or all of his workers).

(7) In this regulation –
"benefit" does not include any benefit awarded to a worker by virtue of his ceasing to work for A.

          EMPLOYMENT EQUALITY (AGE DISCRIMINATION)
                         REGULATIONS 2006 – reg. 32
           ➥ **EQUALITY ACT 2010 – Sch. 9**

Rolls-Royce plc v   **[2009] IRLR 576 EAT**
Unite the Union

Length of service as a criterion for redundancy selection is capable of constituting a "benefit" within reg. 32, in the absence of any statutory definition which inhibits the word from otherwise having its wide dictionary definition.

Contractual redundancy scheme

MacCulloch v   **[2008] IRLR 846 EAT**
Imperial Chemical Industries plc
In a contractual redundancy scheme, where there is a standard set of rules identifying the amount of redundancy payment to be paid, and no discretion in the amount of payment, it would be an error to examine the application of the scheme to the individual as though the scheme was irrelevant to his or her position. The reason for the individual's treatment is linked inextricably to the aims of the scheme. Accordingly, whilst the proportionality test must focus on the extent of the disadvantage to the individual, the balancing exercise must have regard to the impact which a different scheme would have on the whole range of employees.

MacCulloch v   **[2008] IRLR 846 EAT**
Imperial Chemical Industries plc
It cannot be assumed that because a scheme in broad terms achieves certain business objectives that this necessarily establishes the justification for differentials in pay linked to age. The reasonable needs of the business must be balanced with the discriminatory effects on the claimant.

Loxley v   **[2008] IRLR 853 EAT**
BAE Systems (Munitions & Ordnance) Ltd
It may be justified to exclude those who are entitled to immediate benefits from their pension fund from the scope of a contractual redundancy scheme since preventing a windfall can be a legitimate feature of a scheme. However, such an exclusion is not inevitably and in all cases justified. Ultimately, it must depend upon the nature of both schemes. The tribunal must ask whether the treatment of the claimant achieves a legitimate objective and is proportional to any disadvantage which he suffers.

Kraft Foods UK Ltd v   **[2010] EqLR 18 EAT**
Hastie
A cap on awards made pursuant to a voluntary redundancy scheme was justified, notwithstanding that it disproportionately adversely affected employees closer to retirement. The cap prevented employees from recovering more than they would have earned if they had remained in employment until retirement age, thereby preventing a windfall. A provision which prevents an employee recovering more than they would have been entitled to earn is necessarily justifiable whether the amount of the windfall is large or small.

Equal Opportunities Review (EOR) is the UK's leading monthly journal focusing on equality, diversity and discrimination law and practice. It translates this fast changing and complex area of law into easily accessible news, feature articles, diary, case studies and surveys to help make your daily job as easy as possible. It also includes legislation and case reports from the UK tribunals and UK and European courts. Published monthly, **EOR** includes:

- **Expert commentary** – contributions from key people in the world of discrimination law and diversity.
- **Legislation** – reviewed and explained clause by clause, with analysis of potential problem areas.
- **Case reports** – expert analysis of key cases from the UK employment tribunals, EAT and appeal courts, and the European Court of Justice.
- **Case studies of named organisations** – an insight into best practice, and guidance as to how others are addressing legal compliance.
- **Surveys** – providing guidance on current employment practice across a wide cross-section of organisations.
- **News** – keeping you up to date with everything in the field of equal opportunities, diversity and discrimination law.
- **Diary** – a regular column by Michael Rubenstein providing an insight into what's happening in the world of equality, diversity and discrimination law.

What does your subscription include?

- **12 issues of the journal**, delivered to the destination of your choice.
- **Access to the online service** — **www.eordirect.co.uk** — which offers a fully comprehensive archive of all past issues.
- **Discrimination: A Guide to the Relevant Case Law** which is published annually and is worth £90.00 if purchased separately.

I already subscribe to IRLR, why should I subscribe to EOR?

- Unrivalled analysis from Michael Rubenstein of new equality legislation.
- **EOR** contains outstanding commentary and explanations of key employment discrimination cases.
- In-depth features and research from **EOR's** editorial staff pinpoint innovative developments in the world of equality and diversity.
- Analysis of important current issues from leading experts in the field such as *Darren Newman,* In-Company Training Services; *Rachel Krys*, Employers Forum on Age; *Gail Cartmail*, assistant general secretary, Unite the Union; *Gloria Mills*, national equalities officer, Unison; *Marian Bloodworth,* partner, Berwin Leighton Paisner LLP.

Michael Rubenstein is editor of Industrial Relations Law Reports, publisher of **Equal Opportunities Review** and general editor of **Equality Law Reports**; each product has been specifically designed to complement rather than compete. For more information, go to **www.rubensteinpublishing.com/eor**

Michael
Rubenstein
Publishing

The UK's only series of discrimination law reports

Equality Law Reports (EqLR) delivers, direct to your desktop, case reports on all areas of discrimination law. **EqLR** gives you comprehensive coverage of all key employment discrimination cases, as well as reports on non-employment discrimination cases, including access to goods, facilities and services, housing, education and the public sector equality duty. **EqLR** is supplied monthly in PDF format, with the extra option of receiving it in print too.

As the UK's first and only series of discrimination law reports, EqLR will allow you to:

- See how the courts are interpreting discrimination law - from the EAT, the UK appellate courts, and the European courts.

- Give effective advice across all areas of discrimination, not only relating to employment, but also non-employment.

- Access the information wherever you are, whenever you want, as **EqLR** is delivered to you via PDF and supported by **www.eqlr.co.uk**, our growing online service of all discrimination cases.

Authoritative commentary and headnotes come from **Michael Rubenstein**, General Editor, and Editors, **Katherine Tucker** and **Sarah George** (General Editors of Sweet and Maxwell's *Discrimination in Employment*).

I already subscribe to IRLR, why should I also subscribe to EqLR?

- **EqLR** covers not just employment but the whole world of discrimination law: the expanded public sector equality duty; access to goods, facilities and services; human rights and discrimination; discrimination in education and housing.

- Because **EqLR** is delivered electronically, it provides considerably more comprehensive coverage of key employment discrimination cases. **Some of the cases it uniquely reports could be of key importance to you.**

- **EqLR** provides systematic unique coverage of employment tribunal decisions, with summaries and a link to the full text.

*Michael Rubenstein is editor of Industrial Relations Law Reports, publisher of **Equal Opportunities Review** and general editor of **Equality Law Reports**; each product has been specifically designed to complement rather than compete. You will find more information about how **EqLR** complements IRLR and **EOR** at* **www.rubensteinpublishing.com/eqlr.**